Teach Your Children Well

Also by Madeline Levine, PhD

Viewing Violence: *How Media Violence Affects Your Child's and Adolescent's Development*

See No Evil: *A Guide to Protecting Our Children from Media Violence*

The Price of Privilege: *How Parental Pressure and Material Advantage Are Creating a Generation of Disconnected and Unhappy Kids*

Teach Your Children Well

Parenting for Authentic Success

Madeline Levine, PhD

HARPER

An Imprint of HarperCollins*Publishers*
www.harpercollins.com

HarperCollins books may be purchased for educational, business, or sales promotional use. For information, please write: Special Markets Department, HarperCollins Publishers, 10 East 53rd Street, New York, NY 10022.

The names and identifying characteristics of individuals discussed in this book have been changed to protect their privacy, as have the locations of certain events.

FIRST EDITION

Library of Congress Cataloging-in-Publication Data has been applied for.

ISBN 978-0-06-182474-6

12 13 14 15 16   OV/RRD   10 9 8 7 6 5 4 3 2 1

This book is dedicated to my mother, Edith Levine, who blessed me with unconditional love. Passed from generation to generation, her gift to me is also my children's inheritance.

You who are on the road must have a code that you can live by.

—*Graham Nash*

CONTENTS

PART THREE
THE RESILIENCE FACTOR:
SEVEN ESSENTIAL COPING SKILLS   185

PART FOUR
WALKING THE TALK   241

INTRODUCTION

Courageous Parenting–Taking the Long View

When *The Price of Privilege* was published in 2006, I thought I had written a substantive, if modest, book. After all, I was reporting on the unexpectedly high rates of emotional problems documented among a relatively small group of teenagers, those from families with high levels of income and education. While I assumed my audience might be small, I knew the findings were important and counterintuitive. Privileged children, long assumed to be protected by family resources and opportunities, are experiencing depression, anxiety disorders, psychosomatic disorders, and substance abuse at higher rates than children from socioeconomically disadvantaged families who have traditionally been considered most at risk. In addition, while these privileged children often perform well on tests, they are frequently wily but superficial and indifferent learners in spite of the congratulatory e-mails and fat acceptance envelopes many of them receive from prestigious colleges.

Based on a substantial body of research, *The Price of Privilege* suggests that our current fashioning of success, with its singular emphasis on easily measurable achievement, is a significant contributor to the high rates of emotional problems among affluent youth. Many academically driven kids take stimulant drugs to neutralize the exhaustion of excessively long hours of homework, cheat regularly to maintain the high grades that have come to be viewed as matters of life and death, and resort to unhealthy ways of coping with overwhelming anxiety by substance abuse or self-mutilation. Just as this narrowly defined and hyperfocused system stresses many students (and their families), so does it marginalize many more who either cannot or choose not to participate in a highly standardized, pressure-cooker education. These children find the interests and talents that they do have either ignored or trivialized, and disengage from school feeling unsupported and devalued. This leaves them vulnerable to high-risk behaviors such as substance abuse and petty crime, or a hopelessness that keeps them from succeeding even on their own terms. I proposed then—as I have again in this book—that the system responsible for these poor educational and emotional outcomes needs to be reexamined and reconfigured.

I expected to take a few months off for a book tour and related speaking engagements, and then return to the psychotherapy practice I had maintained for close to twenty-five years. That's not what happened. Five years later I have returned to my clinical work only part-time. *The Price of Privilege* was reprinted seventeen times before it was released in paperback. The small group that I had anticipated would find the book relevant has morphed into an extensive and diverse collection of parents, students, business executives, clergy, educators, university administrators, and public policy experts. Apparently, many of the problems identified in *The Price of Privilege*—stress, exhaustion, depression, anxiety, poor coping skills, an unhealthy reliance on others for support and direction, and a weak sense of self—are problems faced by large numbers of children across the country regardless of the socioeconomic status of their families. It turns out that many of these students are reporting high levels of stress whether they are trying to pass a high school exit exam or are juggling multiple AP courses.[1] While historically children have cited either family discord or peer problems as being their greatest sources of stress, school is now identified as the number one stressor in their lives.[2]

Major governmental studies report that one in five American children and teens shows symptoms of a mental disorder and one in ten suffers from "mental illness severe enough to result in significant functional impairment."[3] These numbers are expected to increase by 50 percent in the next decade.[4] The reasons for this are complex and varied. However, our children are increasingly deprived of many of the protective factors that have traditionally accompanied childhood—limited performance pressure, unstructured play, encouragement to explore, and time to reflect. Too many of our children are simply not thriving. We know it. Yet many parents are unsure about what to do.

To begin with, we must embrace a healthier and radically different way of thinking about success. We need to harness our fears about our children's futures and understand that the extraordinary focus on metrics that has come to define success today—high grades, trophies, and selective school acceptances from preschools to graduate schools—is a partial and frequently deceptive definition. At its best, it encourages academic success for a small group of students but gives short shrift to the known factors that are necessary for success later in life. It makes the false assumption that high academic success early in life is a harbinger of competence in many spheres, including interpersonal relations and sense of self. Sometimes this is the case; often it is not. Perhaps of even greater concern, because it involves far more kids, is the fact that our limited definition of success fails to acknowledge those students whose potential contributions are not easily measurable. If we insist on a narrow and metric-based definition of success then we maddeningly consign potentially valuable contributors to our society to an undervalued and even bleak future.

The "authentic success" that is the subtitle of this book sees success and its development in a different light, one based not on anxiety, but on scientific research, clinical experience, and a sprinkling of common sense. This version of success knows that every child is a work in progress. It recognizes that children must have the time and energy to become truly engaged in learning, explore and develop their interests, beef up their coping skills, and craft a sense of self that feels real, enthusiastic, and capable. Authentic success certainly can include traditional measures of success such as grades and top-tier schools, but it broadens the concept to include those things that we intuitively know are critical components of a satisfying life. While we all hope our children will do well in school, we hope with even greater fervor that they will do well in life. Our job is to help them to know and appreciate themselves deeply; to approach the world with zest; to find work that is exciting and satisfying, friends and spouses who are loving and loyal; and to hold a deep belief that they have something meaningful to contribute to society. This is what it means to teach our children well.

You will often come across the words *well-being* in this book as one of the hoped-for outcomes for our children. There is a reason why I've chosen *well-being* instead of *happiness*. Of course we'd all like our children to be happy, but we also know (albeit reluctantly) that life will throw curveballs at our children regardless of how hard we may try to protect them. The growth (emotional, psychological, cognitive, and spiritual) needed to make one's way through life comes out of challenge, and challenge can bring disappointment, anger, and frustration. It would be foolish to want only "happiness" for our children. This would leave them stunted and poorly prepared for life's inevitable difficulties. What we really want to cultivate is well-being, which includes as generous a portion of optimism as our child's nature allows and the coping skills, and therefore the resilience, that make adaptive recovery from challenge possible. As an added bonus, researchers tell us that the very characteristics that are most likely to encourage our children's emotional well-being are the same ones that will make them successful in the classroom.[5] Not surprisingly, optimistic, resilient, engaged kids report high levels of happiness.[6]

The precursor to authentic success is the growth of a sense of self that feels robust and genuine. Your child's "self" is not lost or in hiding, waiting for you to flush it out. Rather, it is in development. Your child develops a sense of self not simply because you've paid attention to and cultivated every interest and talent your child has. If our notions of child development stopped there, we'd continue to see the entitled, narcissistic kids with poor self-control who worry us now. The bigger and more accurate picture is this: A strong sense of self develops through a process that includes a combination of genetics; the influence of family, peers, and mentors; the opportunities presented; and the culture we live in. It certainly is informed by the way you support the particular strengths and interests of your child, but it also includes the ways in which your child interacts with the outside world, and, particularly, the values that are communicated in your household and in your community. Authentic success is being "the best me I can be" not simply in isolation, but as part of a community, and it always includes a component of meaningful contribution and connection with others. We would do well to start thinking about success not in terms of today, the next grading period, or the next year, but in terms of what we hope for our children ten or twenty years down the line, when they leave our homes and walk into their own lives. Yes, it requires both courage and imagination to parent with this long view, but it is also the most effective way to ensure that our children have satisfying, meaningful lives.

We've spent years being bombarded by the press about the competition for prized academic spots, told by corporations that we weren't doing our jobs as parents unless we made every effort to give our kids a competitive "leg up," and immersed in a culture that celebrates obvious and measurable performance over all else. When I first began traveling around the country, many parents found it difficult to take a clear-eyed look at the cost of too much involvement, too much "enrichment," too much stress, and too little recognition of the real needs of children. Thankfully I no longer encounter much skepticism: the toll of a narrow version of success has become painfully obvious to most parents. What parents are clamoring for now are solutions. "What should I do?" has become the collective mantra of my audiences around the country.

Teach Your Children Well is my answer. We must shift our focus from the excesses of hyperparenting, our preoccupation with a narrow and shortsighted vision of success that has debilitated many of our children, and an unhealthy reliance on them to provide status and meaning in our own lives, and return to the essentials of parenting in order for children to grow into their most healthy and genuine selves. I will not shy away from providing concrete answers for concerned or confused parents when research is clear that children are most likely to benefit from one course of action over another. Parents are often willing to make changes faster than the institutions around them. The pace of institutional change can be positively glacial compared with the vigor of a parent who feels his or her child is in jeopardy. No matter where I speak in the country, the worried questions tumble out in predictable sequence.

- All the kids in kindergarten are reading. My son isn't. What should I do?

- My eight-year-old son has been called a "gifted" chess player, but he's refusing to go to a chess camp this summer. Instead he just wants to hang out with his friends at the local "adventure" camp. What should I do?

- My twelve-year-old daughter has three hours of homework a night and is exhausted. What should I do?

- My son seems content to get B's, even C's in high school. He works hard on his schoolwork but spends a lot of time puttering around in the garage. His counselor says he'll never get into a good school. What should I do?

All of these questions are driven by the same concern: if we don't get it right, our children may pay an intolerable price because of our uninformed, inaccurate, or poor decisions. Never before have parents been so (mistakenly) convinced that their every move has a ripple effect into their child's future success. Depending on where you are in your own child-rearing cycle, some of these questions may seem foolish, others quite pressing and important. But even though there are always exceptions, it is easy to answer questions like these based on what we know from the scientific research. In other words:

- Many children can't read in kindergarten. Don't worry about it. Three years later there is no difference in reading skills between those who learned in kindergarten and those who learned a year or even two later.[7] Finland, generally considered the world's exemplar when it comes to education, doesn't begin school for children until they are seven years old. Your child will feel bad only if you or the school turns normal development into pathology.

- Two of the major developmental tasks of middle childhood are developing friendships and sampling a wide range of activities. Kudos to your son for knowing his own mind. Having your child called "gifted" can be a siren song to parents' ears. But remember that both Bill Gates and the

Unabomber, Ted Kaczynski, were considered gifted. These two men had very different relationships to their gifts. You can certainly encourage your son's talent, but ultimately you need to follow his lead on how much time and involvement he wants to put into chess. Certainly parents can force their children to cultivate a talent and rightfully insist that they have perspective their children lack. On occasion this works out, particularly if your child has a genuine talent. It's rare, however, and it always puts your relationship with your child at risk.

- Research is clear that junior high students derive academic benefits from about an hour of homework a night, but not from more. Find out from your daughter's teacher if she is having difficulties that are slowing her down. If she is, then she needs a lighter load and some help. If not, then talk to the teachers and school administrators about bringing homework time into line with known benefits. Get your community involved in a discussion about healthy amounts of homework. Kids who aren't getting enough sleep are likely to be less engaged learners, and crabbier family members. Your first job is to guard your daughter's health.

- In spite of grade inflation, a B is a good grade and a C is an average grade. We are all average at many things. With almost 4,000 colleges in the United States, college placement is about making a good match, not about winning a prize. Steve Jobs's grandfather often talked about the long hours his grandson put into "puttering" in the garage. As long as your son is putting in effort, he's probably doing the best he can. Your son will feel like a loser only if you treat him like one. Ask for another counselor.

Although this book will provide these sorts of concrete answers, its goals are far more ambitious. *Teach Your Children Well* aims to help you identify and strengthen the basic strategies that are known to promote effective parenting. This will make it easier for you to stay on target as you guide your children through the different stages of development and help them strengthen the coping skills that they will need to move successfully from one level to the next. Think of child development as a scaffold. A scaffold needs a sturdy base in order to support its higher rungs. It is important that we respect this progression as our children climb rung by rung, and not push them to the top prematurely or without adequate support. Good parenting skills make this climb safer, more satisfying, and ultimately more successful for our kids.

Additionally, by carefully examining the capacities and the challenges of children at different ages, *Teach Your Children Well* will give you the tools to differentiate between minor and expectable transgressions and more concerning problems. A normally diligent child who forgets a homework assignment is not the same as a child who makes a habit out of it. One needs little intervention from us, the other needs more, and we need to know if that's a discussion, a reprimand, a consequence, or an evaluation. *Teach Your Children Well* will help you figure out when to hold back and when to intervene, when to compromise and when to stick to your guns so that you are a more confident parent.

The other major goal of this book is to help you clarify and prioritize your values and your definition of success so that there is greater alignment between what you believe is important and what is emphasized in your home and communicated to your children. Nowhere is the issue of values more alive for parents today than in our conflict over how hard we push our children to be academically successful, since we also recognize that their healthy development takes more than high grades. Do we believe in the importance of playtime but schedule our youngsters with a boatload of extracurricular activities because we worry that they might "fall behind"? Do we value spirituality but find ourselves measuring success by material possessions? Would we allow our child to compromise his integrity, say by cheating on an important test, if it helped him gain admittance to a prestigious school?

By applying the information, the relevant research, and a series of paper and pencil exercises in this book, you will be able to construct a personal definition of success that is in line with *your* family values, and with the skills, capacities, and interests of *your* particular child. Of course, no book, no matter how comprehensive, can possibly address more than a fraction of the dilemmas that are part of the everyday experience of parenting. But what *Teach Your Children Well* will do is help you construct and formalize a set of principles, grounded in research but unique to your particular family, that you can use as a compass to guide you through the inevitable thicket of parenting choices and challenges.

This book will ask a lot of you—it will ask you not only to recognize problems, but also to work diligently to change their causes. I'll also ask you to do some psychological work of your own. This is critical; children thrive when their parents thrive. You will need to dig down deep and examine your own motivations, ambitions, and distortions. This is not easy work, but if you are willing to be both reflective and honest, I promise that not only will your child benefit, but you and your family will as well.

Here's how *Teach Your Children Well* will proceed:

- The first section starts with an overview of our current high-stakes, high-pressure culture. How does this culture affect kids and families? What are the realities and the myths embedded in this lifestyle? Who stands to benefit and who stands to lose from a narrow view of success? Should this view be modified, and if so, why has this been so difficult to do?

- The second section deals with the particular challenges that children and teens face as they grow up and move from elementary through middle and high school. Understanding that children and teens have multiple tasks—growing up, figuring out their particular interests and talents, making friends, managing risk, and so on—can help us have a healthier perspective on academic achievement and a broader perspective on success.

- The third section presents seven coping skills that are known to be protective of children's well-being and integral to the development of a sense of self. The more coping skills children have at their disposal, the more likely they are to successfully meet the challenges of growing up and finding their own definition of success. While some coping skills are more inborn and others are clearly an outgrowth of interaction with parents and the world, they all can be strengthened. Specifics on how to do this effectively (and what gets in the way) are presented at the end of each coping skill section.

- The fourth section is directed at you, the parent. It includes a series of exercises designed to help you clarify your values and carve out a specific action plan for bringing more of what you value into your life, your children's lives, and your home. In order to optimize the chances of making real change, this section also focuses on helping you evaluate your own history and explore how unresolved issues in your past may be contributing to current parenting issues or your reluctance to make the kinds of changes you would like to implement.

Teach Your Children Well refuses to accept the false dichotomy that in order to be successful children have to be physically run into the ground and emotionally disengaged from themselves, their families, and their studies. We do not have to choose between our children's well-being and their success. Both are inside jobs. They are developed when kids are guided and encouraged to build a sense of self internally. To not be overly reliant on others for definition or validation. To trust that their parents are on their side and have their back, as they go about figuring out their interests, skills, capacities, identities, and values. Certainly externals matter. Kids have to follow the rules, master content, learn appropriate behavior, and conform when necessary. However, our kids have had a huge helping of external expectations and demands that have crowded out the time and energy needed for the exquisite and necessary internal work that is the bedrock of a healthy sense of self.

We know far too much about promoting healthy child development to continue to tolerate the myth that success is a straight and narrow path, with childhood sacrificed in the process. The truth is that most successful people have followed winding paths, have had false starts, and have enjoyed multiple careers. Academic excellence will always matter, and parents are right to maintain a high bar for their children. But there are other skills that are likely to be particularly important to success in the twenty-first century— creativity, innovative thinking, flexibility, resilience in response to failure, communication skills, and the ability to collaborate.

Unless success is experienced internally, in alignment with one's interests, skills, and values, it never feels truly owned and can't confer either the pleasure or the protection that real success provides. Many kids have become proficient at image management. They have high grades or special talents, and a quick read of them suggests that they are successful. However, a deeper examination of these children shows that their external success is superficial and even meaningless to them. "I am only as good as my last performance" is what they really believe. Success that is not authentic, that doesn't feel real or "owned," never feels like success at all. Not to us. Not to our children. The "imposter syndrome" that all of us feel from time to time becomes a permanent state of affairs for our children when success feels inauthentic. Ultimately, it is only our children themselves who will pass judgment on their success, or lack thereof, in their lives.

This book is about choices and courage. Choices about how we view success, raise our children, and expend our energies and resources. It is also about the courage to make the changes we believe in even in the face of collective pressure to act otherwise. We live in a culture that has had a great deal to say about raising successful children. Much of it is dead wrong. Too often we are asking the wrong questions. Which school? How many AP courses? Which extracurricular activities? It's not about whether kids should study more or less. It's not about "rigor" versus play, where we score on international testing, or whether children should be indulged more or have their feet held to the fire.

Rather, the real questions are broader and more long-term. How do we create environments in which children thrive? How do we help them find, and keep, the sparks that kindle deep interest and real engagement with learning? How do we help them to live up to their potential? Advance their abilities to contribute? Find meaning? Develop their most genuine selves? These are the questions we need to ask, to think about, to work on. Given all the time, money, concern, and love we expend on our children, let's make sure that we're focused on the questions that really matter. Children cannot be defined by their grades, trophies, or "fat envelopes." Not even by the sum of these things. They are whole people, and to see them as anything less is a form of parental blindness.

It's time to reassert our parental prerogative. We need to decide for ourselves what we value, which activities denote real accomplishment, and which are superficial. We need to insist that the schools that serve our children be committed to developing the potential of every student and be just as vigilant about their physical and mental health as they are about their test scores. It's time for us to reclaim our good judgment as well as our children's well-being, and return our families to a healthier and saner version of themselves.

PART ONE

AUTHENTIC SUCCESS

*It's Not About Bleeding Hearts
Versus Tiger Moms*

· CHAPTER 1 ·

The Kids Are Not Alright
(and Neither Are Their Parents)

A dad and his son sit together on the sofa opposite me. They are not in my office for any pressing psychological crisis. As a matter of fact, I have known both of them for many years. Dad and I have served on various school committees together, while his seventeen-year-old son, Daniel, played lacrosse with my youngest son. From time to time I see Daniel in my office when he is wrestling with a problem. They have come, at Dad's request, to discuss college options. Consultations like this have become rather routine, as parents seek opinions from a wide range of experts about their child's college potential and choices. I know that Dad is a well-meaning, hard-driving guy and that Daniel is a great kid, well liked by his teammates, athletic, academically gifted, and surprisingly laid-back. I know before we begin that he is most likely headed to a "top-tier" school and am curious about the kind of school that he envisions for himself.

Daniel talks enthusiastically about his interest in the environment. He likes math and science and could be interested in engineering, or possibly environmental science. He hopes to find a college where teachers are interested in "mentoring." He seems completely at ease with his lack of clarity about exactly what will ultimately interest him, but he's adamant about one thing;

he has to go to a school where the kids are "nice." He's tired of the constant competition and stress at his high-pressured private school and talks sincerely about looking forward to a school that values cooperation over competition. Olin College pops into my mind, a small, extraordinary engineering school in Needham, Massachusetts, where learning is almost entirely project based and collaborative.

But we've just begun to talk and I ask Daniel if he has any specific colleges or universities in mind. Being a California kid, he starts with Berkeley, UCLA, and Stanford, the expected trinity of schools for high-achieving kids in suburban communities like mine. He then moves on to the usual suspects outside of California. Dad listens intently. Daniel mentions small liberal arts schools like Williams and Amherst, but also large prestigious universities like Georgetown and Tufts. As Daniel talks about the pros and cons of each of these schools, his father leans in closer, increasingly attentive to Daniel's choices. Finally, Daniel brings up the Ivy League schools. At the mention of Harvard, Dad nearly jumps off the sofa and says, "Now there's a school I would give my left testicle to get my son into." Daniel's animated face turns listless. My jaw drops.

There is so much at play here. On the surface, it looks like Dad is a jerk and his son has somehow managed to grow up thoughtful and grounded. Daniel at seventeen has a host of typical adolescent issues to consider—who he is, what he likes, how to make good choices, and what kind of future he would like to begin crafting for himself. Preserving his father's gonads is not one of them. But at the heart of this interchange between father and son lies something more basic than Dad's boundary misstep. When he was younger, Daniel and his father had more or less the same perspective on what constitutes success, but their perspectives are diverging in notable ways as Daniel approaches college. This is a common and generally positive developmental milestone because it means Daniel feels secure enough in his family to examine issues of separation and identity, two of the most pressing psychological concerns of adolescence. The resultant divergence of opinions, however, can temporarily throw parents, their teenagers, and often the whole household into a tizzy. None of us wants our children to pick a college simply because they are "asserting their independence" (actually, a potentially better reason than "I hear the girls are easy" or "It's a great party school"). And parents rightfully insist that they have a perspective about long-term consequences that their teenagers can't possibly have. But for the moment, what would make Daniel's dad so adamant about a school his son has little interest in and that is unlikely to meet the criteria that Daniel has clearly articulated?

Daniel's dad grew up in the late 1970s, a bright child whose parents divorced unexpectedly when he was twelve. He and his brother lived primarily with their mother, who found herself in limited financial circumstances after the divorce. Dad worked very hard at school, was able to attract a scholarship from a top-tier college, although not an Ivy League school, and went on to make a great deal of money in finance. When Dad married, he vowed that his family would never suffer the kind of deprivation and instability that he, his brother, and his mother suffered after the divorce. In fact, he lived his life very much "on track" with a high degree of driving ambition. It served him well. He liked his work, felt like a good provider, and was very proud that his oldest son seemed to be following in his footsteps. He was sensitive enough not to push his son overtly, and had encouraged Daniel to consider many different schools. His spontaneous outburst on the couch was really a reflection of his deeply held belief that his son, like himself, was most likely to thrive and prosper under particularly competitive circumstances, specifically attendance at arguably the most highly recognized and prestigious school in the country. Like every parent, Dad wanted his child to be successful and to have advantages that had been denied to him. His particular version of success, rooted in company loyalty, conformity, diligence, hard work, competitiveness, and academic excellence, has had a long run in this country. His own success stood as a testimony to this particular paradigm.

Daniel, on the other hand, had grown up in a particularly loving and stable family. His father and mother had succeeded in providing the kind of environment in which Daniel's emotional, physical, and academic growth could proceed unimpeded by either financial or emotional instability. Smart, motivated, and hardworking, he was able to take advantage of the resources provided by a family, school, and community that placed a high value on academic achievement. Like many high-achieving kids, Daniel was particularly adept at presenting himself well, even when he was struggling with normal and predictable adolescent worries. Because he was private by nature, it was sometimes difficult to spot Daniel's conflicts or distress. From our occasional sessions together I knew that he had been struggling with issues of academic integrity for quite some time. Daniel's singular insistence on going to a school where kids are "nice" suggested that, at this particular time, he was more concerned with social and ethical issues than with the academic issues that preoccupied his father.

Daniel had spent most of his young life in highly competitive academic schools. During elementary and middle school, Daniel had little reason to question this view of success, since he found it easy to thrive under demanding academic circumstances.

Things began to change for Daniel when he entered high school. He continued to do very well in school but noticed the toll that the pressured environment exacted on some of his good friends. During his sophomore year, a close friend was carted off to rehab for alcohol abuse, and a girl he had been friendly with since elementary school was hospitalized for an eating disorder. At the beginning of his junior year, many of his friends began taking Adderall, a stimulant medication generally used for attention deficit hyperactivity disorder, in order to stay up nights and complete the excessive amount of homework they were given. Cheating was the norm at his school, and Daniel always felt uncomfortable when people copied his homework or even his test papers. He felt like a "mean person" and a "bad friend" if he refused to participate, but he also felt bad about himself when he colluded with his friends around cheating. He never discussed this with either his parents or his teachers, for fear of being forced to be a "snitch."

This was just the beginning of a series of conflicts around academics that culminated during Daniel's junior year. Daniel himself began copying his friends' homework, "in order to keep up." After years of discretion, Daniel was stunned when he was anonymously reported to the school "hotline" for cheating. Expecting to be excoriated for his dishonesty, Daniel was shocked when his only consequence was a brief discussion with his counselor and a halfhearted warning not to do it again. Daniel kept a journal and brought in the following entry for me about their meeting.

> *I realized today that everyone, including the school, understands that students are engaged in a battle. A battle for grades, SAT scores, and big-time college acceptances. The rules I had been brought up to believe in no longer seem to apply. Kids I have known for years have become thoughtless and cruel to each other. I feel myself retreating from all this. I love learning, so my grades stay high, but I have lost interest in being part of a community that values a grade over integrity or friendship. I now know that the college I go to will have to be a very different kind of place, probably not the high-*

*prestige, dog-eat-dog school everyone else has in mind for
me. I'm afraid that I'll hurt my parents who have worked
so hard to give me so many advantages. But if they really
understood what was happening, I don't think they'd
disagree. I just don't know how to explain it without
making it sound like I'm slacking off or being ungrateful.
Sometimes I just feel like throwing in the towel around
this whole college thing.*

Daniel was appropriately crafting his own version of success.
Fortunate enough to grow up in a family of plenty, Daniel was less
focused on scarcity and avoiding deprivation and more focused on
collaboration and personal growth than his father. Certainly Daniel
had internalized many of his family's good values—perseverance,
effort, and loyalty—but he was also intent on adding teamwork,
curiosity, moderation, and honesty to the things he valued. This
was a kid who truly believed that a well-earned B was superior to
an ill-gotten A. Daniel reminded me that it wasn't that long ago
that teenagers in my office spoke frequently and passionately about
moral issues. Whatever happened to that?

Daniel was right that his father was having a hard time understanding why Daniel would even think about attending a less
prestigious school when he had all the credentials for a highly selective school. Dad, like many high-achieving men, had been greatly
relieved that his son seemed headed for a life of financial success.
For Dad, this meant he had done a good job preparing his son for
the eventual responsibility of raising a family of his own. To think
that Daniel might be drawn more to the "soft" value of "niceness"
rather than the "hard" (or as Dad would say, "practical") value of
being an "alpha dog" made Dad question whether he had done his
job well enough.

In this respect, Daniel's dad and mom both needed to understand that they had done a good job in raising a son who was not particularly vulnerable to the opinion of others and whose motives were internally driven. Since internal motivation is highly correlated with all kinds of positive outcomes—notably higher academic success and lower levels of emotional distress—Daniel was well positioned to be successful regardless of the college he ultimately would choose. After just a couple of sessions, Dad came to see that Daniel's admirable view on what constitutes success, effort, persistence, and good values was highly aligned with his own. There is an interesting body of research that shows that involved, engaged fathers have a significant effect on their child's social and moral behavior.[1] Knowing this made Dad proud and more tractable about understanding that, while he and his son were both ethical, ambitious, and hardworking, Daniel was more realistic about the kind of environment in which he would thrive. Dad was given credit for his involvement and he appreciated being recognized for his contribution to Daniel's healthy development.

Daniel's story illustrates the cost that even the most competent and well-adjusted kids face whether they opt in or opt out of our current success-at-all-costs paradigm. Daniel felt compromised both emotionally and ethically when he was in the system, and faced disapproval from both his parents and his school when he considered opting out. He ultimately chose a well-regarded smaller college with the kind of teacher-student support that he valued and a student body known for being particularly collaborative; he turned down several more prestigious schools, including one in the Ivy League. Daniel continues to do well academically, but just as important, he feels at home at his college. He studies and socializes (not necessarily in that order) with students who also place a high premium on creative, collaborative work. Daniel chose well. Unfortunately, too many students today lack the combination of internal resources and external support needed to make good, healthy choices about where to go to school and even what to study.

To be clear, this book is not about downplaying academic success, high grades, or prestigious colleges. *On the contrary, it is a book about how to optimize conditions so that a far greater number of children can actually be successful without the accompanying high levels of distress that have become so prevalent.* There is currently a spirited debate in this country about how parents and schools can best encourage success. Because the media like simple and controversial coverage (particularly when the topic is complex and nuanced), we are frequently presented with what seems to be diametrically opposed views on how to cultivate success in our children. On the one hand, "tiger moms" (of all stripes) insist on "rigor." They exert constant pressure on their children to perform at the highest levels, from the earliest ages, and are seemingly oblivious to the social and psychological needs of their children. In spite of this, their children turn out to be well-adjusted, high achieving kids who perform at Carnegie Hall and make the rest of our kids look like slackers. This plays to the fear of more lenient parents that their children will be working at McJobs while the "tiger cubs" will be sought after for the best and most lucrative positions. Alternatively, there is perceived to be a posse of softhearted academics and child development experts who seem inordinately focused on "well-being." They are so concerned with the emotional development of children that they will coddle them right out of any viable economic future. Their kids may be well-adjusted, self-reliant, and kind, but they'll be living in the basement or sleeping on the living room couch after college. This plays to the public's general mistrust of academics as living in "ivory towers" and being removed from the real-life struggles of parenting.

This kind of bifurcation is not only unfair, it's inaccurate. While there are some clear differences in parenting practices between these two points of view, there are many more similarities. All parents want their children to be happy, to be able to love, and to be loved. To be competent at some things and expert at others. To find joy and meaning in life, be a good person, and contribute to society. There is no disagreement about the fact that all students have to master content and that effort and practice are the keys to learning. Or that children, particularly young children, need a great deal of parental involvement and guidance. Real disagreement seems to be about whose needs take center stage, but there are things to be learned from both sides. Letting go of our children prematurely is tied to a host of problems, as is the inability to tolerate a child's moves toward independence. No parent strives to bring up an emotionally impaired child. And of course, most important, every child is different and we need to tweak our parenting style accordingly. There is no faster way to dispel a one-size-fits-all theory of child rearing than to have a child.

Is it important to keep the bar high for our children? Absolutely. We know that parents who have high expectations that are in line with their children's capacities have children who tend to academically outperform those whose parents do not have high expectations. Kids live up or down to the bar we set for them. But we need to make sure that we are keeping our eye on the right bar. Our bar should focus primarily on effort and improvement, not performance. Kids' capacities differ, and they change across time and across subjects. If you keep the effort bar high then good school choices make themselves reasonably clear. For one student that might be Princeton, and for another it might be a community college. *Both of these options carry the possibility of success and neither guarantees it.*

There is something crazy about a system that takes a well-adjusted kid like Daniel and flirts with turning him into a dropout while disrupting the equilibrium of his otherwise healthy family.

According to Garrison Keillor, all the children in Lake Wobegon are above average. But that's yesterday's news. Today it appears as if, given half a chance, all of our children would be extraordinary. And while that is true in deep and profound ways, it is not true in the narrow and frequently superficial way that most schools and standardized tests measure. Reality is set aside as parents overestimate their kids' capacities and insist that average students have disabilities, good students are actually excellent students, and excellent students are geniuses. The cost of this relentless drive to perform at unrealistically high levels is a generation of kids who resemble nothing so much as trauma victims. They become preoccupied with events that have passed—obsessing endlessly on a possible wrong answer or a missed opportunity. They are anxious and depressed and often self-medicate with drugs or alcohol. Sleep is difficult and they walk around in a fog of exhaustion. Other kids simply fold their cards and refuse to play.

An academically talented patient of mine lies in bed for days after being rejected from one of the most competitive schools in the country. She will not get up, and when I visit her at home, all she can say through her streaming tears is, "It was all for nothing. I'm a complete failure." And one of my street-smart patients, the kind of kid who is a C student, with terrific interpersonal skills and a hands-on style of learning, refuses to apply to college, fearful that he will experience the same rejection there that he felt "every day when I walked into school." He has made himself scarce as his friends' acceptances and rejections come in, calling the whole process "stupid." I hope that with some confidence under his belt, he will reconsider next year and apply to the kind of school that knows how to teach hands-on learners and will value his talent for communication and his practical skills. For kids like this, a year off, with the opportunity to feel capable at a job, often takes the edge off their lack of confidence.

Once measurements become the standard of achievement, for every above-average child there is a below-average child; this is a reality my audiences typically don't like to consider. But it's a problem only when we don't allow ourselves to see that there are many different kinds of potential in our children and that standardized testing looks at only a narrow range of possibilities. Our job is to help encourage our children to find and nurture that potential whether it's in math class, in art class, in music, out in nature, in relationships, or in any one of the hundreds of possibilities for deep learning and meaningful engagement that exist out in the world.

Every child has at least one "superpower" and usually several. These are the skills, talents, and interests that come naturally to children and that give them pleasure. While we may rejoice over a kid who has a superpower in math and worry about the kid whose superpower is being on the phone for long periods of time figuring out the social problems at school, both of these aptitudes have the potential to contribute to a life of meaning and satisfaction—whether you're an engineer, a mathematician, an organizational psychologist, or a mediator.

Charles Darwin was a mediocre and "lazy" student who loved fiddling with minerals, insects, coins, and stamps—hardly the kind of interests most of us assume to be precursors to changing the world. And yet he did. Name and celebrate your child's superpowers—it will feed his sense of being known and understood, will encourage him to stay engaged with learning, and will fortify his relationship with you.

I've walked into hundreds of schools in this country, and usually what I see most prominently displayed is a plaque with the names of students who have made the honor roll and a cabinet full of athletic trophies, often going back decades. The unvarying placement of these things—close to the front entrance—makes it very clear what accomplishments these schools value. But other schools take a different approach, one much closer to the reality of almost any student body. In these school entrances one can find an art exhibit; a photography exhibit; disassembled automobiles; textile and clothing designs; architectural models of buildings, bridges, and parks; as well as evidence of academic and athletic accomplishment. Schools like this make it clear that they encourage curiosity and effort, and value a wide range of talents.

Schools have many functions in addition to teaching content and preparing students to take standardized tests. They are the incubators for the workforce, training grounds for informed participation in a democracy, and transmitters of perspective and culture. Hopefully they also function as places of nurturance in which a child can develop skills, interests, ethics, and a sense of identity. Until we are willing to enlarge the tent so that more children feel that school is a safe place open to the diverse talents of its students, school will continue to be the single greatest source of stress in kids' lives. *In the real world, success has all kinds of different faces in all kinds of different fields of endeavor.* It would be nice if we could acknowledge as much to our kids.

We'd like to think that educational systems are designed to optimize the potential of each student. But in reality, educational systems have always been designed to turn out the kinds of workers that our economy needs. Sitting still, rote memorization, and unquestioning allegiance to one's teacher were traits well suited to turning out the kind of "organization man" that was in great demand in the 1950s. Every educational system has had its pluses and minuses, and the kind of system that encouraged conformity produced workers who remained loyal to their companies for years, but it generally neglected creativity and critical thinking.

Such a system is completely unsuited to the needs of an expanding global knowledge economy, where problem solving, innovative thinking, adaptability, and initiative promise to be of far greater value than the ability to know the "right" answer, because that answer is not likely to be static. We may think that students with straight A's or perfect SAT scores have the best future prospects but most business leaders are saying that content and technical skills are a distant second to skills like problem solving, communicating well, and asking good questions. Of course, good grades are important. They are evidence of analytic intelligence, hard work, and mastery of content. But focusing *only* on knowing the right answer leaves little time or energy for thinking about the right question. A major study conducted by IBM found that the single most sought after trait in CEOs is creativity.[2] This all suggests that in addition to wreaking havoc with our children's emotional development, our current system is leaving them woefully unprepared for the work world they will inherit.

Misconceptions about what success is, and how to get it, abound. Let's start with some of the myths about raising a successful child that have come to resemble gospel.

Smart kids get high grades:

Some do, some don't. There are many different ways to be "smart," not all of which lend themselves to paper and pencil evaluations. There are reasons for the bromide that the world is "run by C students." Many of the characteristics that lead to success, particularly interpersonal skills and a robust sense of self, are never assessed in school.

Kids need all kinds of extracurricular activities to "keep up" with their peers and to look good to prospective schools:

Kids, for the most part, need what kids have always needed: love, support, limits, and responsibilities. In this respect, the kids that I treat now are no different from the kids I treated thirty years ago. Child development simply does not change—it's biologically encoded—and no amount of extracurriculars makes up for a kid who feels unloved or entitled, both of which are poor predictors for success.

Attending a prestigious school gives kids
added advantages in life:

This is really the big one. Most of us believe that if only our kids went to Yale, or a comparable top-tier school, they would have unimaginable advantages when they go out into the world. Interestingly, two researchers, Alan Krueger, an economist at Princeton University, and Stacy Dale, a senior researcher at the Andrew Mellon Foundation, have done a comparative study of students accepted at Yale who actually attended the school and those who were accepted but ended up going to less prestigious schools for family or financial reasons. Down the road, they found no difference in job advancement or pay between these two groups.[3] For the right kid, going to Yale is a terrific choice. While it will offer opportunities, it is not likely to determine the trajectory of your child's life in a significant way (except for economically disadvantaged children or children of color). Bright, hardworking kids tend to do well regardless of the school they attend.

Yes, but won't my child get to make connections at
prestigious schools that will open doors in the future?

Probably. A disproportionate number of kids at prestigious schools come from families with both money and social connections. There certainly can be valuable networking opportunities at these schools. The issue isn't whether prestigious schools offer tickets to opportunity. They often do. The issue is the price you are willing to have your child pay for these tickets. There are kids who belong at the most prestigious schools in this country and who find their way in through a combination of academic talent, hard work, and a bit of good fortune. But there are other kids who give up their childhood, their integrity, their health, and their psychological stability to get into these schools. In spite of parents' rationalization that "they'll thank me down the line," very few of these kids will.

While it's clear that the cost of our current narrow vision of success is unacceptably high for our children, our families are suffering, too. First of all, the preoccupation with our children's activities has squeezed out what little time was traditionally left for parents to enjoy a (typically) meager bit of time each day for their own recreation or friendships. Second, having a stressed-out, anxious, or overwhelmed child can color the whole tenor of the household. Since it's Mom who is more apt to have conversations with the kids about things like homework or emotional glitches, and since it can seem like our kids are frequently teetering on the edge of exhaustion or panic, our work starts to resemble crisis intervention more than it does mothering. Being a mom is a tough enough job without the added stress of premature concern about college, distress about each and every grade, a calendar of (child-centered) activities that would challenge a cruise director, and a pervasive sense that one is *still* not doing enough. Our most important job—to provide a calm, secure, and loving haven for our children as they go about the challenging business of growing up—has been utterly compromised.

Susan is a forty-six-year-old teacher who over the years has come to see me when she wanted some help deciding whether to continue full-time teaching or be a stay-at-home mom. Finances in Susan's household were tight and she needed to bring in some income. Over a couple of sessions Susan decided to become an active substitute teacher and work per diem. On the rare occasions when I saw her, it was clear that she felt she had made the right decision and was able to enjoy her time at home with her children. At least she did the last time I had seen her, six years earlier, when her daughter, Cassie, was ten and her son, Ryan, was six.

The woman who sat in front of me now was clearly not getting a great deal of pleasure out of anything. Frazzled, anxious, and teary, Susan said that she "couldn't keep up." What she meant was that her children's schedules had become so demanding that she felt she could no longer maintain even her flexible job schedule. The specifics are familiar to many of us. Cassie was a junior in high school and in the middle of what had become a frenzy around potential college admissions. Her college counselor kept insisting that with "just a little more effort," Cassie would be considered by some notable colleges. Already working on her homework well into the night, Cassie couldn't imagine where she was supposed to find the time to work even harder. On top of that, she was playing a varsity sport, volunteering at a local food bank project, and taking a prep class to prepare for the SATs. Her brother, Ryan, was part of a traveling soccer team, with many games held on the weekend away from home. Both Susan and her husband attended all of these games, giving up any semblance of their own social life, because they felt it was important to "support" their younger son, who wasn't the student his sister was.

The details here are not what matters. You can fill in your own. For most of the families I see or talk with, the specifics may change, but the frantic pace and the squeezing out of what we used to call "a family life" are pretty much the same. To say nothing about Susan's escalating anxiety and depression about being able to keep up with all the demands being placed on her.

Let's take a step back from the multiple pressing demands on Susan's time and try to look at the big picture. What does Susan, or any of us, need to function optimally? First, we need connections with other adults. Yes, Susan is a mother, but she is also a wife, a friend, a teacher, and a person with interests of her own. How can she function well in any of those capacities if she is perpetually depleted? There is no question that the early years of child raising can be incredibly demanding because of the amount of oversight that young children need in order to be safe. But Susan's kids are twelve and sixteen, and while adolescence brings with it a whole other range of concerns for parents, we no longer have to cover up electrical outlets, put gates across stairs, and keep our eyes on our child in the swimming pool for every single second. The argument can be made that teens need just as much vigilance, and while they do indeed need our attention, availability, and guidance, no, they do not need as much vigilance. That's the point of growing up. Besides, we tend to be vigilant about the wrong things. We know everything about their grades and not enough about where they go and what they do. We monitor their performance, but not their character.

So, is Susan entitled to a life of her own or is it her responsibility to make sure that her children are provided with every possible opportunity even if it means putting her own life on hold? Many women say, "I'll go back to my own life when my kids are grown. For now my job is to give them everything they need to be successful. That's my legacy to my children." You should hear what most kids say about this kind of "legacy." While you think you're giving your kids everything, they often think you are bored, pushy, and completely oblivious to their real needs. But let's look at this very simply: if you're willing to give up your own life and identity, what is the message you have sent your kids about the value of other people, mothers in particular?

On a recent Mother's Day my phone was ringing off the hook. Why? So many moms were feeling hurt and unappreciated. Past the age of school-mandated Mother's Day cards, older kids were for the most part oblivious to the importance of the day for most of us. Thoughtful gifts were practically nonexistent, and the few kids who managed to bring flowers brought, in the words of one of these moms, "the tiredest flowers I've ever seen. I'd swear they came from a Dumpster." The moms who got late-in-the-day phone calls tried hard to feel content with "just hearing my daughter's voice." These kids have been shown that we expect so little, are entitled to so little, that the mere sound of their voice is enough.

While the hurt of these moms was real and painful, this outcome should come as no surprise. If you're willing to give up your life, interests, friendships, and profession so that your child gets to see you week after week passively sitting in the bleachers watching whatever game he's playing; if you spend night after night sitting next to your child, helping with homework or overseeing her efforts instead of going out with a friend or your spouse; if money goes to prep course after prep course, tutor after tutor instead of to a family vacation or even a weekend away for you and your husband, then don't be surprised by "tired flowers." You have taught your kids that the moon and stars revolve around them and that the needs of adults, adults charged with the responsibility of taking care of and supporting a family (and often taking care of aging parents as well), can't hold a candle to a twelve-year-old's soccer game or a sixteen-year-old's math test. Entitled children are the inevitable outcome of time and resources that are wildly and disproportionately assigned to the children and not the adults in the family.

It is possible to feel that things are "normal" when it seems that everyone around you shares a similar belief. To do right by our children we are encouraged to believe that college begins with our preschool choice. Athletic training can't start too early. Summers are for advancing glimmers of talent at specialized camps. Kids need to take every rigorous course offered. Tutoring is to be expected. As for our children, when every grade, interest, activity, and pursuit is a step toward or away from academic success, then everything they do is outer-directed and they can't possibly figure out who they are, what they value, or what kind of life is most likely to be authentic, meaningful, and satisfying to them. They can only parrot a view of success that is a pressured, dysfunctional, one-size-fits-all mockery of authentic success. What led us to this dreadfully eviscerated vision of the successful life?

• CHAPTER 2 •

How Did We Get into This Mess?

Personal space is expanding for the Eight-year-old. He can now return home alone by bus from a somewhat distant point. His walking area within his own neighborhood is so wide that it is sometimes hard to locate him.[1]

Ten prefers to be active, and the outdoors is his greatest love. Tens love most to play outdoor gross-motor games and ride bicycles. . . . Play is paramount in their lives and they enjoy doing almost anything.[2]

Fourteen is pretty much at the helm as far as sleeping goes. As one Fourteen puts it, "I usually go to bed myself. I know enough to go to bed." The hour of bedtime ranges from nine to eleven with the commonest time at nine-thirty or ten.[3]

The quotations that begin this chapter come from a series of books that were the gospel when I was bringing up my three sons. The authors, Drs. Louise Ames and Frances Ilg, devoted each of their books to a particular age, with titles like *Your Eight-Year-Old: Lively and Outgoing.* I read every one of them from cover to cover. They seem like relics to me now.

Yes, my children are grown, but my youngest son just left for college last year. It's not as though I was parenting centuries ago.

And yet, anyone with an even passing familiarity with kids' lives today would acknowledge that children have left one universe for an entirely different one. I recently ran a parenting workshop, and curious about the issue of "personal space," I asked: "At what age would you allow your child to walk around the neighborhood without your supervision?" The most frequent answer I got was twelve, with many parents saying they wouldn't allow their child to walk around freely until even later. Not one parent felt comfortable about having an eight-year-old out and about. I didn't bother asking about the bus. It wasn't that long ago that a New York City mother was accused of child neglect because she let her nine-year-old take a subway alone. Today, referring to an eight-year-old as being "sometimes hard to locate" is enough to make most mothers break a sweat.

As for robust outdoor play for ten-year-olds, it's predictably on the decline, about half of what it was just a decade or two ago. Only 8 percent of kids this age spend time out of doors in physical activities like walking or hiking. Instead of the play that Ames and Ilg observed and considered critical to this age (as do all current researchers on child development), kids are spending more time studying, watching television, playing video games, and being on the computer, cell phone, or smartphone.[4] Many parents are hesitant to tell their ten-year-old to "just go out and play," preferring the perceived safety of organized sports with adult supervision.

And finally, there is something positively quaint about the notion that most fourteen-year-olds are tucked into bed at nine thirty or ten because they have become good self-managers. While the American Academy of Pediatrics recommends nine hours and fifteen minutes of sleep each night for a fourteen-year-old, the average teen gets just over seven hours of sleep with over a quarter getting six and a half hours or less. The documented problems with this include memory issues, irritability, less pruning of brain synapses (necessary for efficient learning), poorer judgment, lack of motivation, depression, and attention deficit disorder.[5] Increased homework time and social networking account for much of the time that is stolen from sleep.

The disconnect between what professionals emphasized a mere decade or two ago and what is currently the focus of our parenting anxieties is unsettling at best. In a short period of time we've moved from childhood and early adolescence as important developmental stages in their own right to considering them a training ground for college admissions, graduate schools, and even careers. We treat our children like young adults, simultaneously acting as if they're small children in need of perpetual oversight. The zeitgeist seems to be that the world is a dangerous place, far too dangerous to let kids run around willy-nilly. We ignore the fact that violent crime, the reason we worry about our kids' safety, has decreased, cut by 50 percent over the last two decades.[6]

We worry that our children will not be able to compete in a future that at present can be only partially imagined. The three brief comments that opened this chapter may have set the stage for success in a less competitive global economy, but now, for many parents, they seem naive. If play or sleep needs to be sacrificed, it's in the interest of making certain that our children will ultimately "do well." While we may not exactly be at ease with this, neither are we so disturbed that we are willing to take a stand. We see the gains as greater than the risks.

Does this mean that all of our kids are secretly on the verge of collapse, hiding a raft of symptoms from unaware parents? Of course not. There are kids who appear to manage well in this system, who don't exhibit troubling behaviors or symptoms. Yet even for them, I would argue, there is still a substantial cost associated with this paradigm: the neglect of aspects of what educators call the "whole child." Youngsters whose free time is closely scheduled, children who are expected to participate in high-level traveling teams, and teens who are perpetually short of time (and sleep) are all bypassing critical developmental tasks. The lack of unstructured play for youngsters is associated with less enthusiasm for learning, diminished creativity, and poorer social skills. For middle school children, premature athletic specialization can lead to physical injury, and it puts limits on one of the most critical tasks of childhood, sampling a range of activities in order to find the best fit. And finally, the overburdened teen has no time to do what teens are programmed to do, which is to develop an identity and begin to experience intimacy. If your reaction to this is "Well, can't these things wait? They'll have more time when they get into a good school, a good university, a good job . . ." here's the psychological reality: they can't wait. Child development proceeds in a predictable sequence. If you haven't learned to sit in your seat and raise your hand in kindergarten, it's very difficult to develop the self-control needed in adolescence.

Young kids need to play for many reasons. Play teaches creativity, resourcefulness, and social skills. Without some success on these tasks, it would be extremely difficult to move on to experimenting with the different kinds of interests we expect older children to be drawn to, such as hanging out with friends and trying new things. Resourcefulness provides the "backbone," the courage that allows kids to move out into the world and test themselves. Social skills and creativity pave the way for successful peer relations in new endeavors. And it is in the process of trying different activities that kids begin to notice that they are similar to their families in some ways and quite different in others. "My mom likes to swim, my dad likes to bike, but I really like soccer" is a nonthreatening start to separation and identity formation. Without these small moves toward autonomy, teens find themselves either too unskilled to begin the process of separation or so frantic about separation that they end up using a weed whacker in order to separate when pruning shears would be far more effective. Our children simply cannot bypass the developmental tasks of their particular ages because we are either dismissive of "soft skills" like creativity or so worried that they will be disadvantaged in the world that we forget the critical importance of psychological and social development. Few of us would make this choice consciously, but our better angels are often derailed by our anxiety.

We can get back on track. But first we need to understand the multiple forces that have contributed to the distressing sense of helplessness, even paralysis that many of us feel about bucking the current system. When systems change, whether the change is in parenting practices, education, social policy, or politics, there are always winners and losers. Children should never come out on the losing end.

America is "the land of opportunity" where hard work, not lineage, is the deciding factor in our destiny. While we are not quite the meritocracy we are fond of believing we are, we can still breathtakingly defy notions of class and race. Hard work, self-reliance, resilience, compassion, and a willingness to take personal responsibility, even in the face of daunting odds, have characterized many of our country's most outsize success stories, from Oprah Winfrey to Barack Obama, from Larry Ellison to Sam Walton.

This particular national story is a good and noble one. It allows for the *possibility* of opportunity and advancement based on well-developed internal traits as opposed to chance or accidents of birth. This is a realistic view of success and one that approximates the trajectory of most Americans who consider themselves successful, whether that's amassing a fortune or simply feeling fortunate about one's life. It also explains the popularity of the "shirtsleeves to shirtsleeves in three generations" idiom. Success is most often earned, not conferred.

But amid the excesses of the 1970s, America's ideas about success took a 180-degree turn. The concept of self-esteem and its relationship to success became absurdly distorted. Making sure that all children receive sports trophies so that there are no "losers," insisting that all children be invited to birthday parties so no child feels left out, giving prizes for "participation" (just showing up), and heaping endless praise on kids for minimal effort are all antithetical to the development of real esteem, which is a healthy regard for oneself born out of competence and a realistic assessment of actual accomplishments. While schools implemented self-esteem curricula and parents devoured books on how to nurture it in their children, a critical fact was overlooked. In the popular but wildly mangled translation of a complex psychological concept, what we ended up focusing on was not self-esteem but narcissism. Feeling appropriately good about one's accomplishments is self-esteem; feeling "special" just because, especially when coupled with a lack of empathy, is narcissism.

Narcissism and self-admiration ("narcissism lite") are *less likely* to make a child successful regardless of whether you're looking at academic performance or popularity. Even real self-esteem doesn't contribute much to success.[7] *But success contributes mightily to self-esteem. Kids have to "do" something, and do it well, to get a self-esteem boost.* When children's apparel starts to resemble nothing so much as an ode to self-indulgence and materialism— "Princess," "Future Ruler of the Free World," "My Parents Went to Paris and All I Got Was This Lousy T-Shirt" (all the better to cultivate a materialistic mind-set early)—and when products from the quotidian shampoos of L'Oreal ("Because I'm Worth It") to Cartier's high-end jewelry ("All About You Forever") encourage us to stay self-absorbed, then competence, hard work, perseverance, and collaboration lose their importance. We're too busy loving ourselves to cultivate our capacities, learn how to love, and be of service to others. Real self-esteem suffers as a result.

Many of today's parents are applying these mistaken notions about self-esteem to their parenting practices with some nasty consequences. What researchers have found is that this excessive focus on the self has led to a substantial increase in narcissism, and its evil twin, entitlement. When the emphasis is on how "competitive" everything is—grades, schools, jobs—then "looking out for number one" becomes the logical response.

While most of us are not suffering from clinical narcissism, try getting up in front of a thousand people and telling them that most of their children are not particularly special. No matter how much empathy I put behind this startling but statistically accurate statement, it is *never* met with polite applause. Most parents today were brought up in a culture that put a strong emphasis on being special. Being special takes hard work and can't be trusted to children. Hence the exhausting cycle of constantly monitoring their work and performance, which in turn makes children feel less competent and confident, so that they need even more oversight. Since self-esteem comes from actual competence, the ever-present parenting hand only breeds dependence, destroys resilience, and as a result, lessens self-esteem. We need to distinguish between the inherent uniqueness of our children, and the unrealistic specialness we insist on when we argue with teachers or coaches or push our children past their limits. The former moves our children forward, the latter only hinders their progress. Our need to have our children be special is, not coincidentally, an outgrowth and an addendum to our own need to be special. "I am a good parent because my child is an honor roll student" simply is not the way to think about parenting. "I am a good parent because my child is a good person" is. Look at how we trick out our cars with bumper stickers related to our kids' academic standing—typically "My Child Is an Honor Student" or occasionally the pushback "My Kid Kicked Your Honor Student's Ass." But all the "values"-type bumper stickers—"Wag More Bark Less" or

"Practice Random Acts of Kindness"—seem addressed to other adults or to the ether. I've yet to see a bumper sticker addressing a kid's virtue in any arena other than his GPA. Is this really the best (or only) thing we consider worth advertising about our children?

Of course the culture of narcissism and its psychological fallout are not enough to fully explain our preoccupation with a short-sighted and narrow version of success. Social change, politics, and economics all play a role. In the past fifty years we've gone from the open-ended, student-driven, grade-free, no-homework, no-pressure days of Summerhill (a creative and permissive type of education, developed in England, that became popular in the 1960s and '70s) to our current narrow, test-driven, grade-focused, homework-overloaded, pressured system. This isn't to say that the Summerhill model was preferable. There are aspects of both approaches to education that are useful and aspects that are dreadful. But the point is that within my lifetime, I have seen a 180-degree turn in attitudes toward education. This drives my hope about reforming our current system.

In 1983, amid concerns that America was losing its competitive edge in education, President Reagan commissioned a blue-ribbon panel to evaluate the condition of our educational system, both public and private, from elementary school through college. After two years of intensive study, the outcome of that investigation was *A Nation at Risk: The Imperative for Educational Reform*. This slim volume contained some of the most forthright and forceful language ever seen in a government report and was extremely critical of America's system of education. Its primary author, James Harvey, famously wrote, "If an unfriendly foreign power had attempted to impose on America the mediocre educational performance that exists today, we might well have viewed it as an act of war."[8] America no longer led the world in successfully educating its students and the report made many strong recommendations, including that high school students be assigned more homework, that standardized achievement tests be administered at "major transition points," and that teacher salaries be increased and based on performance. The first two recommendations were taken very seriously, albeit also misunderstood to some degree, and were integral components of the No Child Left Behind Act (NCLB) of 2001, signed into law by President George W. Bush. The third and probably the most important recommendation (since a critical predictor of a child's learning is the quality of his or her teacher), regarding improving teachers and the teaching profession, was ignored.

While *A Nation at Risk* recommended significantly more homework, it is doubtful that the three to four hours of often mindless homework that many high school students put in on a daily basis is what its authors had in mind. Many countries that score higher than the United States on international tests of achievement give less, not more, homework than we do. And nowhere in that report is the suggestion made that students should be tested annually beginning in third grade, as NCLB has mandated. Major transitions would be at the end of elementary, middle, and high school. The emphasis in the report was on making sure that graduating high school students were competent to go on to college or out into the workforce. President Obama's current Race to the Top, in the tradition of NCLB, continues to penalize the schools that are most in need of resources. Has all of this made us more competitive in the global economy, if standardized testing is indeed taken as the measure of excellence? The answer is no. We continue to perform closer to the bottom than the top when our students are compared to students in other industrialized countries in the world.

This quick look at the past forty years of attempted reform shows that the seeds of our current high-pressure, high-stakes education system, and the parenting practices that logically ensued, were sown many years ago. I will leave it to educational historians to document the pluses and minuses of our attempts at education reform. My interest is different. Does better achievement necessitate stressing out students and panicking parents? Whether you believe America is really falling behind in academic achievement or that what we do best—create and innovate—cannot be measured by standardized testing, the fact remains that we are tolerating, even advancing, a paradigm that is substantially at odds with what we know about healthy child development, enthusiasm for learning, and real-world success.

There are some rather obvious contributors to our current anxiety about how our children will fare in the future. Unemployment is higher than it's been since the Great Depression, and most Americans have seen the value of their assets plummet. Income inequality is at its highest recorded level.[9] This degree of unequal wealth distribution creates a winner-takes-all economy. In uncertain times, especially when the stakes are high, all of us look for pockets of certainty. If that certainty is attached to a degree from Harvard or a profession like medicine, then many of us would be likely to overlook the bags under our kids' eyes, knowing that we have helped them to secure a comfortable future. The problem is that this thinking is flawed.

No school or profession can guarantee success, financial or otherwise. The child who values close connections with mentoring adults is unlikely to feel successful at a large, impersonal school, no matter how prestigious. And the child whose blood runs music is not likely to feel successful in a dental program. While every protective parenting bone in our bodies says, "Yes, but . . ." ("Yes, but there are always jobs waiting for kids who go to prestigious schools"; "Yes, but a dentist can always make a living"), we must also consider the possibility not only that are we wrong, but that we are also preventing the very success we wish for our children.

We need to get a few things out on the table. While each and every one of us feels that our children are special, they are not all academically gifted. Of course, some children are highly academically talented and for them the top schools offer the kind of education that suits their needs. But these top schools can fill their incoming classes many times over with the brightest students. No child should be made to feel that any particular college acceptance is vital. For all the different kinds of brightness that exist, there are multiple schools that will fit the bill. And just like adults, kids can be quite talented in one area and not in another.

Our kids are much more complex, interesting, and unique than their grades, their SAT scores, or the colleges they ultimately attend. One child is an academic whiz with a profound interest in public health; another is a good student with fantastic friends who he considers to be as worthy of his time as his schoolwork; a third is fascinated with music and sound; his grades are passable but his room is like a recording studio. You may look at these three kids and think, "I'll take the whiz kid." But really, aren't they all interesting kids, kids you could easily feel proud of? All of these kids bring enough talent and zest to their lives to suggest that with respect and encouragement they will be successful in their own ways.

This does not mean that grades, college choices, and options don't matter. They do. And while they may start out mattering more to you than to your children, ultimately they have to matter to your children. *They* have to be invested in their own choices, goals, and accomplishments. We should encourage our children to try a range of different activities; we should stress effort and encourage persistence when the going gets tough. Part of feeling successful at something is being good at it and most of being good at something has to do with effort and persistence. But here's the difference: practice enforced by an anxious parent who sees mastery as a matter of life and death is very different from practice encouraged by a parent who understands challenge, who insists on effort and persistence but is not personally affected by her child's performance. Children will be most successful when *they* decide which interests and talents to pour their hearts into. This is the work of growing up, to choose a life's work (or as we go forward, more likely several kinds of work) and to understand that some interests become hobbies and some become passions and ultimately we allocate our resources accordingly. For some kids these passions turn into a medical degree from Harvard, for others a teaching credential from Bank Street College, and for others a stint in Hollywood learning the ropes of the film industry.

There are kids whose aspirations are fully aligned with their parents'. Kids who truly want to go to the schools that have been in their families for generations, kids who want to follow in the footsteps of their parents and grow up to be doctors like their mothers or writers like their fathers. Parents tend to feel they've really lucked out when their kids fall so easily in line with family values and choices. The issue here is to make sure that, even if your child goes to your alma mater and ends up taking over your law practice, these choices are not preordained but rather are truly "owned" by your child. This means keeping a close eye on whether your child lights up at the thought of carrying on family traditions or sees it as an unfortunate but necessary responsibility. I've seen families where one child carries on the family business and another chooses to become a yoga teacher. Healthy families celebrate these different choices.

While economic viability is certainly important, and parents will naturally be concerned about their child's financial future, we have our eye on the wrong ball. If our children have the benefit of a loving relationship with us, a bar set high enough to give them something to reach for, and a sense of being understood and valued for themselves, then we've done the best we can to ensure that grades, schools, and eventually work will fall into place. Most of us know that the constant drumbeat of questions about academics and grades, colleges and SAT scores is wearing not just on our children and on ourselves, but on our *relationship* with our children. I see this in the child who proudly invites his parents to his photography exhibit at a local gallery only to have them say, "I wish you would put half as much time into your physics homework as you put into your photography." I see it in the outgoing, athletic teens who come in depressed or anxious because they know that a big college experience is right for them, yet their parents are pushing the small liberal arts schools they value. And most disturbingly, I see it in the kids who have thrown in the towel, who feel "no one knows who I am," who have a "fuck you" attitude toward school and their parents because it's easier than feeling the pain of not living up to unrealistic expectations. And in spite of knowing all of this and more, most of us still find it hard to pull back, to have faith in our children and in the evolution of their lives. What we see as concern they rightfully experience as a vote of no confidence.

Another contributor to our current dysfunctional system came as the result of a demographic blip in the mid-1980s. During this time there was a drop-off in college enrollment because there were simply fewer kids. Colleges had to master a variety of seductive techniques for appealing to students and parents, including making their school look particularly selective. *U.S. News & World Report* concocted a statistically dubious measuring system for deciding on the "best" schools in the country (best for whom?), and the prestige race was on. Add to that the growing industry of child "enhancement" opportunities, from intrauterine musical experiences (no benefits) to videos that claimed to advance language skills (they don't) to specialized after-school activities for kids (lest they not be "productive" in their few free hours), and you have market forces that play to all parents' fear that they aren't doing enough. Add the increase in households with two working parents who understandably want their child in a supervised after-school environment and the extracurricular industry exploded. Tutoring has now become a $7 billion a year industry. No wonder we worry. From conception through college there are goods and services that promise a smarter, more competitive, higher-achieving child. Who would want to settle for a regular kid when you can engineer a superkid?

The possibility of having an extraordinarily talented child is, in psychology-speak, a "hot" idea. It's seductive on several levels: we would feel gratified; our friends would be amazed, maybe even a bit envious; it would prove that the sky's the limit in terms of what our child could accomplish in life. By contrast, scientific or academic ideas can often seem "cold." Here are two propositions regarding teens and sleep, one from a private tutoring business, the other from an academic journal.

- "Yes, you have to push your children and they'll miss some shuteye. But think of how proud you'll be when they end up with straight A's and a shot at any college in America."

- "Plastic processes occurring during wakefulness result in a net increase in synaptic strength in many brain circuits. The role of sleep is to downscale synaptic strength to a baseline level that is energetically sustainable, makes efficient use of gray matter space, and is beneficial for learning and memory."[10]

Prestigious schools and universities, tutoring services, prep courses and "educational" toy manufacturers, with the help of Madison Avenue's most aggressive marketing firms, have all mastered the language of "hot" cognitions. They know how to downplay risk, say it's okay to "miss some shuteye," appeal to your parenting instincts, imply your kid has a "shot at any college," and play on your narcissism, prophesying "how proud you'll be." There is also the implication, partly because of the personal, friendly style of writing, that this is a no-brainer ("You'd have to be crazy not to see it this way"). And finally, there is the unsubstantiated connection between the service that is being offered and stellar academic performance. Quite simply, it's an offer you can't turn down.

Compare this with the "dry" facts typical of an academic paper. Not only does this kind of research rarely see the light of day, but academic writing doesn't hit us in the gut. And when it comes to our kids, a promise of success, or even just the implication of success, is so much easier to grab hold of than academic ideas with all kinds of caveats and disclaimers.

Parents have always been concerned about their children's future, but the kind of overblown panic that I'm seeing in parents today has its roots in an extraordinary marketing campaign designed to convert normal parental concern into frenzied anxiety about what it will take to be successful in the twenty-first-century global economy. In a relatively short period of time parents have gone from sporadic tutor use for students having difficulty to hiring tutors in the hopes of squeezing a bit more performance out of children who are already doing well. We have been sold a bill of goods and that bill of goods has clouded our common sense and judgment. *Here's the reality: kids who are pressured, sleep-deprived, and overly focused on by parents convinced that without significant oversight and intervention, their children are not likely to be successful are at high risk for emotional, psychological, and academic problems.*

Why have we become so vulnerable to ideas that have minimal value and maximum hype? Yes, some kids need tutors, some kids need special testing for learning disabilities, some kids benefit from being kept very busy, and other kids belong at the most competitive schools. But all these special circumstances involve a *minority* of our children. Currently there are school districts where close to half of all students are labeled as having a learning disability (which allows for extra times on the SAT and ACT), schools where tutoring is the norm, and high schools where the *majority* of graduating seniors apply to an Ivy League school. There are prep courses for *preschool* admission and programs that guarantee admittance to a top-tier college if you sign up as soon as your child hits kindergarten. You don't need a PhD in psychology to know that this is wrong.

There is no way to know what will be a good match for your young child some fifteen years down the road. All you know is what *your* dreams and hopes for that child are. You can rest assured that some of those hopes and dreams will be realized and that many will not. When we construct our children's futures prematurely, the stories we transmit to them become nothing more than fabrications made out of our own interests, hopes, and projections. Assume little. Wait to see the particulars of your child. Concentrate on character and values. Provide opportunities. And then, for goodness' sake, let children grow naturally into their unique selves.

Perhaps we have become so seduced by the possibility of being able to cultivate "outstanding" children because we are a bit lost ourselves. Technology has revolutionized communication. While smartphones, tablets, Skype, Facebook, and LinkedIn increasingly connect us they can paradoxically make us feel disconnected as we devote less time to basic human needs for empathic, resonant communication, eye contact, and touch. Increased mobility robs us of the stable community that once provided the emotional resources to weather the challenges of child rearing. Instead we are immersed in a culture that emphasizes individuality, competition, and self-centeredness. This cannot possibly nourish our own needs adequately, and it often leads us to feel isolated and even a bit desperate. We hunker down and immerse ourselves in our children's activities at the expense of our adult relationships and our own continued development. Decreasing the sphere of our own lives makes us increasingly dependent on our children for a sense of meaning and accomplishment.

Parents have always had to let go of their children, hopefully under optimal circumstances, but often under terribly trying ones. While we certainly do live in uncertain times, it's hard to square the level of anxiety so many parents have about their child's success with the facts of life in the United States in the twenty-first century. We act as if we're terrified of letting our children out into the world without our perpetual involvement and oversight. The reasons for this are complex, varied, and largely *unconscious*. It's laughable to think that any of us are intentionally trying to hold back or debilitate our children. Nonetheless, often we are.

Many of today's parents knew profound loneliness and uncertainty from when their own parents divorced. They confuse overinvolvement with stability. Many have divorced themselves. They bind their children tightly to avoid further loss. Many gave up promising careers and arenas of great satisfaction in order to parent. They want their families to run with the notable precision and success that they brought to their companies. They (childishly) expect to be repaid for their sacrifice. Many have moved far from their roots. They put "all their eggs in one basket," relying exclusively on their children for a broad range of support that used to be offered by the entire community. Many know that upwardly mobile kids can end up living down the block or, just as easily, on the other side of the world. They hold on as long and as tenaciously as they can, fearing that college heralds the end of family life. And many, brought up in a culture that emphasizes science and measurement, feel lost when it comes to "measuring" their success as a parent. They look to their children's achievements as tangible evidence of competence.

And finally, we hold on to our children because it helps us to escape (temporarily) the sadness and grief that are *always* part of transformation and loss. Our own loss of the great love affair we once had with our children. Our own transformations as we age. Our children's transformations as they grow into the young adults we once were. And, of course, the realization that we will not always be there to protect, to soothe, and to heal our children's own inevitable losses and transformations.

None of us wants to raise entitled, fragile children. We know in our hearts that kids need to fail, need to be challenged, need to be left to their own devices, and need to feel the rush of pride when they find that they can manage. The exultant cry of the two-year-old, "I do it myself," and the insistence of the teen that "it's my life" are both celebrations of developing competence, and lines in the sand about whose life it is. Our job is to be emotionally in synch with our children, celebrating right alongside them. Overwhelming anxiety, the kind we're feeling about our children's future, kills this party. It prevents us from being creative and flexible in our parenting. It shuts down our coping skills. We yell when the umpire blows a call instead of exerting self-control. We cry over first-choice school and college rejections instead of showing enthusiasm for acceptances. And we worry endlessly about real or imagined parenting missteps instead of trusting our instincts.

We simply cannot control our children's future no matter how many enrichment experiences we buy and how many tutors we hire. Of course, I'm not talking about throwing pitches with your child in the park, getting a tutor for a kid who is really struggling, or appropriately encouraging interests, hobbies, and talents. But we are so far past "appropriate" that our actions, rather than benefiting our children, are increasingly impairing them. No parent should tolerate what has become a culturally normalized form of child abuse— sleep deprivation, repetitive stress injuries from early and excessive athletics, overwhelming academic stress, and a complete disregard for the known protective factors of child development.

We need to reacquaint ourselves with the basics of healthy child development and the stages that our children predictably move through as they grow up. Best parenting practices for each of these ages will be identified with the caveat that the best parenting practice of all is to know your child in deep and accurate ways. Growing up is a tremendous challenge. We are spending way too much time worried about our children's performance and grades—their heads—and not nearly enough time paying attention to their hearts.

If we don't attend to all the needs of children we will find that our children continue to be denied the very things we wish most for them: meaningful and satisfying lives. The following section on child development will make clear what challenges kids face at different ages and how to optimize their chances of advancing through each of these stages well prepared to meet the challenges of the next stage. We may need to rethink some of our parenting practices while endorsing the benefits of others. It is my hope that by better understanding the nonacademic parts of development we will be able to shift our focus and return to the most critical part of parenting: making certain that our children have been provided with the essentials—the time, the guidance, the psychological space, and the unconditional love—to be able to develop their unique selves, capable of not simply apparent or superficial success, but deep, authentic success.

PART TWO

THE "SCHOOL YEARS" ARE NOT JUST ABOUT ACADEMICS

A Primer on Child Development

CHAPTER 3

The Tasks of the Elementary School Years

Ages 5–11

Earlier notions of middle childhood being a period of "latency"—psychology-speak for "nothing much happening"—have been shown to be profoundly inaccurate. It is over the course of the elementary school years that children begin to hone a sense of self; develop friendships that are deep, loyal, and often enduring; and become increasingly motivated to be competent in multiple arenas, most notably in school and among their peers. This is hardly a time of developmental hibernation. Often, however, it is a welcome break for parents between the vigilance we needed when our children were very young and the fortitude we will need to navigate through their adolescence. If this sounds like an invitation to kick back and glide through your child's elementary school years, it's not. It's simply an acknowledgment that *conflict* between parent and child tends to be reduced during this period of time. Development, however, marches on, and along with it parenting challenges.

It's hard to think that a five-year-old and an eleven-year-old have much in common. Your five-year-old may still be struggling to tie her sneaker shoelaces while your eleven-year-old may be refusing to wear any shoelaces in her sneakers because it's "stupid." Certainly, toward the end of elementary school, issues start to arise that look far more like teen than five-year-old concerns. However, there is a reason why these ages are traditionally grouped together. The overriding task of elementary school children is the move away from near-total dependence on the family for regulation ("No cookies before dinner"; "You have to say 'I'm sorry' for breaking your brother's toy") to increased *self*-regulation of impulses, emotions, behavior, and relationships ("I'll have dessert after dinner"; "Gosh, I'm sorry I broke your toy, it was an accident").

This turning from the dependable structure of the outside world to an emergent internal world for direction is no easy task and will tax your child's resources just as it will demand your oversight and guidance. The developmental direction of the elementary school years is toward children entering a more complex world where they direct and regulate more of their own experiences while still largely under our supervision. It is this period of *coregulation* that lays the groundwork for an emerging sense of self and for healthy independence and reciprocity in adolescence and young adult relationships. But for much of elementary school your child is still holding on to your hand.

Childhood is characterized by multiple transitions. Kids leave the relaxed world of preschool and enter a school that enforces rules and regulations at every turn. Not only are the demands of elementary school broader, but they are also harsher. Missteps in social communication, dress, or athletic ability are not easily forgiven. The fantasy world that was so reassuring and available to younger kids is replaced by a world that is organized and fact-based. Your child may still have an "imaginary friend," but he's apt to leave that friend at home when he crosses the school's threshold. Simple understandings of what is good and bad or right and wrong are being replaced by far more complex ideas about relative values and different perspectives. Bodies are growing, sometimes overnight. The accessible world grows bigger as children learn to move about, ride bicycles, take the school bus, and skateboard. The larger world beckons.

When my youngest son, Jeremy, was six years old he ran away from school. I was at work and received a frantic phone call from the mom doing pickup that afternoon; she couldn't find my son anywhere. I flew out of my office and ran the few blocks to the school. The sight of police cars in the school parking lot took my breath away. The only thing that provided any reassurance was the school secretary saying that not only was Jeremy missing, but so was his best friend, Matt. Phone calls made, descriptions given, the police asked me to wait at home while they scoured the neighborhood. When the police car pulled into my driveway with my son in the backseat, looking for all the world like he was having the adventure of his life (which he was—more on that in a moment), I felt relief and anger as a single emotion. Clasping him to me, teary and hiccupping, I could only repeat, "Where were you?"

Jeremy is my youngest son, and so I'd had sixteen years of parenting practice before this incident. I think that if it had been my oldest, I would have banished him to his room for eternity. Instead I took a few deep breaths and tried my best to focus on Jeremy, who seemed far more worried about my state of mind than about his police escort. Because he was shy and quiet by nature, I knew I'd have to cool my heels and wait for him to tell his story. And his story made perfect sense in a six-year-old kind of way.

School was out for the day. He and his friend Matt were shooting hoops in the school yard, waiting for their ride, when they decided that it would be much cooler to shoot hoops in the high school gymnasium just a couple of blocks away. Jeremy had spent a lot of time in that gym with his basketball-playing older brother. The fact that Jeremy and Matt had to meander the back roads of our town was apparently no deterrent compared with the intoxication of being independent explorers. Thankfully, they arrived without incident, easily scrambled up the metal fence around the high school, and were having the game of their lives when the police found them. Rather than being appalled by the appearance of the police, they both seemed to think that riding in the back of a patrol car was a suitably exciting conclusion to a thrilling afternoon.

Once Jeremy was home safe and I regained my equilibrium we were able to talk about his "adventure" (as he still calls it to this day). By being able to actually listen to his recounting of the story I learned a great deal about some of his strengths and weaknesses, his thinking process, and his temperament.*

One of the most prominent parenting challenges during the elementary school years is figuring out how much oversight and how much freedom to allow our kids. This is as true of the eleven-year-old who wants to go on a "date" as it is of the six-year-old who wants to cross the street. Kids differ in the strength of their curiosity and exploratory drive and we differ in how much anxiety we can tolerate. But this much is certain: in order to do the teaching we need to do, we need to keep our cool, see things through our children's eyes, and then give them feedback and guidance. When safety is an issue we must be able to accurately assess our child's ability to be responsible and we must be firm in our directives. However, this doesn't exclude respectful listening to your child's point of view. This ability to keep your relationship intact, even under duress, is the insurance policy you will be glad you bought when your child is an adolescent.

So instead of banishing my son to his room for eternity, he went there for the evening. But first he and I went over the events of the day, the upset it caused me, the rules about staying on school

---

* When I asked my son's permission to use this story in the book, I also asked him why, in retrospect, he thought he ran away. His answer: "You're the shrink. Don't you know little kids can't plan ahead?" Something to bear in mind.

grounds, and my expectation that he would "think" before acting. I made it clear that "leaving" school was unacceptable and that if it happened again it would result in a serious loss of privileges. By bedtime we had both regained our emotional equilibrium (which is to say I had, which meant he could as well). I read a few pages of his favorite book, as usual, cuddled a bit, and told him I loved him, and he said, "I love you back." It was a pretty undramatic ending to the day. The way most days, even the challenging ones, should end.

It's easy to romanticize childhood. To think about it as a simple and carefree time, particularly if we also have young teenagers who have turned parenting into what most often feels like an endurance test. But childhood is not easy. Children have to become disciplined students when they'd rather be free explorers (see above!). They have to welcome unknown adults and other children into their daily lives when they feel far more secure with their folks and a best friend. They have to learn how to organize themselves, make plans, sit still, attract just the right amount of attention, and learn a seemingly endless number of rules. The tasks of early childhood are demanding and complex. What are some of its greatest challenges?

LEARNING HOW TO MAKE
FRIENDS AND BE A FRIEND

Friendships in preschool tend to develop because of geographic proximity, parental direction, or happenstance. A friend is the kid who lives next door, your parent's best friend's child if he's close in age, another family member, or whatever child happens to be at the playground the same time you are. Developing friendships is rather easy—"Wanna play?" And while some friendships last, most are fleeting, with few ill effects on either child. These early friendships provide a training ground for both cooperation and companionship—"training ground" because anyone who has seen a three-year-old bop his "friend" over the head with a bucket in the sandbox, push him out of line at the sliding pond, or pocket his favorite toy knows that preschoolers have a long way to go before they can engage in the kind of thoughtful, reciprocal, and supportive relationship that we generally call "friendship." It is a necessary beginning because once children enter school they embark on one of the most important missions not only of middle childhood, but of life: the ability to cultivate and sustain reciprocal relationships.

Slightly older children are in school less than half of their waking hours and a good part of the rest of the time is devoted to the development of the personal and social skills needed to be an interesting, trusted, loyal, cooperative friend. When asked about why they've chosen a particular friend, many girls this age respond with "she really understands me." Look at the tremendous complexity involved in a seemingly ordinary exchange between two ten-year-old girls.

STELLA: I'm having trouble with handwriting and the kids in the class are teasing me about it.

ELENA: I heard what they were saying and I don't think they were very nice. I know how you feel. I'm having trouble with spelling and my parents want me to do better.

STELLA: Can you please help me? I hate it when the kids tease me, and I know you have pretty good handwriting.

ELENA: Sure, do you wanna do it at recess?

STELLA: Thanks. That'd be great. You're a really good friend to me.

ELENA: BFF?

STELLA: BFF!

We are seeing the development of emotional intelligence here—the growing ability to identify, understand, and manage emotions. Younger children simply *have* emotions; Stella and Elena are *using* their emotions to solve a problem and deepen their friendship. Elena recognizes and can communicate her internal state of distress in a way that is light-years away from the young child's limited ways of showing distress: whining, withdrawal, or temper tantrums. Her worry about how her folks will react shows that she is aware of how others feel. She also has enough insight to know which of her friends to turn to in order to help her manage her feelings. Stella can both empathize with her friend and relate to her dilemma. She is generous with her time and expertise because she knows that Elena has the capacity to return the favor. Stella and Elena end with "BFF"—a bit of code that cements the intimacy of their relationship. The depth of feeling between these two girls is palpable; they really "get" each other, and as a result Stella's mood is greatly improved.

While girls' friendships tend to be characterized by emotional disclosure and resonance, boys' friendships are characterized by physicality. They push and jostle and engage in lots of rough-and-tumble play. Both boys and girls have strict rules against fraternizing with the enemy and there is virtually no mixed play. It's unclear which sex actually has more "cooties," but what is clear is that boys find girls incomprehensible and dangerous and vice versa. This moratorium serves the function of allowing both boys and girls to solidify their identity with a minimum of confusion because they are surrounded almost exclusively by friends of the same sex.

While boys and girls may have very different ways of relating over the course of elementary school, they both gravitate to kids who are like them. The academically inclined tend to get together, as do the athletic kids, the socially skilled kids, or kids with particular interests—music, the outdoors, video games. Ethnicity also brings kids together. This is a period of time when "like me" is far more appealing than "not like me." It's tough enough to figure out who you are at this age without considering characteristics that are far afield. While we may wish our children had a broader group of friends or interests it is probably best to simply make an occasional suggestion and not push. Give them time to solidify aspects of themselves slowly.

Common Questions Parents Have About Friendships in Elementary School

"My ten-year-old daughter spends all her time with one friend. She's actually a lovely girl, but the two of them are inseparable. They spend every spare minute together and sleep over each other's houses on the weekends. I worry that she's missing out on learning how to interact with a broader group of kids? Should I be concerned?"

Probably not. A period of intense connection with a single friend is not unusual for children this age. Some kids are naturally very social. Others are content with just one or two friends and unless you see other symptoms, like depression or social phobia, then there's no need to worry about this type of relationship. These can be supportive, compatible, wonderful friendships. Sometimes they last a lifetime.

"My nine-year-old son is painfully shy. He does have a few friends, but only because they've reached out to him. I don't think he's ever made a friend by taking the initiative. What can I do to help him become more outgoing?"

Temperament plays a large role in shyness. Some kids are just "slow to warm up." They rarely, if ever, take the initiative and hold back in new social situations until they feel some sense of ease. This can be particularly trying for a sociable parent. However, unless your son's shyness is disabling then it's probably you who need to adjust, to his temperament. Since you say he does have friends, it's unlikely that there is anything to worry about. Kids who are shy need to be guided gently into new situations. You can smooth the way for your son by casually helping him prepare for a new experience, say a bowling birthday party, by preparing him for the sights and sounds and rehearsing what he might say to another child at the party.

"My eight-year-old daughter has no friends. None. She spends all her free time alone and says she is 'sad' and that 'no one likes her.' I try inviting other girls over to the house, but they rarely accept the invitation and when they do come they often want to leave early. Help!"

A child with no friends is cause for concern. Have you observed your daughter enough in social situations to have an idea of what might be causing her problem? This is best done in a relaxed and nonintrusive setting—when it's your turn to carpool or be a parent volunteer on a field trip. You need to know whether your child is actively being rejected because she is disruptive or aggressive or if she is being ignored because she doesn't "fit in" and doesn't seem to have the social skills to be interesting to other children. Some kids are slow to pick up on social nuances and conventions. They stand too close, talk too loud, or interrupt. You probably should speak with her teachers or guidance counselor since they have lots of opportunities to observe kids in different social situations. Playground monitors are another good source of information.

Once you have a better understanding of why your daughter is having so much trouble connecting with other kids, you can start discussing her role in the problem. She's already feeling inadequate, so this needs to be done gently and in a spirit of collaboration. Maybe the next time she says, "No one likes me," you can ask what she thinks she can do differently. If she's not sure, make a suggestion or two.

There are social skills groups for kids who have trouble reading social cues. These can be very helpful if you can find one in your neighborhood. Persistent sadness and isolation warrant consultation with her pediatrician and a referral to a child therapist.

"My eleven-year-old son has plenty of friends. But you should see them. Quite frankly they all look like juvenile delinquents. Their pants are sagging, their hair is straggly, and their language consists mainly of grunts and sometimes even obscenities. My son was always a good kid and I have no idea why he suddenly took up with this group of losers, but I'm afraid that his nicer friends will ostracize him. How do I get him to see that these kids are nothing but trouble? Should I just prohibit him from associating with these boys?"

Forbidding your child to be friends with these boys is likely to backfire. You have no way of enforcing your will since he spends a good part of the day away from you at school. You don't have to like these boys, and you can let your son know that, as long as you're specific about what bothers you. "You know we don't curse in this house. Please ask your friends to respect the rules. Otherwise they'll be asked to leave." A few bad words when they're horsing around in your son's room are best left unremarked.

Consider that there may be less here than meets the eye. Boys this age are starting their prepubertal journey. Experimenting with different "looks" is not unexpected. If your son feels that you're critical and unsupportive, he'll stop talking to you (as much as eleven-year-old boys are likely to talk). Try to get past the sagging pants and long locks; there is a reason why your son likes these boys. Be interested in finding out why. What we may see as troubling—peculiar haircuts, bafflingly odd clothing, daring behavior—can be particularly compelling to kids who have always walked the straight and narrow. You certainly do not have to tolerate bad behavior, but you want to reserve your authority for situations you feel are dangerous to your child or that seriously threaten family values.

Far more than hair length or pants fit, you want to know if your son's new friends are actually engaged in "deviant" behaviors. Are they failing school or experimenting with drugs? The danger with having troubled friends is that they can "train" your child in deviant behaviors. If your son's new friends are troubled, then you need a clearer idea of what is going on with your son. Is something happening in the house? Divorce? Family conflict? A new sibling? With a child at this age, fathers can be more successful at finding out what's going on through shared activities than moms can through the "talks" they are so fond of. Check out your concerns with others who know your child well: his teacher, another parent, perhaps your pediatrician. If you still feel you have cause for concern set up a meeting with the school counselor.

How Parents Can Help

For some moms there is a sense of loss now that their child is out of the house much of the day and increasingly turning to peers for companionship, support, and comfort. The secrets and confidences that once were shared between the two of you are now being shared with others, and your access to your child's internal life is becoming restricted especially toward the end of elementary school. For other mothers this is a welcome change, allowing them to concentrate more on other siblings, a career, their spouse, or themselves. For most of us it's a mixed bag. There's the drumbeat of eventual separation at the same time that we're extremely involved in our child's burgeoning desire to explore and be active. There are car pools and new schedules, clubs and teams, parties and sleepovers. Since we're handing part of our children's lives over to new people and new friends, we want to make sure that they have the skills they need to form healthy, satisfying friendships.

Think back to your own early friendships. Do you still have contact with any of those friends? Do you remember more the close parts of those relationships or the conflicted parts? Your attitudes, the pictures you pull out, the stories you tell will affect your own child's view of friendship. Share some of your positive stories with your children. Let them also know that friendship involves cooperation and sometimes even disappointment. Keep in mind that the rules, expectations, and behaviors you endorse when your children are young are being internalized and will serve as a template for how they will approach friendships now and in the future. Listen to the nine-year-old daughter of one of my colleagues.

> *It's easy to make friends unless you do not say hello.*
> *To be a friend you should not talk about them behind their*
> *back. That means, do not talk about someone when they*
> *are not with you. Don't say mean things like "You are*
> *stupid." And you should always smile when you introduce*
> *yourself. That's the number one thing. Also you should*
> *behave properly—even when you're angry. And never*
> *shout at your friend. If you're that angry, go get your*
> *mom.*

You can practically hear this young girl's mom in the background encouraging her to be friendly, not to be rude, and to get help when things are blowing up. This is exactly how kids become socialized. They have warm, supportive relationships with their parents that make them open to advice and guidance and allow them to internalize parental values. "Be nice. Say hello. Don't yell." This is Friendship 101 but assume little when it comes to emerging social skills for elementary age children. They still have a lot of learning to do.

Here are some additional points to keep in mind.

- Researchers have found that parents who use "reflective messages" with their children have kids who are more socially adept. This means that parents encourage their children to think about the impact of their actions on others as well as on themselves. "When you didn't thank grandma for her present, how do you think she felt?" When they comfort their children, they encourage them to express their feelings. Children who are parented with this emphasis are both more likely to be chosen as friends and less likely to be rejected.[1]

- Having an involved father is a strong predictor of a child's eventual level of empathy. Optimally this involvement should begin when children are starting elementary school. Moving from preschool to elementary school is a big transition for kids. Dads, who often take the lead on making the outside world enticing, appear to grease the wheels and make this transition easier. This effect is equally marked for young girls and boys alike.[2] Kids who are less preoccupied with the transition may have more energy to relate to and empathize with other children. This makes them desirable friends.

- Don't underestimate the complexity of social interactions for children. What seems like a walk in the park from an adult point of view may be absolutely terrifying for a child who is socially unsure or shy. Just walking into a new classroom involves deciding where to sit, knowing how to acknowledge other children in the room, and figuring out the social hierarchy. Don't downplay difficulties by trivializing them. "Oh, don't be ridiculous. You're just moving to the classroom next door." To your kid this can feel like moving to the other side of the world.

- Help your child find and develop "islands of competence." A musical child who feels "left out" socially at school might benefit from an after-school program focused on music, where he will meet other kids who are musically inclined and gain confidence from the recognition he gets for his efforts there.

- Remember that your family life serves as a "staging area" for your child's understanding of how people relate to each other. Warm, responsive, supportive households send out children who know how to be warm, responsive, and supportive. Harsh, dismissive, unpredictable households send out children with knowledge and practice in skills that are not conducive to friendships. Pay attention to how people speak to each other and interact in your home. Get help if you need it, especially if you feel depressed. Depression in mothers has negative consequences for many aspects of your child's life, including the ability to socialize well.

BECOMING COMPETENT AND
EXCITED ABOUT LEARNING
···

I used to watch, in rapt fascination, as my four-year-old son learned how to tie his shoelaces. Over and over he would take those two laces, turn them this way and that, wrap them around each other, tie knots, or approximate a bow that would collapse as soon as it was pulled. It took hundreds of failed attempts and yet his persistence never wavered, nor did his good humor. He never asked if he was slower or faster than his older brothers. Nor did he seem in the least distressed by the slowness of the process. He was actually indignant when I suggested maybe Velcro sneakers would be a good option (you can see who had trouble with the slowness of the process), telling me "it's important to be patient with little kids." In retrospect, these early years were the golden age of learning—self-motivated, curious, flexible, and joyful.

Think of the amazing learning accomplishments of the first few years. Crawling, standing, walking, feeding, toileting, running, catching a ball, drawing, skipping rope, hopping, climbing, getting dressed, identifying objects, learning names. There is more learned in these early years of life than any years that follow (even if you're wrapping up your PhD in aeronautics and astronautics at MIT!). Young children are positively driven to learn and because they are unencumbered by fear of failure, comparison with others, or notions about being more or less "smart," they approach learning with zest and an unshakable belief in their capability to master challenges. Once they get the hang of something, they are quite satisfied with themselves and think they've done a good job, no matter how lopsided the bow or if their shirt is on backward. *Until they enter elementary school most youngsters are motivated by the challenge itself, not by stars or grades or rewards. This is called mastery motivation and is the form of learning most likely to lead to both engagement and persistence, and ultimately to expertise.*

So what happens to our ecstatic young learner in the years between preschool and middle and high school? To begin with, there is a radical shift in thinking that begins around age seven. Early in elementary school, children come into a whole new mind, one that has the capacity to think logically, realistically, and strategically. This shift happens so dramatically and so consistently to children all around the world that it is often termed a "cognitive revolution." It allows children to tackle all kinds of problems that were beyond their reach just a year or two earlier. They can classify categories accurately—hence the single-minded attention to sorting and arranging baseball cards, rocks, or Barbie accessories. They are leaving the magical world of preschool behind as they become increasingly adept at distinguishing reality from fantasy. They understand symbols, so that math and reading advances become the portals to other academic skills. They have a greater understanding of what's important and what they need to pay attention to, and they can develop strategies for memorizing important information.

So it would seem that all of these additional abilities would just add to the excitement about learning. Yet while most children maintain enthusiasm in the first few years of elementary school, there is a precipitous falloff in both excitement about and engagement with learning as kids approach the end of the elementary school years. Why?

Learning stops being fun:

Young children learn in ways that are primarily *fun*. "Where is your nose?" "What sound does a doggie make?" Life is a constant pop quiz for young kids and they don't get F's for pointing to their eyes instead of their noses or saying "Moo" instead of "Woof." They're more likely to get a laugh, a gentle correction, and encouragement to try again. There's very little work involved in keeping curiosity alive in children.

Kids begin to compare themselves with each other:
Young kids are too busy learning, too egocentric to care much about how they "stack up" to the kid next to them, and they overestimate their competence. While their positivity may seem unwarranted, it helps them infuse learning with enthusiasm and optimism. Starting at about age eight, kids begin to compare themselves with others in earnest. This is because they can now classify, sequence, and observe similarities and differences. Kids no longer see themselves as "the best" or "the greatest." They are now forging a sense of self that is more realistic, but also more vulnerable.

They suffer the negative effects of
excessive standardized testing:
All kids have to master material in order to continue to move forward in school and eventually out in the world. But our current system of standardized testing looks at only a limited number of skills, primarily math and English, and as a result, much in-class time is taken up preparing students for assessment on these two categories alone, cutting significantly into the class time needed to introduce other content and to develop critical thinking skills. It is primarily rote memorization that is tested and not the far more important and complex skills needed for difficult problem solving. School budgets depend on kids scoring well but this preoccupation has communicated an unfortunate message about learning and metrics. "No matter where your talents, capacities, and interests may lie, if it can't be easily measured, we're not interested." Physical education, music, arts, theater—all these programs have been cut or radically reduced as a result. Most worrisome is that the ability to think critically is being neglected and therefore has eroded. No wonder that researchers find a steady dropoff in engagement with learning (75 percent of kids say that they are "disengaged" with learning—that

is, they are "going through the motions" without enthusiasm or real interest) as our kids move through our education system.[3]

What Does It Mean to Be "Smart"?

There are two ways to think about intelligence. Carol Dweck, one of the country's leading researchers on how intelligence is conceptualized, calls these two different points of view "fixed" and "growth" mind-sets. A fixed mind-set is assumed not to be amenable to modification. Either you were born "smart" or not. The other way to think about intelligence is that you "get smart" at something because you work hard at it. In the growth mind-set, intelligence can be developed.[4] The enthusiasm of the very young child came about partly because of his self-centeredness, partly because no one was categorizing or measuring him, and partly because learning was predictably fun and rewarding. We were so thrilled with every advance our toddler made that we were not standing on the sidelines criticizing: "What, you fell down again? Can't you do anything right?" but rather waiting at the finish line to swoop him up when he took his first steps, declaring, "Yay! That was terrific, big boy!" Young children have faith in their ability to master a new task by sheer persistence. In fact, we can all master a surprisingly wide array of problems, tasks, and materials by putting in the time, effort, and practice.

This doesn't mean that anybody can do anything. We also have a genetic inheritance. But it does mean that we can do so much more than is readily apparent, particularly if we feel that our strengths are of value. Of course, there are kids who can do multiple things well. Who can play an instrument and field a fly ball. Who write for the school paper and build bicycles. Who ace their tests but are happiest at the piano. But many kids have valuable talents that we are too quick to dismiss, often because they are hard to quantify. The child who has little interest in or capacity for visual spatial learning but has a real knack for understanding and getting along with people, given encouragement and the sense that his skill is of value, can become competent, even expert, in a whole range of fields. He might not become an engineer. Perhaps he'll become a businessman, a psychologist, or a lawyer. He's certain to be a good friend and a terrific dad. But if his interpersonal skills go unrecognized or are dismissed ("Yeah, he's quite a talker, but that won't get him into college"), he's likely to become discouraged and less apt to pursue the very thing that might yield great satisfaction. Cultivating authentic success means that we readily and happily recognize our children's strengths and let them know that these strengths are genuinely valued and valuable. You can't fake this. You may have dreamed of having a doctor in the family but your child's talents and interests may be far afield of the sciences. Allow her to grow into her strengths and dreams.

I have yet to find a healthy child whose interests are dead ends. The kid in my neighborhood who seemed oddly obsessed with plants as a youngster is now a professor of plant biology, specializing in ferns, at one of the leading universities in this country. The child who didn't much like school but loved imaginative play and constantly had his "characters" speak became the voice of one of Pixar's best-loved characters. These are vivid examples, but of equal importance are the many kids who pursued their interests, idiosyncratic or not, and ended up being happy with their work. Unfortunately, we are knocking both the potential and the spark out of far too many of our kids when we insist that only a narrow range of skills and interest are valuable. Here are two things to pay attention to:

The difference between performance and mastery

- Children who are interested only in performance, that is, being positively evaluated by others, have narrow goals. Their focus is on the grade more than the material. They are so afraid of failing that they challenge themselves far less, take fewer risks, and therefore limit opportunities for growth. They are also at risk for perfectionism, a well-documented precursor of depression.

On the other hand, mastery-oriented kids are in it for the learning experience. They are internally driven to succeed. They relish challenge, and getting recognition is a distant second to their own pleasure in their efforts and accomplishments. Interestingly, when work is not challenging, kids in these two categories achieve at pretty much the same level. However, when difficult material presents itself, the performance-oriented kids do poorly, while the mastery-oriented kids do well. The best way we can help our children welcome challenges is to encourage them to work just outside their comfort zone, stand by to lend a hand when needed, and model enthusiasm for challenging tasks.

Intelligence comes in different forms

- The most highly regarded researchers in the field of education agree that there is little value in thinking about intelligence as a single, static entity, whether it's Howard Gardner's concept of multiple intelligences (logical, verbal, interpersonal, kinesthetic, visual/spatial, existential, intrapersonal, naturalist, and musical), Robert Sternberg's theory of triarchic intelligence (analytic, creative, practical), Peter Salovey and John Mayer's emphasis on emotional competence, or Carol Dweck's concept of fixed versus growth mind-sets. At any given Mensa meeting of extremely high-IQ individuals you will find professors, surgeons, researchers, engineers, cops, firefighters, cooks, cabdrivers, and waitresses. We've all known people who seem really bright but who have floundered in their careers and others who seemed rather ordinary but have become wildly successful. In fact, conventional IQ tests predict only about 10 percent of the reasons why your child will be successful in school and the workplace.[5] There are plenty of books and enrichment programs that focus on that small contribution; this book is focused on the other 90 percent.

How Parents Can Help

When your child says, "Grace is really smart," your response needs to be "In what way?" From the beginning it helps our children to know that there are many ways to be smart, many ways to be successful, and many ways to lead productive, meaningful lives. Here are some other ways that parents can encourage their child's intellectual development.

STAY CURIOUS WITH YOUR CHILD

For your child the world is a miraculous place. Sit with her while she watches the clear liquid you poured into the bathtub turn into a burst of colored bubbles that dance and disappear with her slightest breath. We can recapture some of our lost sense of wonder by seeing what has become ordinary through the fresh eyes of our children. Resist hurrying your child through fascination. Don't dictate what is valuable and what isn't. Try not to squeal at bugs. Your child is both awakening to the world and becoming a trained observer. Curiosity and observation are at the heart of learning.

ENCOURAGE QUESTIONS

We are so trained to respond to the "right answer" that we forget that it's the "right question" that has the most potential for learning. Many leading educators and psychologists believe that it is the ability to ask good questions that characterizes both intelligence and creativity.[6] Children are prolific question askers. This helps them to understand and navigate their way through a world that they understand only meagerly. "Where does the sun go at night?" "Why can't I sleep outside?" "Where does God live?" "Why can't I have ice cream for dinner?" The fastest way to gather the endless amount of information that kids need to understand and manage themselves and the world around them is to ask adults. Our job is twofold:

- To provide answers

- To help children learn the process by which they can answer their own questions

Imagine needing outside help many, many times every day, whether it's to figure out how to satisfy a basic need ("Mom, where's the bathroom in this restaurant?"), how to solve a social problem ("Mom, Rachel never does her homework and she always wants to copy mine. What should I do?"), or how to complete a homework assignment ("I don't understand fractions. Can you help me?").

How we answer our children's questions plays an important part in encouraging their curiosity and advancing their critical thinking. Let's also be realistic about the fact that no parents can always provide optimal answers to their children's questions. We have many demands on us over the course of the day and there are bound to be times when the best we can muster is "I don't know. Let's talk about it later" and the worst is "Stop asking so many questions." None of us will be exemplary at all times.

Let's take the copied-homework question. What's the best approach to take? While this looks like a simple question about Rachel's impropriety, it is about much more. Your daughter is dealing with a social problem, an integrity issue, and an identity issue, at a minimum. You might be tempted to tell her to "figure it out," but she can't; she needs adult input to make sense of her experience.

You could say, "Tell Rachel to stop it," but you really need to help her look at the broader issues of friendship and trust so that she can think about the many permutations this question will have in the future—someone copying on an exam, not returning her blouse, or stealing her boyfriend.

The best approach is to brainstorm with your daughter by asking her clarifying questions. Does Rachel cheat often, is something going on with her at home, does she understand what's going on in the classroom? Encourage your daughter to come up with possible explanations and possible solutions, and offer one or two if she's stuck (tell the teacher, offer to help Rachel understand the assignment, stop being friends with Rachel). Help your daughter evaluate the consequences of her ideas. "What would it be like if you and Rachel weren't friends anymore?" "What might happen if you tell the teacher?"

If you can respond along these lines, then you've given your daughter the skills required to answer any complex social, personal, or academic question. Your message to her is that her questions are valuable, that actions have consequences, that friendships have limitations, and that a collaborative approach to everyday problem solving can be most productive.

VALUE ACADEMIC RISK TAKING

Kids who are more willing to take academic risks do better on tests, are more engaged in learning, and are more interested in taking on increasingly challenging intellectual problems. It can be hard to imagine "academic risk taking" for our eight-year-old. But this is exactly when kids are endlessly interested in why things are the way they are. Risk taking at this stage often involves focusing on the questions rather than the answers. Most kids can do rote memorization, but if they come to see this as the best way to learn, we have taken away the driver of lifelong learning—real curiosity, persistence, and engagement with the material. It isn't enough to simply be able to classify living and nonliving things as taught in a third-grade science curriculum; the engaged learner will have many more questions.

Taking some academic risks is also important because it provides opportunities for developing perseverance and resilience. Kids who are told that their answer is "wrong" will react quite differently from kids who are met with "Interesting answer. How'd you come up with that?" This is not an endorsement for giving kids A's when in reality they've flunked a test. But mastering content is the easier part of learning. What we really need to attend to with elementary age children is keeping their interest alive and helping them figure out multiple approaches to thinking about content. It is the ability to creatively and enthusiastically persist in the face of difficult problems that is the hallmark of our most talented students.

GET YOUR CHILD OUT INTO NATURE

The natural world is probably a child's favorite classroom. Our preoccupation with danger has deprived our children of what have traditionally been some of the most nurturing and instructive experiences of childhood. Young children learn through their senses. They love to walk through mud, water, or puddles not because they enjoy making you cart out the vacuum cleaner one more time, but because this is how they most easily and enthusiastically take in information.

Children have a natural affinity for nature. In psychological testing we expect children under the age of seven or so to populate their drawings more with animals than with people. There are few things more tender than the young child who brings home a bird with a broken wing and nurses it back to health. The natural world offers unparalleled opportunities for developing our children's powers of observation, compassion, self-esteem, and self-reliance. Try to conjure up the "secret" place you retreated to when you were distressed as a youngster. For me it was an oak tree, for my two oldest sons it was the brambly lot behind our house, and for my youngest it was the neighborhood creek. Nature nourishes our children's minds and spirits and generally moves at the slow pace that children are most comfortable with. Just watch a couple of kids spend hours at the water's edge—looking, skipping an occasional stone, or picking their heads up as a flock of geese passes by. No child is better off in front of a computer or practicing the times tables. Childhood is precious. It is not preparation for high school, college, or a profession but a brief and irreplaceable period of time when children are entitled to the privilege of being children.

DEVELOPING A SENSE OF SELF: WHO AM I?

All children think about themselves, but changes in thinking shift dramatically as they grow up.

> *Four-year-old*—*"I'm the best singer."*
> *Nine-year-old*—*"I sing well, but not as well as my friend Amy. She's really good."*
> *Fifteen-year-old*—*"I can sing, but I'll never make it to Carnegie Hall. That's okay, singing's fun, but math and science are really my thing."*

The young child is exuberant and positive, not necessarily tied to reality, and too egocentric to compare herself with anyone else.

The middle-age child, who is now logical and grounded in reality, can reflect on her ability and compare it with another child's ability usually one dimension at a time. Adolescents can think in complex, abstract, and mostly adultlike ways. While beginning elementary school children still have miles to go before constructing a realistic, multifaceted, and solid sense of self, they have begun the journey.

By the end of elementary school, most kids have a reliable sense of self and self-worth. "School's okay, but I prefer hanging out with my friends. I worry a little about how I'll do in middle school, but when I need to buckle down I usually can. I'm pretty good with challenges. But mostly I feel that I'm a good friend and a good person." This ten-year-old girl is well into developing a sense of self that she feels good about. She has perspective on that self, is aware of her strengths and weaknesses, and has high, appropriate self-esteem. Her coping skills are deepening and expanding to include self-reliance, realistic self-esteem, a work ethic, and self-efficacy.

One of the most unhealthy outcomes of our current preoccupation with having "exceptional" children is that it is very difficult to maintain a consistently positive sense of self when you are expected to be exceptional at all things. Listen to how different these two nine-year-old girls sound:

TAYLOR: Jeez, I got a C again in math. My parents aren't going to like it. But I tried my best. Math is really hard for me. I'm really smart in most of my classes, especially English and history. I guess it's not so bad. Overall, I'm pretty smart. I'll just have to work a little harder in math. Doesn't matter that much because I want to be a journalist not a computer programmer when I grow up.

GRACE: I can't believe I got a C again in math. I studied half the night. My dad says that math and science are the most important subjects. Yeah, I'm good in English, but he says that won't count for much when I go to college. I'm such an idiot. I might as well give up.

Taylor is able to see her strengths and weaknesses. This ability to hold contradictory opinions about oneself is a critical part of developing a comfortable and robust sense of self. Younger kids see themselves as either "all good" or "all bad." As our children grow they increasingly understand that being a person is a complex business and that, internally, they have to make room for many different points of view about themselves. While both Taylor and Grace are critical about themselves, Taylor's acknowledgment of a weakness doesn't affect her self-esteem, because *she* does not place particular importance on math. Grace doesn't distinguish between what matters to her and what matters to others. As a result, she's vulnerable to outside criticism, seriously affecting her self-esteem and sense of self. There's a hint of why they rely differently on outsiders in the way they describe their parents' reactions. Both Taylor and Grace will need to develop adequate math skills. It's just a lot easier to meet any challenge when you don't feel like a loser.

The "self" that children develop over the elementary school years is the outcome of many factors: temperament, cognitive advances, emotional growth, peer relationships, opportunities to advance competency in all of these areas, and a supportive family environment. Parents need to be tuned in to the delicacy and vulnerability of their child's emerging sense of self. Remember that every opportunity for growth and advancement also carries the potential for relapse and disappointment. Development can be quite uneven over the elementary school years, with kids zooming ahead in one area and having difficulty in another. This is normal.

Ultimately, we all want our children to have a sense of self that is vital, grounded, realistic, generous, and nourishing. We help them develop this self when we set appropriate expectations and limits, encourage them to push themselves a bit, make clear that we will be accepting and nonjudgmental when they need our guidance, and underscore our unconditional love.

How Parents Can Help

Elementary school age children have significant cognitive limitations on how they can think about their "selves." In the early years of elementary school, they do not yet have the capacity to be either introspective or self-reflective. Asking a six-year-old to think about why he ate most of the cookies you prepared for the school bake sale is likely to be met with the explanation "They were just sitting on the counter." Young kids certainly are curious. But they are primarily curious about the outside world, which they scrutinize like scientists. Their internal world is of little interest to them. That is, until they realize that this inside world is of great interest to you. Here is where the construction of the self begins in earnest. You care about feelings and thoughts, accomplishments and infractions, and as a result your child will come to care about these things. Your children's selves develop in the crucible of their impulses and your evaluations and responses.

Your ability to be clear about what is and is not acceptable behavior is one of the most critical ways in which your child constructs a self that is in line with your family's values. You can't get your young child to think through consequences and reflect on values, but you can act as a surrogate for these more advanced ways of thinking by using reinforcement, discipline, direct instruction, and modeling. The endless discussion with young children about why they behaved this way or that is, in general, a waste of time. Your youngster steals a candy bar from the corner grocery because he wants it. Your job is to let him know that this is unacceptable and to march him back to the store to either return or pay for the candy bar. Of course you're telling him why stealing in unacceptable. But what he's really picking up on is your distress. Gradually, and in large part to avoid your distress, he will internalize your rules and they will become his own.

Our willingness to take a stand about what matters to us helps our children develop a "story" about who they are. If every time your child is nice you notice and praise him, and if every time he is sneaky or mean you discipline him, then your value system will become clear. Parents help their child's growing sense of self by providing a general narrative about how much they value their child and a specific narrative about the qualities and behaviors that are most admired. In part, this is the function of having family pictures around the house, making videos of family vacations, and instituting family rituals. "See how you could walk when you were only eleven months. Always a go-getter." Or "Remember when we went on vacation and your sister was really afraid of the water and you helped her get used to it? What a great big brother." This is how children come to forge a sense of self that is weighted toward their particular strengths and is in line with family values.

BECOMING AN EMPATHIC PERSON

Would you rather your child was smart or good?

My übersharp colleague Denise Pope poses this question often when she talks to groups of parents. When I first heard it, I thought, "Oh, come on. How smart? How good?" I found every reason not to answer the question. It wasn't specific enough. It was silly. It was hypothetical. I'd drum up the most enigmatic scenarios—what if the child is smart enough to end world hunger but is a serial killer—all to avoid confronting the wise heart of her question. What do we value most?

On a perfectly ordinary day, I got a call from my youngest son's calculus teacher. "I'm sure you know this, but I just wanted to call and let you know what a really nice kid Jeremy is. I swear he doesn't have a single mean bone in his body. He's kind to everyone." The calculus teacher? I knew my son was barely passing calculus. But his teacher didn't have a word to say about his work, only about his character. Of all the calls and conversations I've had in more than twenty-eight years of raising three sons, this remains the sweetest call of all. The call that tells me I've done the job that matters most to me. The call that finally allowed me to answer Denise Pope's question. Sure, I want my kids to be smart, but more than anything it matters to me that they are good people. That their "mean bones" are few and far between. That they are kind.

I also realized that there was a real difference in how much more effort most of us put into "smart" as opposed to "good." We watch our kids' academic progress closely (sometimes hawkishly), we read progress reports, troll standardized testing percentiles, meet with teachers, find academic enrichment programs, and hire tutors when necessary. However, our children are not evaluated on their "goodness." We don't seek out special experiences designed to encourage "goodness" (sending your child to build a water treatment plant in some developing country in a few years in order to beef up her résumé doesn't count) and I've yet to hear of tutors hired to raise a child's character.

Still, all of us want our children to be good people. We want them to be kind and caring, to be able to communicate their concern about others, and to value honesty and integrity. We want our children to be intolerant of bullying, involve themselves in good causes, question unfair treatment, and generally behave in ways that consider the needs of others as well as their own. We know that being kind and empathic will stand them in good stead in their friendships and their intimate relationships and eventually out in the work world. In order to have kindness, compassion, and empathy be part of our children's selves we have to put as much effort (I would suggest more) into strengthening those qualities in our children and modeling them in our homes as we do into issues of academic or athletic performance. Emphasizing goodness should be a daily exercise for us as we "catch" our children being good at small things—sharing a cookie with a friend, helping a younger sibling with a math problem. It is the expectation of good behavior and the rewarding of it in its minor forms that accumulate and turn our children into good people.

Many of the ways we can encourage our child's academic proficiency are reasonably straightforward. Know your child's interests and capacities, underscore the importance of effort and improvement, and applaud deep learning, not superficial performance. But how do we know whether our children have greater or lesser capacities for empathy and how do we help them hone these skills? The explosion of bullying that is taking place in elementary school, with three-quarters of students saying it is a problem and a third of students being victims, suggests that with all of our oversight we have not been as successful in teaching basic human values as basic academic skills.[7] Empathy in even young children is highly associated with being able to make friends, being popular with peers, being more likable, and being seen as particularly competent by teachers.[8] While experts on child development often call the years between five and eleven "the school years," they are also the years in which the foundation of character is laid down. This happens both in and out of school, and is a critical component of both childhood and ultimately of the type of person your child becomes. Let's look at some of the ways that we can help our children develop their capacity for empathy.

How Parents Can Help

A girlfriend is driving in the car with her ten-year-old when I call to find out from her son what the insult of the day is at his school. My boys are older and some of the insults I remember so well have taken on a new cast. *Geek*, which used to be a searing insult, is now a cross between a popular television show and the possibility of being named *Time* magazine's Person of the Year. The sting is gone. But I live across the street from a middle school and a couple of blocks away from an elementary school and know that taunts and bad language are still rampant. Yet my son's friend can't come up with a single "bad" word. Not because his mom's in the car with him, but because he simply doesn't know any. With some encouragement, the worst he can come up with is "idiot." He says that in his school, which he describes as "bully-free," any and all infractions of this policy are referred to the principal.

This young boy goes to an outstanding Jewish day school. The school has an active antibullying program, a strong emphasis on character as well as academic achievement (as do many parochial schools), and parents who I suspect struggled less with the "smart/good" question than I did. They have many areas of social commitment in their own lives, a strong grounding in religious faith, and a belief that what you model in your home is what your children will come to internalize. They are unequivocally committed to making sure that their children are as well educated in matters of character as they are in matters of math or science. They keep the bar high, whether it's figuring out who gets invited to a birthday party or how much effort goes into a history report.

Character is the end result of many things, including genetics, temperament, opportunity, and parenting. No one has been able to assign relative values to these components. But parenting is the one we have control over so here are some well-researched ideas about what you can do to encourage the development of empathy in your child.

POINT OUT THE EFFECTS OF YOUR CHILD'S BEHAVIOR ON OTHERS

As you wait in the courtyard to pick up your eight-year-old from school, you hear him taunting one of his best friends. "No wonder you always get picked last. You're such a spaz. Even I wouldn't pick you to be on my team." Mortified, you hustle your son into the car and in exasperation demand, "What's the matter with you? James is one of your best friends." Your son looks back at you with something resembling blind incomprehension.

While none of us like to hear our kids being cruel, there are reasons for your young son's lack of tact and you're in the perfect position to educate him. Children are naturally self-centered. If a friend, even a good friend, blows a catch on the ball field, then he's fair game for humiliation. Why? Because young children have difficulty standing in the shoes of other kids. Often the best they can do is stand in their own shoes. And their own shoes tell them just that they're not about to win the game, because someone else bobbled the ball. Kids learn how to be empathic because we *teach* them how to be empathic. We can't ask enough "How would you feel if . . ." Empathy is a skill like any other. We need to provide opportunities for our children to practice it and we need to "catch" them being good at it. At this age, your being proud of your children's behavior is typically motivation enough for them to become kinder.

TALK ABOUT MORAL ISSUES

One of the many reasons that it's important to have dinner with your child most nights of the week is that this is a great time to discuss issues. Research shows that parents who encourage their kids to think about how people feel in different situations help kids become more empathic and more moral. Hopefully a good moral compass is a strong part of your life. Talking about good morals regularly and seriously lets your kids know that you think this is an important part of life, a part they should pay attention to. These kinds of discussions are most helpful when they relate directly to your child's life. At this age, talking about the responsibility of Wall Street is nowhere near as compelling as talking about the responsibility of the kid who copied your child's answers on his math test. Supportive, back-and-forth discussions and encouraging your child's independent thinking are the best approach.[9] Simply providing information or lecturing is far less effective.

PROVIDE PLENTY OF OPPORTUNITIES FOR YOUR CHILD TO PRACTICE EMPATHIC BEHAVIOR

Whenever practical, take your child with you when you're involved in community service. Donating or sorting clothes, cooking or delivering meals, visiting the elderly or the needy are all opportunities for your children to learn that thinking past their own needs is a good and expected part of life. It also helps them to feel competent. Kids want to be like their parents—whether that's a two-year-old singing to her "baby," or a ten-year-old teaching a younger child how to swing a bat. Ultimately these children turn into young adults who are more likely to be committed to social justice and to work for worthy causes. Not surprisingly, these young adults report having parents who were "excellent" models of prosocial behavior and who frequently included their children in related discussions and activities.[10]

REMEMBERING TO PLAY

Play is the most efficient driver of learning for children. This is as true of their cognitive development as their physical and emotional development. As a matter of fact, it is so essential for healthy child development that it has been recognized by the United Nations as being a *right* of every child.[11] Certainly younger elementary school children seem to have more time to play than their older counterparts. But play has ceased to be a major activity of childhood as the demands of academics, extracurricular activities, and technology increasingly impinge on playtime. In many schools, even recess has been eliminated. As one misguided superintendent proclaimed, "We are intent on improving academic performance and you don't do that by having kids hang on monkey bars."[12] Ouch! Aside from being wrong on multiple levels—physical, emotional, and social—it is mostly wrong because children are entitled to a childhood. In our highly educated, highly industrialized, highly resourced country, to essentially say that in order to "keep up" we need to ignore one of the most important contributors to children's well-being shows a profound misunderstanding of the basics of child development. Every stage in life proceeds on the reasonable completion of the stage before. Development is a scaffold, with kids getting to the next rung because they've successfully climbed the previous one. Kids crawl, then stand, then walk, then run.

Seven-year-olds Tyler and John are playing "chase" on the playground during recess. While this may look simply like a good way to burn off energy and calories—which alone is enough to recommend it—it is also a highly sophisticated social transaction. In order for the game to continue, each boy has to be willing to be both the chaser and the chased. In other words, both boys have to be willing to cooperate in order to participate in this game. Chase is a reciprocal activity and ends the moment one of the boys stops reciprocating. This ability to play reciprocally is a powerful predictor of academic success, as is the ability to empathize and cooperate.[13] Boys need plenty of rough-and-tumble play because it has been shown to help them manage aggression. You can wrestle with your friend, but if you beat him to a pulp, then he will most certainly not be up for wrestling with you again. A boy who learns to manage his aggression in play comes to feel that he is "a good friend" and "fun to fool around with." This is just one of many ways that play functions to help our children define themselves.

Over the last twenty years, kids have lost close to two hours of play every day, most of that unstructured play. And it is unstructured play that provides the greatest opportunities for kids to be curious, creative, spontaneous, and collaborative. In unstructured play, kids have to negotiate, they have to figure out how to settle differences, they have to cooperate, make the rules, and most important, learn how to "play by the rules." Unstructured play, which should be part of every child's life on a daily basis, lays the groundwork for social competence. The reasons for the decline in play are not surprising. What is surprising is that parents who are consistently vigilant about helping their children "achieve" are neglecting perhaps the most effective ways to advance achievement. After all, it is unstructured play that stimulates imagination, and it is imagination that is the underpinning of creativity, and, ultimately, innovation. Taken together, these are the exact skills most likely to be sought after in the twenty-first-century global economy.

Why We Have Downgraded the Importance of Play

- We hesitate to interfere with our kids' preoccupation with a dazzling array of technology. While most of us are comfortable limiting some screen time, particularly television time, we are far more reluctant to limit screen time that we see as "productive" computer time. Parents are afraid that their kids won't be able to keep up with other digital natives, and see curtailing use as hampering potential. Certainly there's a difference between playing Angry Birds and creating a family montage on the computer. But both take time away from unstructured play.

- So much seems to be riding on these early years that parents don't want to waste any time on something that is not educational. The outdoors, which is free, is rarely considered a learning environment. But in fact, it is one of the most important learning environments available to our children. "Go out and play" may have gotten us out of our own mothers' hair, but it also encouraged us to figure out how to socialize with our own "tribe" as well as how to appreciate the natural world. No educational toy in the world can hold a candle to creek walks and abandoned lot expeditions. I don't remember much about third or fourth grade, but I do remember meeting my best friend, Leslie, after school every day and walking home together, stopping off at the corner grocery for red pistachios that stained our fingers, and eating them under the tangled brush in the neglected lot behind our houses as we dreamt about the people we hoped to become.

- We have forgotten how to play ourselves. How can we communicate that play is a necessary part of a good life if it's missing from our own? Most of us are too rushed and overwhelmed, too busy multitasking and chauffeuring, to find any "playtime" for ourselves.

A harried young mom who is also a pediatric oncologist is in my office falling apart because of the multiple demands on her time and energy. All of the options we are talking about are logistical. How many hours can she effectively work? When will her two kids be old enough for her to return to work on a full-time basis? Can her husband be recruited to take responsibility for some of the children's extracurricular activities? I feel like we should put poster board on my office walls so that we can draw a flow chart. It hits me that no one can be expected to spend every minute of every day attending to the needs of others. This is why so many of the mothers I have seen over the years have taken to private guilty pleasures, from cocaine to alcohol to overeating; these things could be done quickly and took little time out of an overscheduled day.

Experts recommend two hours of unstructured play for every hour of structured play. While your child is playing take half that time for your own play—a craft project, a good novel (or a bad one), looking at catalogs, sitting outside, dancing. If the very idea of "playing" as an adult confuses you, think back to your own childhood and the things that you spent time on and enjoyed doing. Try them again. As with everything else about children's behavior, there's nothing like a good role model. If you value play, your child will, too.

How Parents Can Help

UNPLUG

Limit the amount of time your children are allowed to sit in front of a screen. In elementary school, this probably should be no more than two hours a day, which includes all screens: TV, video games, computers, smartphones, tablets, and whatever other electronic device your child may be looking at by the time you read this book.

ENCOURAGE YOUR CHILD TO PLAY OUTSIDE

Introduce freedom gradually. If you're in a safe neighborhood, your children should be outside playing (without you hovering nearby) around age nine if they've demonstrated an adequate capacity to be responsible. If they come when called, follow directions, and cross a street safely then they are probably quite capable of navigating the neighborhood. If you're nervous, have a chat with a local police officer, who can give you an objective view of the dangers of your neighborhood. Many parents don't feel comfortable giving their kids permission to simply hang out in the neighborhood until about age thirteen. To put this in perspective, the average teenager in America has sexual intercourse at age seventeen. Let's be real. Our kids need more than four years between crossing the street and putting on a condom.

STAY AWAY FROM "EDUCATIONAL" TOYS

They're not.

DON'T OVERPROGRAM YOUR CHILD

Understandably, extracurriculars are a good way to broaden our kids' experiences and make sure that they have structure after school, especially when both parents are working. But David Elkind, the godfather (well, actually the maven) of healthy child development, says that children of this age should, *at most*, have three extracurricular activities—one social (Scouting, church or synagogue youth program), one physical (Little League, dance), and one artistic (piano lessons, drawing). Playing MLB 12: The Show on a Sony PlayStation does not count as a physical activity. At this stage, extracurriculars, for the most part, are not daily activities.

Kids who are overprogrammed often show signs of stress, particularly physical signs like headaches and stomachaches. If your child is complaining of these kinds of symptoms, have him checked by your pediatrician. If all is well, take a close look at his schedule and, with your child, whittle it down. One way to do this is to ask him to rank the importance of his activities. You may find that the soccer team you thought he loved is way down on his list. Keep his top two and suspend the rest.

GENERAL RECOMMENDATIONS FOR PARENTING YOUR ELEMENTARY SCHOOL AGE CHILD

Pay attention to the ways in which your child is critical of himself:

"Chris doesn't like me" is very different from "Everybody hates me." Kids this age can move quickly from observing specific deficits to making global conclusions about their own worth. This can be particularly notable when a child has a learning deficit or attentional problems. If your child is reasonably specific in his self-criticism—"Math is hard," or "I make too many mistakes when I read," or "I always get picked last"—the first order of business is to assess whether he is being realistic. An occasional critical comment is nothing to worry about. Kids can be dramatic. Remind your child that few people are equally good at all endeavors. Emphasize his strengths. Teach patience. If you're uncertain, ask his teacher if his observations are accurate or his expectations are unrealistic. If he's accurate, then ask the teacher for suggestions. Maybe he needs a bit more work at home, or some time set aside with a teacher or tutor after school, until he's caught up.

Kids who have reached global conclusions about their lack of worth need a different kind of intervention. Once kids feel bad about themselves, it can be very tough to change their point of view. Typically, when kids reach this kind of conclusion, they need more than a parent reminding them of their strengths. While this is a place to start helping your child have a more realistic view, it is likely that some work with a therapist is the fastest way to get your child back on track. Having a child who believes that he is worthless is a red flag.

Do not compare your child's achievements with those of other children:

Kids this age are making comparisons in earnest and they make them about everything, most especially academic performance, athletic ability, and popularity. This opens the door for a few high-performing kids to feel really good and many more to feel bad. Teachers and parents both intentionally and unintentionally make comparisons between a child and classmates, siblings, peers, and other family members. "Your sister got all A's, why can't you?" "If you don't keep up in math, you and your best friend, Dylan, won't be in the same math group anymore." "Emma and Jessica seem to have such nice friends. Couldn't you try a little harder to be friend-lier?" While these kinds of comparisons are hurtful, kids often say they feel the worst when their parents "look" disappointed, angry, or sad. Kids are exquisitely tuned to their parents' emotions and if you're disappointed that your child can't hit a ball, wasn't invited to the popular girl's sleepover, or isn't in the top reading group then your "look" is enough to tell them that they don't measure up. When you've just begun the process of learning a world of new things, the best medicine is encouragement. Applaud effort and improvement. And while it's fine to acknowledge that another child excels at something, let your own children know that you love them whether they bat first, fourth, or last.

Don't pigeonhole your child:

Children are meant to explore. One of the most disturbing trends in child rearing is early specialization. This prematurely cuts off options for children. It can be very seductive to have your athletically talented youngster join the traveling team at age eight. But it also means that you will be spending every weekend in transit (and in too many musty motels to count) while your child never gets to find out if he's also musically inclined, an avid naturalist, or a budding artist. Even when my kids were older, and had clear interests and talents, they railed against being categorized. My middle son, Michael, who has been a theater rat for most of his life, didn't like my frequent description of him as the "creative child." In one of those not uncommon moments, when our children are our teachers and not vice versa, he said to me, "If I'm the 'creative' child then I can't be the 'smart' child or the 'practical' child. But I'm all those things and more. I'm me. Drop the labels, Mom."

Think about the labels you were given in your own family. Were you the good girl, the difficult child, the kind one, the mean one, the pretty one, or the responsible one? Think about how those labels affected your sense of self not only as a child but as an adult. A patient of mine was the "selfish" child in her household mainly because her needy and dependent mother interpreted her moves toward independence as selfishness. "How can you be so selfish and go out with friends when you know I'll be home alone?" As an adult, this woman practically devoted her life to "proving" that she wasn't selfish. She bought gifts for family and friends that were well beyond her means, worked overtime doing community service, was the go-to person when her friends had difficulty, and denied herself even small indulgences. In spite of it all, she still felt selfish and came to see me when she found herself holed up in the back of her car treating herself to an ice cream sundae, terrified that someone would spot her "being selfish." Labels stick.

* * *

The elementary school years are characterized by a sense of wonder both for parents and for their children. Children who just yesterday grabbed our hand for help with the slightest tasks are now aching to try their own hand. While we are still front and center in the lives of our elementary school children, the writing is on the wall and we know that the direction they are moving in is toward separation, independence, and the creation of their unique selves. We have been fortunate to witness their initial launch and hopefully have come to know our children in the kinds of profound ways that will sustain them, and us, as we move into the rockier years of middle school.

· CHAPTER 4 ·

The Tasks of the
Middle School Years

Ages 11–14

Is there a parent alive who hasn't felt blindsided by the rapid, unexpected changes in his or her child who entered middle school as a loving youngster only to be turned, seemingly overnight, into a prickly, if not downright nasty, preadolescent? Most of us are prepared for the ups and downs of high school. It's part of our culture's lore that teens are a handful. But when your twelve-year-old demands privacy while she's on the Internet, insists on wearing tank tops that skim the top of her newly defined breasts, and rolls her eyes when you suggest a visit to Grandma and Grandpa, most of us wonder where we've gone wrong. We haven't. But neither have we shown the interest and enthusiasm for understanding this stage of development in the same way that we have when our children were younger or even older.

Middle schoolers are not as cute as children or as fascinating as teens. They are gangly, acne-stricken, often sullen and intensely private, pubertal creatures. Many of us would just as soon close our eyes and be woken up when puberty is over. Because the emotional demands on us are particularly great during this period of time, we sometimes lack the imagination that is so helpful in raising both younger and older children. However, viewed with eager curiosity, young teens are some of the most interesting folks around.

I promise I'll sympathize with you in a moment, but let's start by looking at what middle schoolers face. The average sixth-grade girl is adjusting to an alien body at the same time that she is trying to master her graphing calculator, hanging on to her American Girl doll, and contending with the fractious and often downright abusive social stratification of the school cafeteria. The smaller middle school boy is cowed by bigger boys and bigger boys find themselves commanding the attention of girls when they'd generally prefer the safety of their male friends. Boys have to furtively test their unpredictable voices before they risk being betrayed by a high-pitched squeak when they open their mouths. They have to sit still for unbearably long periods of time when their entire biology is urging them to move. In spite of a leg that has a mind of its own and unfamiliar stirrings down below, they are expected to pay attention not to their wayward body but to why they need to avoid the passive voice in writing.

Our system of education for this age group is largely a misery, and the middle schoolers' well-documented needs for adequate sleep, flexible study time, multiple breaks, and quiet, restorative time are ignored. Add to this a stew of hormonal and brain changes. Mix in difficult issues like sex, drugs, and academic pressure, issues that were previously reserved for high school students with more coping skills. And don't forget that researchers have documented a host of negative effects simply from the transition into middle school, including lowered achievement, destabilized social relationships, and reduced self-esteem. Given all this, one can get a pretty good picture of why middle school is perhaps the most difficult transition our children will be called on to make.

Transitions, no matter how welcome, always carry an air of both expectation and anxiety. Clearly the transition into middle school is no exception and affects not only the young teen, but the entire family as well. Science tells us what we already know—that there will be disequilibrium in early adolescence, peaking at age eleven or twelve for girls, thirteen or fourteen for boys.[1] What to expect? High drama? Screaming matches? Well, occasionally perhaps. But *bickering* is the word most frequently used to describe these normative but still unpleasant conversations/confrontations in homes with young teens. And these episodes, contrary to decades of press about a looming "generation gap," are most likely to be about rather ordinary issues like curfew, clothing, and what is the lowest possible bar for considering a bedroom "cleaned up," rather than substantive issues like values, education, or career choices.

Yes, there is likely to be more conflict as well as a decrease in closeness between young teens and their parents. The family is reorganizing itself and trying to accommodate to the changing needs of everyone involved. Your child's sense of self is thrown into turmoil by her increased need for separation, privacy, and reassessment of who she actually is. Conflict is most likely to come to the fore when expectations are challenged on either side. For example, most of us are accustomed to having our children listen when we speak. "Honey, hand me that glass please," then "Sure, Mom" was an easy transaction for many years. In early adolescence that transaction may look more like this:

MOM: Honey—

JESSICA: [*Interrupts.*] Stop calling me honey, I hate that name. Why won't you stop?

MOM: Okay, sorry—

JESSICA: [*Interrupts.*] If you're sorry, then why don't you stop?

MOM: Let's start over. Could you hand me that glass—

JESSICA: [*Interrupts.*] You're just as close as I am, why don't you get it yourself?

MOM: Well, I'm cooking right now and—

JESSICA: [*Interrupts.*] I'm not your slave, you know.

About this point Mom either loses her temper or sighs in disbelief and frustration and gets the glass herself. But what's really going on here? This is not a conversation about a glass; rather it is a conversation (or more accurately a series of interruptions) about who calls the shots, who's in charge. Mom was perfectly happy with her prior relationship with Jessica, generally one of closeness and collaboration with Mom in charge. Jessica, on the other hand, is fighting to redefine that relationship so that it is no longer characterized by mother's authority and daughter's compliance. But the middle schooler's lack of experience defining herself in a new way makes her attempts almost unbearably irritating and, if we can keep just a thread of goodwill, also rather poignant.

Power struggles are a big part of early adolescence as growing teens are driven to exert more control over the trajectory and details of their lives. There will be conflict over clothing, music, curfew, grades, friends, and almost every other aspect of their lives. But in early adolescence, the first striving toward being recognized as a "grown-up" paradoxically takes the form of immature behavior such as whining and interrupting. Unfortunately, as in the example above, these conflicts tend to be resolved not through collaboration or compromise but through surrender. After a long day's work, Mom is generally too tired to enter the fray and simply throws her hands up. *This perhaps explains why it is actually parents, rather than teens, whose mental health is most negatively affected during the early adolescent years.*[2] Moms in particular bear the brunt of their teens' irritability but teens report spending more time with their mothers, talking more to them, and feeling closer to them than to their fathers.[3] Moms and their young teens have more intense relationships—both for better and for worse.

One of the things that years of treating preteens and young teens has taught me is that often less is more with this age group. Therapists can easily excuse themselves for just listening and not jumping in with solutions. This particular stance is helpful when the energy of a young teen around some matter of life and death, such as wearing the wrong shoes to a party, sucks all the air out of my office. It's impossible to be dragged into the drama of their daily lives; it will leave you too exhausted for the times when you really are needed. Think of yourself as a sociologist. Keep your distance. Observe. Resolving the vast majority of high-drama crises that unfold over the middle school years is exactly the kind of challenge that your youngster needs to strengthen her confidence in herself. Conserve your energy for those few instances—bullying, sexual manipulation, harassment—that are really beyond the capacity of your child.

The child who enters middle school will, in a few short years, emerge as a distinctly different life-form—a teenager. What are some of the major tasks that underpin this transformation?

NAVIGATING PUBERTY

A Day in the Life

- Brandon heads out to the playground for lunch with the rest of his eighth-grade class. Because he is almost a foot taller than most of the other boys, one could easily mistake him for a student teacher. Not only is he so much taller, but he also has the physique of a young man: muscular, broad shoulders, slim hips. The uneven patches of stubble on his chin attest to the fact that he has not quite mastered the art of shaving. But he wears his "manliness" comfortably, and it's clear that the bevy of girls that surround him, chatting and vamping, are delighted to have Brandon in their midst.

- Tyler is in the same grade as Brandon. The "shrimp" of his class, he shows no signs of being anything other than a young boy. He sits in a corner of the playground with one or two other prepubescent boys perched on their backpacks reading. Most of his male classmates wolf down lunch and quickly engage in some physical activity, shooting hoops, tossing balls around, or general rough-and-tumble play. Tyler doesn't move off his backpack until the school bell rings, signaling a return to class.

- Ashley is in the sixth grade. It is early in the day but she is just itching to show her best friend, Hannah, her new bra and give her a glimpse of the attendant breasts that almost fill the cups. Most of the girls are already wearing bras and Ashley has waited with great anticipation for this day. As soon as the teacher turns her back to the class to write on the board, Ashley leans toward Hannah, pushes her breasts together with her upper arms, and proudly pulls her T-shirt forward. Hannah peers down Ashley's shirt and in a tone of surprise says, "Is that really all you have?" Ashley can feel the redness creep from her disappointed breasts all the way up to her cheeks.

One of the (many) problems with puberty is that it is both inevitable and unpredictable. Breasts can start to develop at eight or at thirteen. First periods can come at ten or at sixteen. Similarly, the growth spurt in boys can be seen at ten or at sixteen. All these variations are normal, but they are likely to have significantly different psychological and emotional consequences.[4]

Take our early developing Brandon. Boys like Brandon tend to be popular, to feel good about themselves, and to be generally happy.[5] In adolescence, however, they tend to get into more trouble and be more prone to substance abuse than their later maturing peers. This does not mean that if your son is an early developer he's headed for a life of cheerful delinquency. However, it's probably a good idea to make sure that early developing boys (and girls) hang out with their own age group, as opposed to older teens, who are more likely to introduce them to sex and drugs.

Because Brandon looks older than his age, he will be assigned to positions of leadership and responsibility. Interestingly, this is likely to make him good "marriage material" down the line since boys like Brandon typically grow up to be responsible, cooperative, and self-controlled. On the other hand, research also shows that too much responsibility, too soon, may interfere with becoming a spirited adult. Parents need to remember that even if their thirteen-year-old looks like a man, he's still only thirteen and needs to be treated accordingly. Physical maturation is not the same as emotional or cognitive maturation.

Tyler is at the other end of the pubertal development scale. He's a late developer and while this will be problematic for him in adolescence, it may be advantageous to him as he moves into adulthood. While Tyler is unlikely to be the most popular kid in his class in early adolescence, once he catches up (which he will) he is likely to be more intellectually curious, show greater social initiative, and, perhaps most important, have better coping skills, both in later adolescence and in adulthood, than his initially more successful early developing counterparts.[6] *With all the push on kids to grow up quickly, there is evidence that they benefit from an extended childhood rather than a precocious adolescence.* Even a year or two of less social, physical, and sexual pressure seems to give kids the much-needed time to prepare for the intense demands of early adolescence. It appears that crafting a sense of self in the middle of cognitive, physical, and psychological upheaval benefits from every extra unpressured moment.

Finally, Ashley's normal middle school self ensures that she is particularly vulnerable to negative comparisons. While young teens can seem terribly moody to us, research shows that this moodiness is less a function of "raging hormones" and more a function of environment.[7] Had Hannah been wowed by Ashley's breast development, it's likely that Ashley would have skipped home feeling buoyed by her friend's admiration. Instead Ashley's parents find her sobbing in her bedroom later that night. When asked about her upset, Ashley is likely to be at a loss to explain. "I don't know," she may wail, closing her door or pulling the covers over her head. In fact, Ashley may well be clueless about her upset. Over the course of a day—depending partly on where she is in puberty, but more strongly on what activities she's engaging in and how smoothly her personal relationships are going—Ashley is likely to have multiple shifts in mood, too many to keep up with or remember. Parents would do well to be empathic, show interest, and not be overly concerned about these shifting states. Ashley may wake up the next morning still upset, or just as likely cheerful and oblivious to her previous night's meltdown.

The Vulnerability of the Early Maturing Teen Girl

Flip open a magazine, something like *Seventeen*, *Teen Vogue*, or even *Girls' Life* (pitched to girls "ages ten and up") and look at the girls inside. They are young, fashionable, made up, and tricked out. But most of all they are thin. Achingly thin, worrisomely thin, often pitifully thin. American middle-class white girls define the perfect body as 5´7˝ and 110 pounds (a body that is considered medically underweight).[8]

The average, healthy American teenage girl is, in fact, about 5´4˝ and weighs somewhere between 110 and 135 pounds.[9] So just as young adolescent girls are becoming acutely aware of their changing bodies, they are bombarded by images that they believe represent the pinnacle of physical perfection but are more likely to put them under a doctor's care.

Female puberty is heralded by weight gain and particularly a shift toward fat as opposed to muscle. So girls who enter puberty early find themselves putting on weight and looking notably different from their friends. While early development may bring a certain amount of admiration for these girls, particularly from boys, it also makes them "different" at a time when most teens are desperate to fit in. For the most part, they are no longer "thin," they struggle with their new body image, and, all too frequently, they go on unnecessary diets.

As we've seen with boys, early maturation carries some initial benefits and some potential challenges down the line. Researchers find that early developing girls are at increased risk not only in puberty but in adulthood as well. Imagine being in the fifth or sixth grade and fully developed. You're in middle school, so there are boys two and three years older than you who are attracted to you. Your girlfriends for the most part have retained boyish figures and if you happen to go to a particularly cliquish middle school, you may find yourself ostracized by them because you're no longer "thin" and you're being pursued by older boys.[10] Not surprisingly, girls in this situation tend to experience lower academic achievement, low self-esteem, anxiety, depression, eating disorders, and panic attacks.[11] Like early maturing boys, early maturing girls are also more likely to engage in delinquency, substance abuse, and early sexual activity.[12]

Parents need to remember that our kids live in a specific cultural context. In Germany, where thinness is less idealized and attitudes toward sexuality are less ambivalent, early maturing girls are found to have *higher* levels of self-esteem.[13] In general, being supportive, emphasizing attributes other than the daughter's physical development, protecting her from experiences she is simply too young to handle well (such as parties with older kids), and maintaining a relatively conflict-free home (a boon to all teens, but especially to those whose resources are already stressed) are all beneficial for these girls. Interestingly, early maturing girls in all-girls schools appear to enjoy a level of psychological and emotional protection not apparent in coed schools.[14]

Is Anything Predictable During This Unpredictable Time?

It is important to keep in mind that most kids make it through puberty just fine. Yes, it is a highly charged period, one that challenges even the most robust young teens and their families. But ultimately, teens adjust to their new bodies and parents adjust to reconfigured relationships with their teens. While the progression through the physical changes of puberty is so variable that it is virtually meaningless to say what is "average" or "normal"—some kids are completely finished with puberty before others have even begun—the psychological and social effect of puberty is relatively consistent. In other words, regardless of whether puberty begins at eight or at fourteen, we can expect our previously temperate child to be moody, sleepy, withdrawn, and profoundly affected by even the most negligible peer interactions. On average, going through puberty takes about three years. While it can feel endless, puberty is a temporary state of affairs.

How Parents Can Help

Twelve-year-old Madison creeps in from school. From your vantage point in the family room, you can see that she is upset: the hunch of her shoulders, the unwavering gaze, the slight shuffle of her feet. You've got a report to finish for work but are uncomfortable about another day with little communication between you and your daughter, particularly since she's in the middle of her first menstrual period. So you call her in with the hope that she might confide in you, like she did just a few months ago. Your conversation may sound something like this:

MOM: Are you okay, Madison?

MADISON: Fine.

MOM: You seem kind of upset. Did anything happen at school today?

MADISON: No.

MOM: I know you had that tough math test today. How'd that go?

MADISON: I don't know.

MOM: [*getting just a bit desperate now*] Well, if you don't know, then who does?

MADISON: I don't know.

Anyone who has a middle schooler knows how this conversation will go. Mom will continue to interrogate and Madison will become increasingly linguistically challenged. If, seemingly overnight, conversations have morphed from dialogues to monologues, how in the world can parents talk about something as sensitive as puberty—talk about breasts and ejaculations and desire? How can we help our children manage what is probably the most demanding transition of their young lives when their vocabulary has been reduced to a handful of noncommittal words and phrases?

In fact, conversations with your middle schooler about puberty and sex are mandatory. They need information, support, empathy, and guidance. But if they're so needy, why does Madison shut her mother down and how exactly does her mom approach sensitive topics?

Let's stand in Madison's shoes for a moment. Whatever had bothered her at school is "private business." Kids at this age are often vigilant about protecting their privacy, a first step toward emotional independence and increased self-reliance. The sense of self that children in elementary school were so eager to share ("Mom, we had gym today and my teacher said I'm such a good runner") has given way to uncertainty about the self. ("No way I'm getting undressed in gym with my period. What if one of the girls notices?") Madison didn't come home asking for help or wanting to "discuss" the events of the day with her mom. That work will be done on her own, perhaps with the help of her girlfriends. Mom's well-intended questions are simply seen as prying. I used to make it a habit with my sons that if I got three (and in retrospect it should have been one or two) *fine*, *nothing*, or *whatever*s in a row, the "conversation" was over. It helps to maintain a sense of humor when stretching the definition of conversation to include repetitive questioning and responsive mumbling.

At twelve, Madison has heard all kinds of sexual references

online, in the media, and among her peer group. While she is quite capable of talking about "being nailed" or giving a "BJ," in fact, her knowledge about her changing body is fragmentary and incomplete. I've had young girls in my office tell me that they've scoured everything from the Internet to the tampon box trying to gain more information on something as basic as their period. For many kids in puberty there is too much bravado and too little information. The emphasis on plumbing in many sex education classes often gives short shrift to the equally pressing questions about emotional and social realities. Menarche can be seen as an achievement or an embarrassment. Feelings of sexual arousal and questions about sexual identity can preoccupy the young adolescent. Romantic feelings are both exciting and disquieting. "Nothing about me is normal anymore," says an anxious thirteen-year-old who has her first crush, her first period, and her first acne outbreak all in the same week. Worry is the territory in which the young teen has set up camp.

Given these realities, parents need to be proactive in bringing up issues of physical change and romantic feelings. Uncomfortable for your kid? Yes. Uncomfortable for you? Probably. But as my sons used to say to me when I waffled on something difficult, "Man up, Mom" (when you have a husband and three sons communication tends to be testosterone-laced). We guide and model for our children in hundreds of different ways; we can't afford to pull back on some of the most critical issues our children will face—making friends with their new bodies, the sexual choices that are part and parcel of physical maturity, and the intimacy that will ultimately characterize their most meaningful relationships. Your children will have to integrate all of these issues into their sense of self. Remember that if you're not a significant source of support and information, then information is likely to come from their equally confused peers.

Some conversations will go well, and some will be met with stony silence. You will have moments of both intense connection and intense discomfort as you engage in conversations that can be profoundly uncomfortable for your child and may reactivate some of your own early adolescent difficulties. The following tips are generally found to be useful when talking to your middle school child about puberty and sex.

- Start early. Sensitive conversations are less sensitive when you've had a history of them in your family. But it's never too late to start. Middle schoolers may find it easier to start talking about sexual activity once removed than about their own. Portrayals in televisions shows, movies, or magazines give us great opportunities to bring up touchy issues. A movie like *Juno*, about a pregnant teenage girl, would give you an easy opening for questions like "How did Juno decide what to do when she found out she was pregnant?" "How" questions are always more likely to be answered than "why" questions that just put kids on the defensive.

- Figure out when your child is most receptive to discussion. Almost every important talk I had with my sons was in the evening around bedtime. Probably because everyone was relaxed. Don't ambush your child when he first comes home from school or when she has a big test the following day.

- Don't be oblique. Preteens and young teens are confused enough about what is going on with their bodies and so questions like "Have you had any new feelings?" are incomprehensible (and anxiety provoking) to them. Much better to be direct and say, "You're probably getting pretty close to having your first period. Let's make sure you're prepared." Often it's easier to ease into feelings after logistics are attended to.

- *Do not* impute feelings to your teen. "You must be worried about when you're going to look like the other boys." This is probably the fastest way to shut down communication. The feeling part of these discussions has to come from your kid; otherwise he or she will feel misunderstood, controlled, and even judged.

- Let your kid know you're available for conversation. "At some point you might want to talk about the changes in your body or about sex. If you do, I'm here to listen." Provide openings but don't push if you get no response. Most children will come to you for information and guidance when they're ready.

There are few inevitabilities in life. Puberty is one of them. Do try to conjure up your pubertal self. Dozens of women over the years have said to me, "I don't know how my mother was able to stand me when I was thirteen." Of course, as mothers ourselves now, we understand that they stood us because they had the experience, wisdom, and love to know that breaking out of a chrysalis—leaving one body for another—is a challenging, disorienting, and miraculous transformation. It is also, thankfully, time limited.

STAYING HEALTHY

When I was five years old I had polio. What I remember hazily about that time was my parents' stricken faces and the large open ward filled with youngsters and teenagers tethered to a nightmare collage of tubes, fluids, and iron lungs. One month after I was sick, the Salk vaccine became available and parents once again allowed their children out to play, to swim in pools, and to drink from public water fountains. Fifty years ago, this was the face of child and adolescent health. Most teenagers who died, died from disease: more than twice as many as those who died from injury. Today the reverse is true with 72 percent of adolescent deaths attributable to injury, primarily car accidents, unintentional injury, suicide, and homicide.[15] In other words, the vast majority of adolescent deaths are preventable. Thankfully, adolescent deaths are rare. But the same factors that can contribute to fatalities—impulsivity, underdeveloped judgment, inexperience, social pressure, and lack of parental monitoring— also contribute to a host of risky behaviors that compromise a far larger number of young teenagers' health. These include bullying, violence, eating disorders, substance abuse, reckless driving, unsafe sex, and self-mutilation.

The relatively new field of "adolescent medicine" focuses not only on the traditional medical model of diagnosis and treatment, but, perhaps more than any other subspecialty of medicine, on education and prevention. The odds are good that a large percentage of serious adolescent health problems could be avoided if, in addition to effectively providing information to teens about the consequences of unhealthy choices, we also provided the environments that are known to be effective in suppressing risky choices. Unfortunately, this is easier said than done. Health messages have trouble competing with teenagers' strong inclinations toward risk taking, their limited and often faulty judgment, corporate advertising, and the strong social pressures that surround them. We have yet to address teens effectively on some issues, though we have made headway on others. Teen smoking and drinking and driving fatalities are on the decline, but teen pregnancy, eating disorders, and self-mutilation are all on the rise. The health habits laid down during the middle school years—diet, exercise, smoking, drug use—typically persist into high school and adulthood for better and for worse.

When our pediatrician gives us the timetable for inoculating our children against measles, mumps, chicken pox, diphtheria, tetanus, whooping cough, and, yes, polio, few of us ignore the advice. Medical science has made astounding strides in protecting our children from diseases that were once the thieves of childhood. So why has it been so difficult to change the health habits of young teens? Changing human behavior may seem easier than changing basic physiologic processes. Yet, overall, we've had more success in altering the physiologic basis of many diseases of adolescence than in changing risky adolescent behavior.

To shed some light on why changing the young adolescent's health choices has been so difficult, I enlisted the help of Emily, who said that I might not "really know what goes on behind the scenes." She was right. Adults, even adolescent psychologists, typically see only part of the reality of day-to-day life for young teens. Emily's description of what her day is like helped clarify why developing healthy habits can be daunting for middle schoolers.

As soon as Emily wakes up at six thirty she starts grappling with difficult issues. Apparently getting dressed when you're twelve years old is an exercise worthy of *Project Runway*. Because Emily's body is changing rapidly, clothes are being discarded in rapid succession. Still growing by leaps and bounds, Emily finds that the pants that were perfect just a few weeks ago now look like "floods" or "high-waters." She can sift through four or five pairs of pants before finding one that she feels comfortable in. The issue for Emily is greater than any single article of clothing; it is an issue of identity and acceptance. Not only is she rifling through articles of clothing, she is rifling through "looks." One of the popular girls, Emily is aware that she has to both fit in and be on the cutting edge of what is fashionable at her school. Her mother only complicates matters by bringing home clothing that is unwearably lame and then looking hurt when Emily refuses to wear any of it. Often she takes Emily to task for being messy or provocative. Emily wishes her mother was aware of how "slutty" many of the girls look and how much attention they seem to get from the boys.

This process of becoming presentable for school takes Emily the better part of an hour every morning. She shrugs off my sympathy by saying, "That's just the way things are." I am someone who pulls on black yoga pants, white sneakers, and a gray sweatshirt every single morning, so to me Emily's early morning decisions seem unthinkable. For Emily they are serious business.

Emily arrives at school at 7:45 so that she has time to see her friends briefly before school starts at 8:05. Her breakfast consists of an Eggo waffle, eaten in the car, often because she has to quickly finish a homework assignment. Her first class is math, a difficult subject for her, and most days she finds herself nodding off about fifteen minutes into the class. Fortunately, she sits in the back of the room and so her teacher rarely notices this unless Emily's head drops to her desk. Emily has figured out how to catch a bit of sleep with one hand propping up her cheek and a pencil in her other hand, giving the illusion of paying attention. She will get notes from one of the other kids in the class later. If she needs to cheat on her next test, she will.

The morning passes by quickly. By about ten o'clock Emily is feeling more alert and as a result contributes quite a bit to her favorite class, language arts. Lunch is pretty much the highlight of the day when Emily can get together with her friends and sit at "their" spot in the school cafeteria. Rumors fly around the cafeteria, outfits are scrutinized, male attention is either highly regarded or dismissed depending on the status of the boy. Over the course of months, weeks, and sometimes hours a few girls are granted permission to enter Emily's group of friends and a few girls are banished. Again, when I try to sympathize with Emily about how difficult it must be to always be on guard about her status and popularity, she once again shrugs her shoulders. According to Emily there are winners and losers in the "social survival" that is middle school. Knowing Emily fairly well, I'm surprised by her lack of empathy with girls who are cut out of her circle for seemingly trivial offenses like laughing at the wrong joke or talking to the wrong boy. Apparently little things easily become big things in the halls and cafeterias of middle school.

Although Emily has little sympathy for those who are socially banished, and admits to "being careful" about what she says at the lunch table, she genuinely seems to enjoy the feeling of camaraderie she has there. Eating, however, is a complex issue since several of the girls are getting "chubby," and as a result they are all very careful about what they eat. Once a week, they pull out the lettuce from their sandwiches and eat only lettuce for lunch. Many of them are "dieting." Some days Emily is "on a diet"; most days she is not.

Toward the end of the school day, Emily once again is feeling lethargic and takes a 5-Hour Energy drink out of her backpack. She and all her friends keep a good supply of these (or Red Bull) on hand. School ends at three, but most days Emily has soccer practice until five. Emily blows in from soccer practice leaving a trail of dirt from her cleats as she races into her room to talk with her friends. Dinner is a quick and often confrontational experience, a far cry from the pleasant dinners her family had enjoyed for many years. Emily returns to her room, quickly downs another 5-Hour Energy drink, and works on her homework from seven until nine thirty or ten. Although her parents have decreed lights out at ten, Emily is contemptuous of this ("What do they think I am, eight years old? When am I supposed to talk to my friends?") and continues to text her friends under the covers until her parents go to bed at eleven. Because she finds it "impossible" to go to sleep until later, most nights she pads out of bed to her computer and spends an hour, sometimes two, texting, IM'ing, talking to friends, and being on Facebook.

Sometime after midnight Emily finally falls asleep.

The Costs of Too Little Sleep

The American Academy of Pediatrics recommends that preteens and teens get slightly more than nine hours of sleep a night. And the percentage of teens that actually get adequate sleep? That would be 15 percent, leaving 85 percent of teens sleep-deprived.[16] The image of the sleepy, perpetually yawning, moving-like-molasses young teen is not ill-founded. In fact, the vast majority of preteens and teens are so sleep-deprived that research has found impairment in almost every area of functioning, from the trivial to the potentially lethal. Rather than minimizing sleep deprivation as being just another inevitable part of adolescence like acne or crabbiness, we need to understand that its consequences are serious, health compromising, and preventable.

Sleep deprivation is associated with a host of academic difficulties, including poorer problem solving, attention, concentration, and school performance. Kids who are sleep-deprived are less capable of modulating emotions and more prone to depression. While younger teens don't yet drive, they can be in cars with older teens who are sleep-deprived and therefore at heightened risk for accidents. While we worry endlessly about drinking and driving, almost as many serious and fatal car accidents are caused by fatigue as by alcohol. To round out this miserable picture of the problems associated with sleep deprivation, there is also an increased likelihood of eating disorders and substance abuse.[17]

The reasons for sleep deprivation at this age are relatively straightforward. More than anything, puberty itself drives a change in sleep patterns. Melatonin, which regulates our sleep-wake cycle, is secreted later and later in the evening in these youngsters. As a result, most teens don't feel tired until late at night, usually around midnight. They aren't being difficult or oppositional when they say they can't sleep at ten o'clock. They really can't. This change is called a delayed phase preference and since we can't change biology, we need to optimize their sleeping environment and minimize their biological tendency toward being night owls.

Interestingly, young teens more often report being aware that they are not getting enough sleep than do their parents. This may be partly because we're often long asleep while they're still up texting. But it also may be that we have normalized parts of adolescence that are more a function of sleep deprivation than anything else. A well-rested teen is far more likely to be enthusiastic, capable, helpful, and even cheerful than one who is constantly on the verge of exhaustion. With eighth graders getting on average only seven hours of sleep a night, more than two hours short of what is needed, it's small wonder that they are cranky and difficult.[18]

Think of how you feel when you don't get a good night's sleep. Now think about how that would feel if it went on for years. Yes, I know it has for many of us, especially when our children are young. I suspect that chronic fatigue did not enhance your personality any more than it enhanced mine. More than any other aspect of my health, I now guard my sleep zealously, knowing full well the difference between a good night's rest and the lingering fuzziness and unwelcome irritability of too little sleep. Sleep restores us physically, emotionally, and cognitively. It should be at the top of our list of parenting priorities.

How Parents Can Help

When biology, school schedules, and the allure of social networking all conspire to ensure that our children are sleep-deprived most nights of the week, what can parents do?

JOIN WITH OTHER PARENTS AND LOBBY YOUR CHILD'S SCHOOL TO PUSH BACK THE START OF CLASSES

The problem, of course, begins with a school start time that is completely out of synch with the young teen's biology. Left to their own devices, most teenagers naturally would go to sleep around midnight and wake up at around ten. Many teens sleep until all hours on the weekend in an attempt to make up their sleep deficits. While it may seem initially daunting, many school districts around the country have made adjustments to their start times. These adjustments don't have to be radical in order for students to benefit.

In one of many studies showing the benefits of a later class start time, as small an adjustment as changing class start time from 8:00 to 8:30 gave most teens an extra forty-five minutes of sleep. (Interestingly, good sleep begets better sleep: kids felt so much better with the extra half hour that they went to bed fifteen minutes earlier.) The number of students getting eight hours of sleep a night improved from 16 percent to 55 percent, and the number of students who slept less than seven hours was reduced 80 percent! Not surprisingly, researchers found a significant improvement in classroom motivation, less fatigue, less depressed mood, fewer somatic complaints, and parents who felt their kids were easier to live with.[19]

LIMIT, SHUT DOWN, OR ELIMINATE ELECTRONICS IN THE BEDROOM AT LEAST A HALF HOUR BEFORE BEDTIME

Even though young teens are getting up at about the same time that they did thirty years ago, they are getting far less sleep. This is because they are going to bed much later. Teens are taking advantage of the changes in their brain's sleep center to stay up late plying their social networking skills. Many teen bedrooms resemble nothing so much as a mini Best Buy filled with mandatory and esoteric paraphernalia—television, computer, smartphone, iPod, iPad, and video game console. Because the light from this potpourri of electronics depresses melatonin production and therefore sleep, teens have acclimated to later and later bedtimes. Shut down both the light and the stimulation and teens will have an easier time going to sleep. Keep at least the television and the cell phone, if not all electronics, out of the bedroom.

TEACH SLEEP HYGIENE

(Yes, it's a slightly funky name. But it's the preferred term of experts.)

Health curricula in middle school emphasize the importance of healthy eating, regular exercise, and safe sex. Large public health campaigns have highlighted these issues for the general public. Yet the basics of sleep—its importance, the consequences of sleep deprivation, and how to create an optimal sleep environment—barely get a nod. Parents have to pick up the slack. Here are some of the most important points to teach (and model for) your children around sleep hygiene:

- Have a consistent bedtime.

- Have a quiet half-hour ritual before bedtime. Find out what relaxes your child—music, reading, diary writing, a hot shower—and encourage it as his or her pre-bedtime activity. This can also be a good time for a bit of quiet conversation with your child.

- Dim the lights a half hour before bedtime.

- Ban caffeinated drinks in the afternoon or evening. Check

labels. Some stimulant drinks market themselves as "nutritional supplements."

- Shut off all electronics a half hour before bedtime.

- Figure out together what might be a good time for your middle schooler to engage in social networking. Networking is not relaxing, despite what your child might say. Middle schoolers have a lot of drama in their lives and having one more iteration of the day's calamities right before bed is not likely to encourage sleep.

DON'T ALLOW YOUR CHILD TO BE OVERSCHEDULED

As we've seen, the biological, cognitive, social, and emotional demands of early adolescence are enormous. Extracurricular activities are very important to middle schoolers, as they contribute to many of the skills kids are developing—self-esteem, self-reliance, enthusiasm, and a good work ethic, to name a few. Middle schoolers benefit from participation in extracurriculars that interest them and provide an expanded social network. "Who am I?" is partially answered by finding the activities that one excels in or just enjoys. But as with so much of our parenting, we've decided that if a little is good, then a lot must be better. It isn't. One of the most common complaints I hear from middle schoolers is that they have "too much" on their minds. It's enough to worry about what body you will find when you wake up in the morning, who will sit with you at lunch, and whether you really understand algebra. Worrying about memorizing your lines for the class play while trying to improve your time in the 25-meter butterfly and practicing for soccer tryouts is simply too much. Most middle schoolers participate in a host of extracurricular activities that would do justice to a Junior Leaguer. A moderate amount of extracurriculars certainly benefits kids. But in order to be able to relax, to put the day on hold, kids need some clear space in their heads and clear time in their days. If the above points on sleep seem daunting to you, the quiet before bedtime, for example, then your child is doing too much. Leave some time every day for reflection and solitude. Your child will sleep better and so will you.

Learning to Eat Healthy for Life

Is the fact that girls diet and boys spend their allowance on protein supplements to help them bulk up just part of the normal trajectory of young teens' concerns about their rapidly changing bodies? How concerned should we be about a girl like Emily who eats lettuce for lunch once a week or thirteen-year-old Ryan, who dumps enough protein powder in his orange juice to sustain a triathlete? Body image dissatisfaction (something we don't want incorporated into our child's sense of self) and poor eating habits developed in early adolescence both tend to endure, so they need to be taken seriously as soon as they surface.

Disordered eating ranges from unnecessary preoccupation with weight and body image to full-blown disorders like obesity, anorexia nervosa, and bulimia. Girls and women in our culture are singled out for an unending barrage of media images stressing thinness; this is one of several factors that make dieting ten times more frequent among girls than boys. In spite of a great deal of recent press coverage that suggests that anorexia and bulimia are "epidemic," they are not. Less than 0.5 percent of teens, almost all girls, are anorexic and 3 percent are bulimic. While these numbers are hardly incidental, especially since nearly 20 percent of anorexic teens die from starvation, neither do they constitute an epidemic. They should, however, alert us to worrisome signs of a serious eating disorder like signifi-cant weight loss, excessive exercise, vomiting after meals, or use of laxatives. Spending a lot of time in the bathroom after meals can be a clue that a girl is throwing up her food.

The real epidemic in America for teenagers today is obesity.[20] More than one in three teens in the United States are either over-weight or obese.[21] Back to Ryan for a moment. Is he simply bulking up or packing on pounds? This will matter, because a child who is obese in middle school has an 80 percent chance of being an obese adult.[22] Is Ryan sticking to protein powder or does he also have a stash of anabolic steroids? Anabolic steroid use among middle school boys is low, about 1.0 percent,[23] but its consequences can be serious, including testicular atrophy and breast development (here's where a little education can go a long way!). Be alert for major changes in body musculature, severe acne, increased irritability, or aggressiveness.

Disordered eating, like so many complex problems, has genetic, cultural, and social roots. So how do we separate these factors out and limit their influence? Parents can have a substantial effect on educating their young teens about healthy eating choices and creat-ing the environment that is most likely to support both good nutri-tion and a positive body image.

How Parents Can Help
MODEL

Being active and making healthy food choices is something we get to model for our children not just every day, but many times a day. This doesn't mean that you need to always choose carrots and wheatgrass but it does mean you can't always choose soda and ice cream. Our job is to educate our children about food choices, bring them along to the grocery store, have them participate in meal preparation, and make healthy snacks easily accessible. Teach them to read labels. Make them participants in their own food preparation.

Early adolescence is a period of explosive physical growth. Your child will definitely be eating more. It can be just as easy to reach for fruit or peanut butter as it is to reach for Ho Hos and Ding Dongs. Don't make a big deal out of occasional lapses. Who among us has not sought solace in a container of Ben & Jerry's? Better to take a moderate view about food choices than an extreme one. Young teens are prone to being oppositional; you don't need to provide them with additional fodder by being unnecessarily rigid. Keep the big picture in mind. We want our kids to feel good about their bodies, to enjoy food, and to generally make healthy choices.

DON'T USE "HEALTHY EATING" AS A COVER FOR YOUR OWN FOOD ISSUES

Margo is brought to me by her mother, who is worried that Margo might have an "eating disorder." Mom is very clear that she keeps only healthy food in the house and that she has "caught" Margo hiding candy bars under her bed. As soon as the mother leaves my office, Margo nails the problem. "My mom's idea of healthy eating doesn't include anything with more than one hundred calories. I play lacrosse every day and I'm friggin' hungry when I get home. Carrots and celery just don't do it for me. At least the candy bars give me some energy and some calories. My mom's been brainwashed about what healthy eating is. It's her problem, not mine." In fact, a little exploration with Mom uncovers her preoccupation with eating healthy as a way for her to stay slim and to keep the "chubbiness" off her daughter. It is not unusual in my practice for "patient" and parent to change seats. Try to be very clear about what is your issue and what is your child's.

DON'T USE FOOD AS REWARD OR PUNISHMENT

Like many parents who lived through the Great Depression, my own parents insisted that I "clean" my plate because there were starving children in the world. In spite of all the time and thought I put into this injunction, I never understood how my gagging on canned peas could help some starving child halfway around the world. I still can't eat peas and as far as I know, no lives were saved by my being force-fed canned vegetables.

Food is fuel. It is not meant to be, nor should it be, commingled with reward, punishment, or saving starving babies. Food as a reward encourages overeating and since it's usually sweets that are offered, it also encourages unnecessary weight gain. Similarly using food as a punishment ("No dessert for you tonight—you were so mean to your sister") only breeds resentment and rebellion. We don't use sleep or exercise as arenas in which to exert control. We shouldn't exert control with food, either. It encourages the kind of baggage attached to food that therapists routinely help unpack in their offices years after the fact.

REALISTICALLY COMBAT BODY DISSATISFACTION

What could possibly make the majority of adolescent girls, most of whom are of normal weight, diet? First of all, about a third of all young teen girls consider themselves overweight when in fact they are normal or even underweight by medical criteria. And 80 percent of these normal-weight girls believe that if they were thinner they would be happier, more successful, and more popular.[24] These troubling findings are not incidental. A sense of self always begins in one's body. It is the first part of our "self" that we are aware of. While generally temporary, girls' dissatisfaction with their bodies is a poor foundation on which to build a healthy sense of self. Boys have much lower rates of body dissatisfaction than girls, but there is increasing evidence that young teen boys feel pressure to be muscular and some are willing to take supplements ranging from the relatively benign (protein powders) to the dangerous (anabolic steroids) in order to develop a more idealized body.[25]

Teens are bombarded by media images of a particular body type that is neither healthy nor attainable for the majority of them, particularly teens in early puberty because of the inevitable weight gain that accompanies this transition. It is little wonder, then, that vulnerable, worried, often socially fixated young teens feel themselves lacking. Because young teens attach so much importance to their peers, a contagion effect is found around disordered eating. The popular girls, who, by the way, are in fact more likely to be thin than not, can bring along a whole group of girls to engage in unhealthy eating behaviors (diet pills, vomiting, fasting). Emily's group of once-a-week lettuce eaters is an example of this type of groupthink.

Body dissatisfaction is the outcome of multiple factors: cultural pressures, family dynamics, genetics, and psychological vulnerabilities to depression and low self-esteem. None of these factors alone ensures that your young teen will develop an eating disorder. But because body dissatisfaction is such a pervasive and potentially dangerous fact of life in middle school, here is a list of concrete suggestions that have been shown to protect young teens from falling victim to an unhealthy and unrealistic view of their bodies.

- Do not dwell on weight—yours, your child's, or people you see on the street. Teach by your own actions that what you notice in others are things like kindness, character, enthusiasm, and attitude, not looks. Out in the world there are endless messages about how a particular appearance (and a particular product) guarantees happiness. Make your family life a sanctuary from corporate brainwashing.

- Normalize your child's weight gain in puberty. Acknowledge that your child is putting on weight as he or she enters puberty. Weight gain is always part of early puberty. It does no good for you to say, "Oh honey, you look exactly the same to me." That's just crazy-making. Better to acknowledge reality: "Yes your body is changing. You're moving into becoming a man (or a woman). Your body needs those few extra pounds to make that transition."

- Fathers play a particularly important role in limiting their young teens' body dissatisfaction. Girls in particular benefit from knowing that their fathers still find them attractive. When your daughter is reaching for a piece of cake, this is no time for Dad to say, "Summer's coming up soon, honey." This is an instance where Dad's feedback can matter more than Mom's.

- Listen. It is so easy to dismiss young teens' concerns about their bodies with bromides about "growing up" and "it's just a stage." Perspective is always good, but don't jump the gun. Remember, when you're in the middle of emotional turmoil, being told "it's just a stage" is worse than useless. It makes kids feel trivialized and judged.

While we can (and should) decry the poor nutrition supplied by Taco Bell or Burger King, let's remember that most of what our kids eat is eaten at home. We need to get our own house in order first. We can start giving our youngsters an enhanced sense of control over their food habits by having them do some shopping or making the dinner salad. Solicit their opinions about different foods and types of meals. The dinner table should be a pleasant experience, not a battleground. Don't be rigid; you'll get much more buy-in if you acknowledge that most of us don't eat "healthy" all the time. It's important for kids to know that occasional indulgences are no big deal. Of course, it really, really helps if you don't keep abundant supplies of chips, candy bars, doughnuts, and the like around the house. Most of us eat what is available. Work with other parents to make sure that lunch offerings at your child's school are fresh and healthy.

How astounding to think that medical science has helped us reach a point where the majority of adolescent health problems are preventable. In spite of all the physical, psychological, and social changes taking place in adolescence, it is one of the healthiest periods of time in the entire life span. There are few things more painful to witness as a parent than a healthy child who is choosing to compromise his or her health. We protect our children against strong negative social, corporate, and cultural influences by maintaining open channels of communication. These channels look quite different in middle school than they did in elementary school and it's up to us to understand the coded messages of middle schoolers. "It's my life" is both a statement of emerging fact and a plea for reassurance. Rolled eyes are both a declaration of separation and a test to make sure that you care even when your child is being difficult. If you can't make it through these normative tests of your middle schooler, consider enlarging your own support group. Parents need each other like never before as their kids traverse the middle school years.

While the challenges of early adolescence test your relationship with your child perhaps more than any other period of development, it is critical to maintain that relationship. The greatest protection you can give your middle schooler against unhealthy behaviors, behaviors that can reverberate far into the future, is your continued love, availability, and involvement.

BUILDING INDEPENDENCE

It's a warm late summer day and you are walking your daughter into middle school for the first time. The swirl of activity that envelops the two of you from the moment you step onto the campus feels very different from the raucousness of the elementary school playground. Yes, kids are running around here—but they're also lounging, sulking, deep in conversation, and engaging in what appears to be flirting. You hold your daughter's hand a little more firmly, wondering how your eleven-year-old *child* is going to adjust to what is clearly an adolescent world. Middle school is light-years away from the consistency of elementary school, with the latter's natural segregation of boys and girls and its reassuring predictability. You can't help but wonder if your child is simply too young for all this. Aren't there places where middle school starts a year later? As you take in the scene with cautious, suspicious eyes, you suddenly realize that your daughter has let go of your hand. It's not that she doesn't seem a bit nervous; she does. But as clear as it is to you that you're in a whole new world, it is equally clear to her. She may not know much, but one look around tells her that this is not a place where you hold on to your mom.

What strange alchemy takes place during middle school? It seems like enough of a feat that, in a few short years, your prepubertal daughter will emerge looking more like an adult than a child. You're prepared for this. You've bought enough books, read enough articles, and watched enough television specials with your daughter to understand the physical changes that she is about to undergo. But it's the hand that she intentionally lets slip that takes you by surprise. Okay, teenagers have always been leery of public displays of affection, but you hardly think of her as a teenager. For close to a decade you've walked hand and hand, first into preschool, and then into elementary school. How did she get the message so quickly that, in this place, being on her own was preferable to being attached to you? What other messages will she get and will she respond to them as easily?

Suddenly you know that the physical changes of puberty are only one part, and perhaps not even the most disquieting part, of this new stage of development. You're not sure you're ready. Up to this point your child's life has been pretty much under your control. Somehow you never fully appreciated that this was a temporary state of affairs, that her drive toward independence would replace her reliance on you. You have a strong urge to gather her in your arms and reassure her that you'll always be there for her, until you realize that you're the one who needs reassuring. Your daughter walks up ahead, then turns to wave good-bye to you with a smile full of excitement and anticipation. You straighten up, wipe the worry off your face, and wave back heartily and happily. Back in your car you can feel the tears well up.

What Drives Independence?

A few days before my oldest son was about to start middle school, I found him on his bed, face to the wall and teary-eyed. "I'm not ready to grow up," he said quietly. I knew that times like this were made for hanging back and listening. But I had a million questions. Was he afraid of the middle school culture? A good athlete, did he worry about losing his "jock" status? Like his mother, he has a poor sense of direction; was he worried that he'd get lost in a big, unfamiliar school? These were my concerns, but were they his? I lay back on the bed and asked the most open-ended question I could come up with: "What's up?" And then with my tongue practically bleeding from biting on it—I waited.

Part of him didn't really know exactly why he felt sad that day, as opposed to excited or nervous. But as he talked, his concerns became clearer and they couldn't have been more different from what I had assumed (hence the oft-repeated "listen" dictum in this book). He'd already been to the school in order to learn his way around before the semester started. He was going with his group of close friends so he didn't worry about feeling like an outsider and he was totally confident that his athletic skills would land him on the basketball team. His concerns were of an entirely different order. He was worried about losing all the prerogatives of being a child before he was feeling ready to be a teenager. He would no longer have one teacher who knew him really well. He was well aware that most of the kids walked to the middle school alone, or with a group of other kids, and not with their mothers. He looked forward to having an "agenda" where he could keep track of all his assignments, but he knew that parents were not allowed to bring forgotten homework up to school. Mostly he longed to be more independent at the same time that he was worried about losing the close family connection that characterized our household. While I was nibbling around the outside of middle school concerns, in mostly concrete ways, he was plunging into the heart of the new middle schooler's dilemma. Would it be possible to be independent without being disconnected?

It is a truism that the job of parenting is to help make our children independent enough to lead their own lives. After all, we won't always be around to help them; eventually, they will have to fend for themselves. But from a child's point of view, why the willingness to give up so much that has sustained them—the affectionate hug, the good-night kiss, the confidences—in the pursuit of their own, singular version of themselves? My son was appropriately sad as he prepared for the transition into middle school. He knew intuitively that he would be giving up his childhood in order to be able to grow into the man he hoped one day to become. There are many reasons why young teens are driven toward independence, perhaps none more powerful than the promise of a competent future self capable of charting an adult life course. Often sadness turns to anger or withdrawal during the middle school years as the safest way to avoid being drawn back into the mother-child symbiosis.

Clearly the drive toward independence doesn't start when your child walks through his first middle school classroom doorway. Remember the baby who spat out food when she had enough, the toddler who insisted, "I do it myself," and the child who begged to have the training wheels taken off her bike as soon as she was able to ride. But yes, middle schoolers ratchet it up several notches and for good reasons. In addition to being able to imagine a transformed, grown-up self, there are both biological and cognitive changes that make young teens strive for independence.

BIOLOGY

In early puberty the hormonal system is being "turned on" and hormone levels are highly variable.[26] Will your child therefore be moodier, less in control of feelings, and more interested in creating distance? Yes. Then again, you may also be more interested in distance from a crabby, unpredictable young teen. It's interesting that monkeys and apes also go through puberty, and scientists have found the same pattern of distancing between mother and child, suggesting some evolutionary basis to the negativity and conflict of early adolescence.[27]

The changes of puberty are bound to upset the status quo because there is an increasing disconnect between how we treat our children and how they are treated out in the world. Dad may ask his twelve-year-old daughter, "How's my little girl today?" but the way boys, especially some of the older boys, are starting to look at her makes it clear to her that she is no longer a little girl. Her middle school environment treats her more or less like a young adult. Dad's innocent question only serves to remind his daughter that it wasn't very long ago that there was nothing she liked more than cuddling with him. With the advent of sexual feelings brought on by puberty, cuddling with Dad becomes verboten. A hissy fit about being called a "little girl" complete with a retreat behind closed doors helps ensure that Dad does not threaten his daughter's vulnerable boundaries again. Being reminded of patterns of parent-child interaction laid down over the years of childhood pulls the young adolescent away from the essential march toward independence. This doesn't mean you're actually treating your young teen like a child; it simply means that your child is on high alert for anything that might pull her back into dependence.

COGNITION

Our new technologies make it possible to look not only at the structure of the brain, but at its processes as well. We've come to understand in previously unimaginable detail how the early adolescent brain functions. We've seen how physical changes move the process of independence forward; now we understand how the brain itself may be wired to do the same.

A revolution in thinking takes place in the early adolescent brain, one that allows kids to think in much more abstract and complex ways. As their thinking moves in the direction of adult thinking, their incessant questioning, criticism, and arguing actually represent a great cognitive leap forward (this is what psychologists like to call a "positive reframing").

We are born with more neural connections in the brain than we need. To become more efficient, the brain "prunes" back these connections from just after birth throughout adolescence and into early adulthood. Depending on where this pruning is most dramatically taking place, we can expect significant changes to those areas of the brain. In the young adolescent, it is the prefrontal cortex and the limbic system that are most actively being pruned. And typically it is in the prefrontal cortex that "adult" thinking takes place. Here future plans are made, alternatives are weighed, risks are evaluated, and impulses are controlled. While there is a lot of pruning going on here, it will not be completed for another decade. The limbic system, closely tied to the prefrontal cortex, is a different matter. The limbic system is involved in the processing of emotions and their regulation, the processing of social information, and the seeking of risk and reward. Here changing levels of neurotransmitters, particularly dopamine and serotonin, make the young teen more emotional, more responsive to stress, and more likely to engage in risky behaviors.[28] It will come as no surprise, then, to learn that the limbic system is outpacing the prefrontal cortex. Since the brain is changing in ways that provoke your young teen to seek risk, novelty, and stimulation before the part of the brain that regulates impulse control and judgment is fully in place, we can see how vulnerable young teens are to doing stupid things. At this point the brain is kind of like a Ferrari being driven by a twelve-year-old.

So given this sensation-seeking brain, what teen would want to hang around with his parents? He knows that his new behaviors are unlikely to meet with parental approval, and he is remarkably sensitive to this. In an interesting study, it was shown that young teens had difficulty attending to a task when they were shown a sad face.[29] Teens are tuned, to the point of distraction, to the emotional tenor of others. So if you want your middle schooler to listen to the content of what you have to say, bring your emotions down. No yelling. Otherwise it's unlikely that your children will actually hear what you're saying, since they're more likely to be thrown off track by your feelings. This isn't to say that we should be robotic with our young teens. And there certainly are situations that warrant a ratcheting up of tone. But for the most part, neurobiology will win the day, and we should try our best for an even emotional keel.

So, were my son's worries justified when he feared that the transition from elementary to middle school would mean choosing between his own independence and his allegiance to the family? Yes and no. He certainly would be pushed in the direction of greater independence—by evolution, the culture, his body, and his brain. He would also find that home was still a safe haven and that his family not only supported but was in fact enthusiastic about his moves toward greater independence. Worry is part and parcel of being a young adolescent. My son was simply preparing himself for the host of transitions he was about to face, including family issues ("How can I get my mom to stop calling me 'sweetie' in front of the other kids?") and pressing social issues ("What are the rules of Truth or Dare?"). Young teens will have to navigate hundreds of compelling and conflicted situations like this over the middle school years. The trivial to you often feels like a matter of life and death to your child. You can help your young, marginally competent teens by being open, sensitive, available, and free enough of your own adolescent issues to truly be helpful with theirs. While perspective is important, our impulse to downplay some of our kids' concerns— "What's the big deal if I call you 'sweetie'? I've been calling you that for years"—is only likely to make them feel misunderstood. In psychology there is an old saw, "Take your patient where he's at." Good advice for the parents of middle schoolers.

How Parents Can Help

Middle school is a complex place. There are pushes and pulls in all sorts of directions on young teens who have barely left childhood. Academics, popularity, puberty, family, peers—the list goes on and on. Every day your middle school child is faced with a host of decisions that would make most of us dizzy. What should I wear? Whom do I sit with? Whom do I stay away from? Should I study? How much should I study? All this unfolds in the context of a changing body and parents who have turned abruptly dull, intrusive, and embarrassing. I have yet to meet a middle schooler who understands that his changing perceptions of his parents are coming primarily from *his* changed perspective. "What has happened to my parents?" is the predictable battle cry. It is in this context—confusion and anxiety—that we need to think how we parent our middle school children. By this point we have at least a decade of parenting experience under our belts and know that when our children are struggling we need to be calm, reassuring, and available. Yet our homes often seem to be anything but calm and reassuring. And our own frayed nerves often make us less than optimally available.

So, what's a parent to do? Puberty is inevitable and so is a period of increased conflict and decreased closeness in the household. It's important to remember that as your relationship with your child changes, you might want to look at other parts of your life that are reliably satisfying, whether that's tennis, a book club, your friends, or your work, and increase their presence in your life, for support, perspective, and renewal.

Here are some strategies that are particularly useful for parents with middle school age kids who are kicking over the traces and declaring independence.

- Keep a sense of humor that excludes mocking in any form.

- Put a sticky note on your mirror that reminds you that this is a temporary state of affairs or that just tickles you. Mine was "Insanity is hereditary. You get it from your kids."

Made me chuckle every morning through more than a decade of raising middle schoolers. Still does.

- Respect your child's need for privacy. Boundaries allow the adolescent to create a space where he or she can be relatively free from the battery of feelings, confusion, and upset that are the hallmarks of early puberty. This need for privacy is also a hallmark of the intense need to find some coherence among the rapidly changing views of the self. Those hours when the child is sprawled across the bed and behind closed doors are both a refuge from a chaotic inner life and a sanctuary for sorting through all the confusing iterations of the self without being distracted by the generally prickly relationship with parents.

- Do not back off from the monitoring that is critical for safety. Know where your kids are, who they're with, and when they're coming home. Trouble lives in the couple of hours after school. Encourage participation in an after-school extracurricular activity most days of the week.

- Provide opportunities for teens to become more independent. For example, don't nag about homework. Unless it's truly unbearable, let your children wear what they choose. Encourage them to take on small jobs like babysitting or coaching a younger child. In these small (and not so small) decisions and experiences young teens are creating a template for self-reliance and self-efficacy. "You try and figure it out. If you have trouble, I'm around."

- Don't sweat the small stuff. Your job is still to keep home a reasonable haven.

- Tolerate irritability and crabbiness, not disrespect.

BUILDING A PEER GROUP

There seem to be two wildly divergent views about the role of the peer group in middle school and how parents can cope with their child's new dependence on friends. On the one hand, peers are seen as potential threats to the sanity of your child and the sanctity of your family. This conflict is considered an inevitable part of the development of early adolescence. The peer group is conceived of as having its own rules and values, most of which are likely to conflict with your rules and values. In the ensuing battle for your child's soul, you are likely to lose. It is peers who will drive your child to sex, drugs, academic underperformance, and refusal to participate in long-established family rituals. Once children come under the influence of peer pressure, all bets are off in terms of understanding your young teens' taste in clothes, music, entertainment, and leisure activities. The one thing you can be certain of is that their choices will differ, and differ profoundly, from yours. This is the "tribe apart" view of young teens and their peers and it is extremely disconcerting to parents who keenly feel that they have lost control over their middle schooler. The best they can do is cross their fingers and hope that in a few years their child will return to her senses.

The opposing point of view holds that while reliance on peers certainly will increase during the middle school years, parents must actively assert their control and limit the effect of the peer group. Parents know that their middle schooler is anxious, confused, and vulnerable. This point of view holds that peers are equally anxious, confused, and vulnerable and therefore are incapable of moving your child's development forward in any positive way. While this "hold on to your child" point of view is reassuring in theory, most parents encounter intense resistance from their children and as a result find conflict is racheted up and implementation is impossible.

It seems to me that these two points of view share a common misperception: that all peer groups function in the same way. In fact, peer groups are no more similar than individual children. There are terrific peer groups that encourage academic achievement; teach social skills; create nurturing places for young teens to feel comfortable divulging all those confused, vulnerable, and anxious feelings; and are perfect habitats for crafting a strong sense of self. Alternatively, there are peer groups that discourage academic achievement, are immersed in antisocial attitudes like bullying, and are likely to have a significantly negative effect on a child's developmental trajectory and emerging sense of self. I have seen some middle schoolers saved by their peer group and a few lost. The vast majority of young teens use peer groups more or less effectively to help them move on to their next stage of development, which includes greater autonomy and the beginnings of sexual intimacy over the high school years.

Research is clear that while peers have considerable influence over your child's cultural decisions about dress, music, and recreation, parents continue to have a strong voice when it comes to factors like values and education. It's good to keep this in mind, because while it's your teens' purple hair or drooping pants that are obvious, it's their values that really count. To keep your relationship strong for those things that really matter, try not to fight about the predictable distastefulness of some aspects of adolescent culture that distance them from the adult world. From your kid's perspective, that's the point. A T-shirt proclaiming Guttermouth (a punk band) may or may not be them, but it's certainly not you!

Function of the Peer Group

I was having dinner with my husband at a local restaurant when a swarm of young teenage girls swept in carrying elaborately wrapped packages. Clearly it was a birthday celebration and it was hard not to marvel at the amount of electric energy these young girls emitted as they careened across the room to their table of twelve. Tall girls and short girls. Girls with the bodies of women and girls with the bodies of children. An assortment of adolescent accoutrements like acne, braces, and glasses marked some of the girls and left others untouched, while the vague odor of puberty wafted behind them all. I guessed that they were fourteen, but they were twelve and thirteen. After all these years of seeing teens, I'm still amazed at how grown-up a twelve-year-old girl can look.

As I looked at them, this is what I remembered about being twelve. I was flat as a board, I wore braces, I was tall and skinny, the world was a complete blur without my glasses, and because family finances were limited, I was never able to buy the "real" Weejuns that I coveted, settling instead for knockoffs, which I prayed no one would notice. And in spite of all this, I was one of the reasonably popular girls, just like the girls in the group seated near me appeared to be. Yet nothing I could remember, close to fifty years later, would suggest that there was anything in the least bit comforting, let alone exhilarating, about that time. As I watched this group of giddy and excited young girls, I knew that I wasn't seeing a new breed of teen girls, happier and better adjusted than I had been. I was simply seeing some of those moments—in between the fear, confusion, and anxiety—when great relief is found among peers. When peers are a blessing, not just because they are going through pretty much the same thing that you are, but also because they are the recreational break, the spontaneous laughter, the lack of responsibility that makes the emotional, cognitive, and physical demands of puberty tolerable.

Certainly our kids had friends when they were younger children, but there is a sharp increase in the amount of time spent with peers when they enter middle school. This is partly because of the additional freedom of, say, walking to school with friends or being allowed to hang out at the mall. The peer group acts as a "way station" between dependence on parents and dependence on oneself.[30] Researchers find that a middle school age child's level of conformity doesn't really change much, but the source of conformity moves from parents to peers.[31] So you are not imagining it when, rather suddenly, it seems like you have ceased to become a reliable source of information for your child, curiously replaced by same-age peers possessed of dubious knowledge and experience. Try not to take this personally. It is your young teen's first move toward being able to figure things out without constantly relying on you. Of course you know more, can analyze risk better, appreciate consequences more realistically, and understand your child better. This is partially—again, only partially—irrelevant to your young teen. Your job is still to keep your child on track, to set limits and consequences, to communicate values, to bring perspective, and to make sure that the dishes are done. With all the demands that are going on, frankly this is a bit of a bummer for your child. Peer group activities tend to be, well, fun. Like the girls at the birthday party, peer group activities are typically about interaction and leisure, dress, music, and media.

So if peer groups function as a break from the stresses of puberty, a place to develop interpersonal skills, and a training ground for intimacy and autonomy, why do we hear so much about the downside of peer groups and especially peer group pressure?

Cliques and Crowds

There is a consensus that kids today spend more time with their peers than in previous generations. There is no scientific agreement on whether this translates into increased vulnerability to peer pressure or even whether this has had an overall positive or negative effect on adolescent development. What is clear, however, is that the social culture of teenagers is largely organized around two similar but not identical structures: cliques and crowds.

In middle school, for the most part, cliques are small groups of five or six same-sex students who have common interests and are good friends. Middle schoolers tend to belong to cliques, girls in particular, but they frequently move (although often with a great deal of drama) between cliques. It is within this small, close group that young teens learn how to be a good friend, how to resolve conflict, or how to assume leadership roles, typically without adult guidance. As a result (and not surprisingly), these skills are developed slowly, often with considerable bruising of feelings.

Because clique members tend to share similar interests, the notion that taking up with the "wrong" friends can spell ruin for your child is simplistic. Emotionally healthy kids don't typically seek out troubled kids. Most of the time, kids seek out friendships with other kids who are similar to them. This is called selection. However, it also happens that kids who are friends can influence each other to become more similar. This is called socialization. Yet the spheres in which both selection and socialization operate are not equally important to adolescent mental health. Kids tend to socialize each other around issues of relatively minor consequence—clothing, hairstyles, music (I know that somewhere during the third hour of headbanger music, this issue doesn't seem minor at all, but really, there are bigger fish to fry than this). Selection, on the other hand, is typically based on shared values, including attitudes toward drinking and risky sexual activity.[32]

Crowds, on the other hand, are composed of much broader and larger groups of teens. One's crowd membership identifies a common image (preppies, drama freaks, jocks, druggies) but does not necessarily indicate close friendship. It may not even indicate the young teen's actual affiliation. One of my young patients, recently arrived from London, was an outstanding athlete. Ordinarily she would have been in the "jock" crowd, but her King's English accent made her sound particularly bright and as a result she spent her years in middle school identified as a "brain." Once in high school, this young girl will find it easier to move between crowds, but in middle school crowds are generally rigidly set.

Mean Girls and Bullying Boys

Rachel McAdams may have brought a wickedly funny flair to Regina, her stunningly nasty character in the movie *Mean Girls*, but mean girls are no laughing matter. Neither are bullying boys. Research shows that the child who is harassed by schoolmates, whether through physical bullying, cyberbullying, or the social aggression that is the primary tactic of "mean girls," suffers from low self-esteem, depression, and academic difficulties, all of which are likely to continue into high school and beyond.[33] Perhaps most notably, kids who are the victims of other kids' aggression have general difficulties around school (not surprisingly, it's awfully hard to pay attention when you're scared, teased, excluded, or threatened).

While there have always been bullies, current studies suggest that bullying has become a normative middle school experience. In addition, it appears that cyberbullying has even more negative consequences for its victims than traditional physical bullying, probably because of the profound sense of helplessness and isolation it engenders.[34] Responses to cyberbullying are particularly worrisome and include somatic symptoms, depression, and even suicide. A spate of recent suicides by young teens who have been relentlessly cyberbullied has made this tragically clear.

Peers, cliques, crowds, and the social vicissitudes of middle school life are to be expected and actually confer some protective value on young teens as they learn to develop resilience and the more complex social skills they will need as they move on to high school. Bullying, however, is unacceptable in any form. It harms the bully, the victim, and the community in which they interact. Parents, in concert with schools, must act to reverse a trend that only promises to increase our already unacceptable rates of adolescent emotional problems. This is one of those places where we don't sit back, where we don't "let them work it out." This is one place where we take action.

How Parents Can Help

Regardless of whether we think that increased reliance on peers is a positive move in social development or a satanic switch in alliances, it is the reality of the middle school years. Here's what really matters: that we stay attached and available to our young teens throughout this demanding transition. While peers certainly do influence our kids, sometimes for better, sometimes for worse, it is detachment from parents that poses the far greater threat to a child's well-being. As our children grow, and move in the direction of increased independence, their list of "go-to" people should also grow. That list should include parents and peers and other responsible adults, such as teachers or coaches or family friends whom your child feels comfortable with.

There are ways to maximize your relationship with your young teen and ways to diminish it. Parents often experience their role as being reduced, which of course it is in certain respects. But more important, our role is being transformed from authority to authority/ consultant (with a gradually increasing emphasis on consultant). Certainly there are times when we retain our roles as authorities, most especially around pressing issues of safety. But it is critical that we are willing to enter into a more collaborative relationship with our young teens and understand the benefits of this. For better or worse, experience simply cannot be grafted. Telling our child what to do is not the same as our children learning, through their own efforts, and sometimes in consultation with us, how to make good decisions. Our willingness to step back, to respect our child's efforts at self-control and resourcefulness, also gives us more credibility for those instances when we must act as authorities. Consultants have a great deal of influence, and just as our kids are adjusting to their new roles, we need to adjust to ours. Here are three real-life examples that illustrate that while the line between consultant and authority is always moving, when our children are in middle school we must be prepared to act in both capacities with an eye toward maximizing what our children learn, minimizing disruptions in the relationship, and always keeping safety our top priority.

- Your eleven-year-old daughter, Kate, announces that this Christmas Eve she will not be going with the family to dinner at her grandparents' house. With great pride she tells you that "Alexis, Kelley, and Olivia, the three most popular girls at school," are getting together on Christmas Eve at Alexis's house, and she has been invited. Her glow lets you know that this invitation is enormously important to her. It has been a hard year for Kate socially. Once part of the popular crowd, she was more often excluded than included in get-togethers in recent months. She makes no mention of the fact that your family has celebrated Christmas the same way every year since Kate was born. You know she will be devastated if she's forced to go with the family, and you're not sure you have the heart to do this. Is this the place to take a stand?

- Your thirteen-year-old son, Jacob, has been hanging out with the same group of boys and girls for most of his last two years in middle school. They're a great group of kids and you've seen little conflict between them. They all come to his bar mitzvah celebration and your only hint that something is amiss comes when the whole group goes MIA for about twenty minutes. Your son is surprisingly low-key at the end of the evening and on the car ride home mentions that his "girlfriend" (the first you've heard of this) was "hooking up" with his best friend, Adam. You're feeling really angry that his best friend would betray him on such a special night. Is this the time for a conversation on what makes a good friend? And are you supposed to ignore the "hooking up" reference in deference to his obvious emotional distress?

- Your twelve-year-old son, William, like most of his classmates, has a computer in his room. While he has always been something of a computer geek, he seems to be spending more and more time on the computer, often with his door locked. When you ask what he's doing he says he has homework. He seems to have lost some of his vitality, complains of stomachaches, and is having trouble sleeping. Your curiosity gets the better of you, and one day while he's still at school you look at his browsing history. You're shocked to find a list of explicit pornography sites. More upsetting, these links appear to have been sent by other kids, some of his good friends, in fact, with the images often Photoshopped so that your son's face appears on the bodies of women, often with some derogatory comment about his being "a queer." Your son hasn't mentioned a word. Isn't this cyberbullying? You're a bit worried about his reaction to your "spying" on his computer, but mostly you're furious and outraged. Do you call the school or the police?

These stories highlight some of the most common challenges kids face in middle school. Kate is still young, and her story reflects concerns about same-sex friendships and the shifting allegiance between friends and family that is so characteristic of this age group. Jacob, just two years older, is now immersed in early boy-girl relationships. Because kids at this age are so new to the workings of relationships, there are frequent moments of confusion, betrayal, and anxiety as they try to figure out how to navigate their romantic relationships while simultaneously maintaining their other friendships. Throw into this the intense sexual feelings that are coming to the fore and you've got the kinds of muddled conflicts about what a friend is that can throw kids into a tailspin. Finally, William's cyberbullying story is unfortunately becoming all too common. While it's clear that he needs protection and intervention, just as with Kate's and Jacob's less worrisome situations, there are more and less effective ways to help children when they are challenged.

So how do we approach the range of peer-related problems that are bound to come up during the middle school years?

EVALUATE RISK

Our first job is to ascertain if there is any real, imminent risk to your child's mental or physical health. Neither Kate's nor Jacob's dilemma poses any imminent risk, although Kate's predicament is certain to produce some family drama. William's story, however, is a whole different matter. The reason that William needs protection is less about his exposure to pornography and more about his panoply of depressive symptoms. Cyberbullying is notoriously toxic because of its anonymity. At what point do you contact school administrators, your child's counselor, or even the police, when your child is being bullied? Because the evidence is so clear on the long-term negative effects of bullying on young teens' mental health, the answer is sooner rather than later. William is at considerable risk and as a result needs his parents to quickly formulate an action plan.

SIZE UP HOW QUICKLY YOU NEED TO ACT

There are few instances that fall into the category of immediate intervention, and you are likely to recognize them if they unfortunately occur. Bullying, physical or sexual abuse, social cruelty, or cyberbullying would all demand immediate parental attention but this is not always the same as immediate action. Should parents get the gears in motion before consulting with their child? Does William's mom walk away from his computer and immediately call the mothers of the boys who have been sending doctored pornography, demand an explanation, and threaten to call the police? Should she call the school and request a transfer? We all think more clearly when we've had a bit of time to get over our initial distress, perhaps confer with trusted advisers, and consider alternative plans of action. There are probably better ways to assure your child that he is being protected than acting without his knowledge. Few things can't wait until your child gets home from school.

TRUST THAT COLLABORATION
IS YOUR BEST FIRST APPROACH

The quickest way to lose ground with your child is with pronouncements. "Young lady, you most certainly will go to the family Christmas dinner." "What is wrong with your friends? Maybe it's time to make friends with kids who know the meaning of the word." "How could you not tell us about this? We're calling the school and the police." This kind of response, no matter how legitimate or well intended, sends a clear message that you're still in charge and that your child doesn't have a say in his own life. This is a message no one is likely to cozy up to, least of all a young teen who desperately needs to feel that he has some control over the way things turn out in his life. These situations and hundreds more just like them that come up during the middle school years are best addressed by respecting your child enough to bring him or her into the process of figuring out how to solve problems. This does not mean that you give up your authority when your child is endangered; it simply means that in order for your child to learn, as well as to be protected, from an unhealthy or distressing experience, he needs to be included in the process.

Regardless of how upset you are, try to approach your child in a concerned but low-key way. Anxiety is contagious and if your children sense a great deal of anxiety from you, they are likely to go into lockdown mode. Neutral statements like "Sounds like we should have a talk about Christmas" or "How did you feel when your friends treated you that way?" or "I hear there's cyberbullying going on—can we talk about it?" are ways to open the conversation and let your child know you're ready to listen, not to pounce. Remember that peer situations—turning down the popular clique, feeling betrayed by a good friend, or being bullied online—can be extremely humiliating. Young teens can find it terribly difficult to talk about things that they are ashamed of. Practice patience if it's appropriate. Assure your kids that you have their back.

By the time your child is in middle school, many things have become negotiable. When there are disagreements, it is important that your kids "win" sometimes, especially when they make a clear and compelling case for their point of view. This assures them that parents are actually listening to them and it models compromise. But some things simply aren't negotiable. To help you make this distinction in your own home, let's look a little more closely at Kate's, Jacob's, and William's situations and how their parents might decide what is and what isn't negotiable. The tact with which the parents engage their children has a great deal to do with how successful they will be in helping their children resolve these situations. Even when there is room for negotiation or compromise, the values that you hold should be in plain sight.

Kate's parents should want to hear why their daughter, who has loved Christmas dinner for years, is willing to give it up this year. One of the most important things that adults bring to kids is a sense of perspective. Kate may fear never being included again if she turns down this invitation. A discussion about popularity versus friendship is probably in order. Maintaining family rituals is very important in early adolescence. On the other hand, a furious, sulking teenager is no great addition to the dinner table. Kate needs to feel that, even if her parents don't agree with her, they can empathize with the difficulty of her dilemma. But be clear that in a family, the needs of all people have to be taken into account. Depending on how important this ritual is to Kate's parents, they might agree to let her go to her friend's, be willing to negotiate a compromise, or insist on her attendance. The process is far more important than any particular outcome.

Jacob's situation is a good illustration of why parents need to step back when it is appropriate. It was unfortunate to have this rather common rearranging of middle school relationships take place on such a special day for Jacob. However, a hallmark of early adolescence is a fluid rearrangement of connections between boys and girls. Just as two BFFs can become mortal enemies overnight, so does one boy's "girlfriend" become another boy's "girlfriend" (and vice versa) in the blink of an eye. Boys tend to generally (but not always) be a bit more stoic about these lapses in friendship. If you want your life to resemble a soap opera for the next few years, by all means step in and start asking how everyone "feels" about what happened. Alternatively, you can take a problem that is well within the coping range of a thirteen-year-old and let him figure it out himself. As for the hooking-up reference, in middle school this usually means some preliminary sexual exploration and not intercourse. But your son has given you an opening to check that out.

William's situation clearly demands the most immediate and thorough attention. All of us know the feelings of anger and protectiveness that kick in when one of our children is threatened. Because we are genetically programmed to protect our young, these feelings push us toward action, but they can also get in the way of being at our most thoughtful. William's mom needs to not simply react, but consider a plan of action. It is obvious that William's mental health is being threatened. Because of the profound feelings of helplessness and shame that cyberbullying engenders, William is showing symptoms of clinical depression. Mom's plan needs to be twofold: to put an end to the cyberbullying and to get her son additional support to deal with his feelings and symptoms. She will need help from many quarters: her spouse or a friend, the school administrator and counselor, her son's pediatrician, and an adolescent therapist.

But first she needs to talk to her son. Already feeling helpless, William is likely to be frightened that bringing this out into the open will only worsen his situation. Contingency plans need to be made for this possibility, including contacting the police. It's a given that the adults in his life will take action to put the cyberbullying to an end. However, it would be most helpful if William doesn't feel that the answers to this problem have all been predetermined by you. Whom does he want to talk to? Does he want to be included in school meetings? Would it help him to confront the "friends" who are bullying him? The absolute here is that the situation be dealt with. An evaluation by a therapist skilled in dealing with adolescents is mandatory. William may be depressed, or he may also be showing symptoms of extreme stress. Tough as it seems, this is an opportunity for William to learn more about how to effectively cope with adversity.

It is also an opportunity for Mom or Dad to encourage the school or, better yet, the school district to consider implementing one of the many successful programs that stress socio-emotional learning, often called SEL. These programs, with their emphasis on recognizing and managing emotions, developing empathy, and learning how to handle conflicts effectively and ethically, have repeatedly been shown to reduce or prevent bullying.[35] Not incidentally, they have also been shown to improve academic performance, reduce substance abuse, and lower stress levels.[36] There is no set of skills more important for healthy development than learning how to effectively and responsibly deal with one's own feelings and the feelings of others. SEL is a twofer. It advances our kids' understanding of themselves, and it helps them get along better with others. Both make it easier to develop a healthy sense of self.

Bullying, cyber or otherwise, has been shown to be so pervasive and to have such negative effects on kids that it is a wonder that more has not been done to reduce its incidence. Your child's school may have excellent teachers and curriculum, spanking-new classrooms, and the latest technological gizmos. But if your sons or daughters are afraid to go to school or are losing sleep or having trouble concentrating because they are being bullied, they can neither take advantage of what the school offers nor produce the kind of work they would be capable of under nonthreatening conditions. Let's get our priorities straight. The first thing our children need, regardless of where they live, is schools that are safe. Schools are a community, and when one child is bullied, every child is under threat of being bullied. Don't step back on this one.

NOTE TO PARENTS
....

Can the middle school years feel heavy with loss—of closeness, of authority, of control, of importance? Of course. Just as our children are leaving their childhood behind, so are we leaving behind years with them that seemed carefree; in contrast, adolescence seems increasingly difficult. Allow yourself time to adjust to these losses; children are not the only people who need time to adjust to transitions. If you're someone who has loved the physical closeness of the early years with your child, intellectual sparring may seem like a poor substitute. But once you've grieved a bit for what is lost, think about all that is gained. A child who is learning to be independent, to make good choices, to carve out an identity, to cultivate multiple relationships, and ultimately to make his or her particular contribution to this world. Don't sell yourself short, either. Many women find middle age to be an invigorating time because of the opportunities they have to pursue passions that had been on the back burner when their children were younger.

When things between you and your child get bumpy, remember that your relationship with your child did not begin yesterday. Parent-child relationships have long and deep roots. The way you and your child are most likely to navigate the middle school years began to be shaped many years ago, and while there will be interruptions and disruptions here and there, if you've had a good relationship the odds are great that both of you will not only survive, but thrive. Advise when you can, rule when you must. Keep perspective and a sense of humor close at hand. Don't expend all your resources. After all, you're coming up to the high school years, years that are as stunningly satisfying and transformative as they are challenging for both you and your child.

• CHAPTER 5 •

The Tasks of the High School Years

Ages 14–18

It's eleven thirty on Saturday night and you're trying to decide whether to stay up for a few minutes of *SNL* or turn in early. It's been a long week, and you're happy that you didn't make plans to go out for the evening. Your ten-year-old daughter is asleep and your sixteen-year-old son will be skidding in shortly, moments before his midnight curfew. Your husband is already sound asleep on top of the covers, still in his jeans and T-shirt. You decide to stretch out next to him with a book that's been sitting on your nightstand for weeks, and you let out a long exhale as you relax and take in the rare quiet in your house. Your cell phone rings and you reach for it quickly, thinking your son might be trying to buy an extra half hour of time at his friend's house.

It's not your son's voice that greets you, but that of a police officer. Panic floods you for a moment until you realize that he already has said, "Your son is fine, ma'am." You instantly love this man who has spoken to so many terrified mothers, he knows to reassure you in the very first sentence. The adrenaline that has been loosed on you prevents you from hearing every word, but this much is clear: your son is being held at the police station, along with his best friend, for possession of alcohol and for public drunkenness. It's all a bit hazy until your son gets on the phone and in a slurred and frightened voice asks you to come down to the station to get him. Then your mother radar switches on and you are clear that your kid is in trouble and needs your help. You wake your husband, give a quick explanation, and ask him to stay home with your daughter. You get into your car, trying hard to imagine your young son intoxicated and stumbling about the streets of your town. Maybe it's a mistake, maybe his friends dared him, maybe it was some kind of initiation. Your son has been straight as an arrow. Responsible, good grades, no drugs (you may have to rethink that one), never out past curfew. Have you missed something? Maybe he's been depressed. Maybe you've been working too hard to notice? You resolve to be a better mother, no matter what it takes, just as you pull up to the police station.

Your ragged son has obviously been drinking. The police say that they can hold him for the night, but they don't suggest it. "He seems like a real good kid. Let him sleep it off and then talk about it tomorrow." Both you and your son are in tears by the time you get into the car, but you are happy to have been given some direction by the officer. His matter-of-fact attitude and lack of harshness help you to feel like maybe this isn't the end of the world. When you get home, you don't bother to remind your son to wash up and instead simply let him slip into bed. His woebegone expression makes you ruffle his hair, tell him that you love him and that you'll work it out tomorrow. He barely manages "I love you, too" before falling into a stuporous sleep. You feel angry, sad, and protective all at the same time and realize that the punishments you're thinking about— "No going out for the rest of the year," "You'll need random drug testing," "I don't know if I can ever trust you again"—might need further consideration.

The next morning finds your son contrite, your husband relatively unimpressed by the night's proceedings, and you still angry. How are you ever going to be able to relax again knowing that your son may be engaging in dangerous hijinks? What in the world was he thinking? How could he have been so stupid, so inconsiderate, so self-destructive? This kind of mistake makes us parents mad with worry and self-doubt. And while you have every right to be upset, there is another way of thinking about the previous night's activities. *What your son did was not about you.* He didn't do it to piss you off, make you anxious, or call into questioning your parenting skills. He did it in order to take a risk, to test the limits of his self-control, to see if he could manage, and to satisfy his curiosity. This is not to say that he made a good choice, or that he should be let off scot-free. It still is very much your job to reassert family rules, to impose consequences, and to help your son think more clearly about the choices he makes. It is also your job to understand what drives his choices so that you can anticipate potential problems and react appropriately to the kinds of similar scenarios that are almost inevitable over the course of the high school years. No teenager will learn how to deal with peer pressure, craft an identity, develop self-control, and avoid risk without missteps.

Teens are driven to behave in certain ways, not because you've been a good parent or a bad parent, but because there is a human drive toward independence. This drive is appropriately heightened for teens as they begin, in earnest, the work of preparing for their adult lives. Certainly there are ways in which we can move this process along and help our teens develop the coping skills known to contribute to good outcomes. But we cannot stop the process. Nor should we want to. A better understanding of what your teens are driven to accomplish, the skills at their disposal, and the roadblocks they're likely to encounter as well as the steps you can take to make their journey safer and more successful will make you a less anxious, more effective, and better parent.

Adolescence is the training ground for adulthood. In a relatively short period of time, your teenager will undergo a metamorphosis. Over the high school years, most teens move from lingering dependence to true independence, from self-centeredness to concern for others and intimacy, from logical thinking to the far more complex abstract and hypothetical thinking, from impulsivity to thoughtfulness, and from a diffuse sense of the kind of person they are to a reasonably defined sense of self. These changes take place at different rates and to varying degrees in teens, but nonetheless, the direction is toward maturity.

As if this weren't demanding enough, teens also have to somehow resolve the illogical task of conforming to social rules and expectations while at the same time freeing themselves from the influence of others. If this were a job description, it would command an outsize salary, extensive benefits, and a Goldman Sachs–type bonus. Instead of kudos, most teens feel that what they get is endless pressure, prying, and criticism, and occasional use of the family car. Fortunately, participation in adolescence is not optional. Like it or not, ready or not, your teenagers will spend several years working on the following tasks as they inch their way toward adulthood.

BECOMING
AN ADULT THINKER

Most of us are likely to think of psychological issues like independence or identity or biological issues like managing sexual development as topping the teenager's task list. But successful management of all the tasks that our teens will confront—feeling comfortable with sexuality and intimacy, becoming independent, refining an identity, strengthening self-control—depends on their being able to think with greater maturity than when they were younger. Fortunately, there is a predictable cognitive revolution that goes on early in high school, one that allows our kids to be able to think much like adults. And being able to think like an adult is a big first step toward being able to act like an adult. This doesn't mean that our high school kids have the maturity or judgment of adults, but they do have a whole new range of thinking skills to draw on, skills that over time will lead to healthier and more thoughtful decisions and behaviors. Here are the remarkable shifts in thinking that take place during the high school years.

Thinking about abstractions and possibilities:
High school kids are able to think about not only what is, but what might be. Their thinking is not bound by what is in front of them; it can also include abstract and theoretical possibilities. This is why younger kids, no matter how talented, can rarely learn advanced math or science. Their brains simply aren't set up yet for complex and abstract thinking. But an interested and motivated high school student can tackle calculus or physics because he or she is capable of the kind of thought necessary to master complex subjects.

Now that teens can think abstractly, they can also imagine their futures in far greater detail than they could when they were younger. Again, because they are no longer tied to the present, they can imagine being in many different schools, careers, situations, and relationships. Teens know that who they are today is in flux and that there will be many iterations before they settle on a final identity.

Thinking hypothetically:
Probably the greatest intellectual accomplishment in adolescence is the ability to think hypothetically, to engage in "if/then" thinking. "If I blow off my math test, then I may fail the course and have to go to summer school." All of a sudden, blowing off the math test is about a whole set of consequences. Clearly this particular skill is a work in progress throughout adolescence as teens consider all

the "what-ifs" associated with things like sex, drugs, academics, relationships, integrity, and risk-taking. Often their ability to think through a what-if situation is greater than their ability to act on their conclusions. Your teens may be quite capable of telling you the consequences of an unhealthy behavior but quite inarticulate about why they choose to engage in it anyway. In spite of the fact that their thinking and behavior are not always aligned, their newly developing ability to consider the future consequences of their actions is an enormous cognitive leap forward.

Hypothetical thinking also allows teens to suspend their own point of view and take another person's perspective. For the most part this is a welcome development, because your teen is no longer solely focused on himself. He can stand in someone else's shoes and understand a different point of view. But paradoxically the ability to be more empathic can also make your teen an unforgiving (and often accurate) adversary. "You're such a hypocrite. You really want me to go to an Ivy League school so that you'll have bragging rights with your friends." Parents often feel taken down a notch or two when their teens—who now have the ability to see us as people, not just parents—point out some of our less than sterling qualities.

Thinking about thinking:

Teens spend a lot of time in internal dialogue. "My counselor is recommending a nearby college, but I think I'll be happier if I go to a school away from home. I'm not sure why I feel this way. Guess I need to think about it." Thinking about thinking, or metacognition, becomes of great interest to teenagers. They are no longer okay with just *what* they know, they also want to know *why* they think a certain way. Early in high school, teens are likely to feel intensely self-conscious as they think endlessly about every minor aspect of themselves and assume that others are judging them harshly. But by the middle of high school most teens put their sharpened thinking skills to use beyond obsessing about their potential, and often imagined, deficits.

Increased interest in their thinking processes helps teens to become more efficient learners, more thoughtful, and more productively self-reflective. Self-reflection is a big step forward for them; it beefs up self-reliance and is a tonic against impulsivity and thoughtlessness. And, of course, self-reflection plays a big role in helping our teens assess their interests, skills, talents, and capacities, allowing them to develop an increasingly realistic picture of themselves. Don't worry that your child is "doing nothing" when he's lying on his bed staring into space or listening to music. It is during these breaks of quiet reflection that much necessary and creative work on the self is being done.

Thinking in complex ways:

Just a few years back, your child would answer questions like "Who's your best friend?" "What is the best thing your parents have done for you?" or "Are you a quiet or an outgoing person?" easily, and often with a single word. In high school, however, thinking becomes much more complex. The teenager might talk about having a number of "best friends" whom she turns to for different reasons—advice, support, or challenge. There is an appreciation that some of the "best things" their parents have done may have involved simply doing nothing. "The best thing my mom did was to stay out of it when I was struggling in math." And self-evaluation is understood to be dependent on context. "I'm quiet in new situations. But when I get to know people and feel comfortable with them, I'm really very social."

The ability to think about multiple dimensions of a problem makes teens much more capable of analysis. Like the development of "if/then" thinking, being able to think about multiple dimensions helps teens understand challenging academic subjects as well as complex personal and interpersonal problems. One of the places that we see this appreciation of complexity is in the teen's new appreciation of major social issues. No longer thinking in black-and-white, high school students are quite capable of organizing a relief effort following a natural disaster or seeing both sides of a political issue. Talking to high school age teens is often fun but also challenging for their parents. Gone are the days of "because I said so." Teens want to know and understand the reasons behind everything. Parents do their teens a great service when they enthusiastically engage in debates, discussions, even arguments with them. While it may seem that there is a moratorium on your child's accepting anything you have to say, in fact your teen is learning to think in more complex and more creative ways as she considers how her own thinking aligns (or doesn't) with yours. But while the endgame is generally quite positive, kids grow up to have values that are more similar to than different from their parents'. They are in fact paying attention to what you are saying and even more to what you are doing.

Putting It All Together

Remember your child's growth spurt, when you were certain that if you just watched at his bedside, you would catch him growing while he slept? And the long period of physical adjustment when he would knock over drinks at the dinner table, stumble over the threshold, and generally career his unfamiliar body off the walls of the house? Given time, practice, and support, adolescents regain control of their limbs and find comfortable ways to live in their new bodies.

The cognitive changes of the high school years are very much like the physical changes that preceded them. While the shifts in thinking continue to be developed over many years, it is exactly the same conditions of time, practice, and support that make the adjustment easier and the outcome more robust. We wouldn't think of mocking our young teen's awkward body; nor should we be sarcastic about our teen's burgeoning reasoning skills. No "Since when did you become an authority on everything?" or "I'll talk to you when you actually know what you're talking about." Abstract, hypothetical, complex thinking doesn't develop overnight. Our kids will need years of practice before they can reliably use their new thinking skills in consistently healthy ways. Just as our kids grew into their adult bodies, they will, over time, grow into their adult brains.

Adult Thinking Is Not the Same As Adult Behavior

Seventeen-year-old Dylan keeps a small amount of pot hidden in his car. Mom, rifling through his glove compartment for insurance papers, sees the bag of pot and confronts him. She's worried both about his frequency of use and whether he drives stoned. Dylan is frank, says he smokes a couple of times a month and never when he's driving. He seems to think that keeping his stash in the car is preferable to keeping it in his room, where his parents might find it and "freak out." Contrary to our first impulse to say that Dylan is just plain sneaky, we should note that he is showing the ability to be able to stand in his parents' shoes and has a good grasp of what their point of view is likely to be. Remember, we are talking about thinking skills right now, not behavior. Ultimately Dylan's behavior will be greatly shaped by his ability to see things from different points of view, but right now he is a relative newcomer to the art of translating thinking into changed behavior.

Mom is less distressed by his casual experimentation than by the fact that he seems oblivious to the potential consequences of being stopped by the police. Dylan says he has had the same concern, indicating that he has also begun to think hypothetically about potential complications. He then sheepishly admits that a policeman had, in fact, stopped him several months earlier and found the bag of pot, but simply told Dylan to "be safe" and sent him on his way. Dylan's conclusion from this experience was that keeping marijuana in the car is fine. Anticipating his mom's objections, Dylan launches into a sophisticated argument about the pros and cons of marijuana use, concluding with the statement that "all things considered," occasional pot use poses no danger to him. This is another sign of a maturing cognitive style, the ability to put together an abstract and complex argument.

Unfortunately, in spite of Dylan's armamentarium of more mature thinking skills, the ability to think abstractly and hypothetically, to take another's point of view, to construct complex arguments, and to anticipate future consequences, he makes the error of generalizing from a single incident. His confidence in his position is strengthened by the fact that it was an authority figure who elected to ignore Dylan's misdemeanor. Since teens, more than adults, place considerably more weight on potential reward than on potential risk, the fact that he was let off so easily only confirms the relative reward of his decision. So, even though Dylan's brain is capable of adult thinking, he lacks experience, and is unduly influenced by his amped-up limbic system, the reward part of his brain that enjoys the feeling of being high. As a result he reaches a different conclusion from his parents' about the advisability of keeping marijuana in his car. Dylan's actions aren't thoughtless; standing in Dylan's shoes we can easily see how he came to his conclusion. So, assuming that the car is not the best place to keep a marijuana stash, and assuming that marijuana use is a more complex issue than Dylan seems aware of, how do we help him become an even more mature thinker?

How Parents Can Help

Reasoned discussion with his parents will help Dylan see the danger of generalizing from a single experience. A calm enforcement of consequences (whether withdrawal of privileges or simply insisting that he not have any illegal drugs in his car) will assure Dylan that while most things in his world are in flux, he can depend on a reasonable consistency at home. Continued discussion about marijuana use, as long as it's not too heated and confrontational, will help sharpen his ability to see the pros and cons more clearly. You may be angry as heck to find your child experimenting with drugs, but your job is to learn the facts, clarify issues, maintain connection, and set limits. Your continued insistence on appropriate limit setting helps your child internalize and advance his own ability to set limits. It helps beef up his self-control.

You also need to be aware of when additional monitoring is necessary. For example, kids who actively experiment with drugs (this doesn't mean an incident here or there), whether marijuana, alcohol, cigarettes, or other drugs, before the age of fifteen are at significantly increased risk for both substance abuse and psychological problems. Kids who experiment with occasional use and are older than fifteen show no negative long-term consequences. Only cigarettes, because they are so addictive, show long-term negative health effects. Of course these are statistics about thousands of kids. Every child is different and some kids experiment early and end up fine, while others experiment late and run into problems. The point is that, in general, the longer your child abstains from using drugs the less likely he or she will be to develop a substance abuse problem.

One of your teen's greatest accomplishments will be not only to think like an adult, but to behave like one. (I mean this in the sense of accrued maturity; there are plenty of adults who continue to behave like teenagers.) Ultimately our kids will need to base their behavior on mature thinking, self-control, and actual practice out in the world. Until these three major advances gel, a process that takes many years, our teens' behavior will from time to time continue to appear distressingly risky. Dylan's mom is not likely to be hoping that her son keeps getting caught until some police officer finally hauls him down to juvenile hall. But the fact is that the experiential part of learning is simply part and parcel of being able to put newly advanced thinking to good use. It is a mistake to intervene prematurely or unnecessarily as teens gather these experiences. *Unnecessary intervention only prevents them from strengthening their coping skills.* It gets in the way of furthering self-control, self-esteem, and self-reliance because it takes the experience out of their hands and transfers it to ours. All this teaches is passivity and a reliance on others to solve problems. Our job is of course to keep our kids safe, but bailing them out of a speeding ticket, for example, works against the very experience they are most in need of: the connection between their choices and real-life consequences.

We are right to be in a "show me" frame of mind when our children are teenagers. In most families, in order to be granted the additional privileges and independence that teens covet, they are expected to exhibit more adult ways of thinking. While this can be frustrating for teens, it is also protective, because it gives them time to practice their newly acquired thinking skills out in the world without too much risk. The sixteen-year-old girl who can't come home reliably with a midnight curfew cannot be expected to manage a 1 a.m. curfew. The fifteen-year-old boy who week after week blows his allowance on yet another video game is unlikely to become a better money manager with a raise. Our teens need practice and they need experience. They need to be reined in when their impulsivity gets the better of them and they need to be reminded often that the rewards of risky behavior are typically small and transient. Equally important, they need to be celebrated for their willingness to be more thoughtful, to take fuller responsibility, to work hard, and to increasingly become the active agents of their own lives.

Next time you hear yourself ask, "What were you thinking?" in either frustration or indignation, listen to your teen's answer. "Everyone was doing coke and I really didn't want to but I thought they'd call me a pussy if I refused." It may not be what you want to hear, but it will give you a handle on how far along your teen is in aligning his behavior with his thinking. Your job is not to go ballistic (which would only ensure that your teen won't confide in you next time) but to appreciate his dilemma, help him put his skills to better use, limit his exposure to real risk, and clarify consequences. Start with questions like "What else could you have done?" or "Was there another way to handle the situation?" If he's stuck, help him along by offering alternatives ("Sorry, can't; my friend had a real problem with cocaine"), encourage him to think through risk and reward ("I know you don't want to stand out, but when kids are high they really don't pay much attention to what other kids are doing"), and remind him of consequences ("Cocaine is a really dangerous drug; for the moment no parties with this group of kids"). Remember, our very first job is to appropriately monitor our teen's safety. After all, if we're not successful at that, then any discussion of cognitive skills is irrelevant. Engage with your teenagers, help them think through challenges, offer alternatives, applaud their ability to think more deeply, and protect them when necessary.

A Note on Discussions and Arguments with Teenagers

Teenagers love to argue, and for good reason. It gives them multiple opportunities to sharpen their maturing cognitive skills. Give teens half a reason (or often no reason at all) and they're ready to engage in verbal battle. Unless all your buttons are being pushed, or if conflict is constant and hateful (a more serious symptom of family problems), try to engage, and even express enjoyment at the process. Don't yell or "lose it." Model how adults can take in and consider different points of view. As we've seen, by the time children are in high school they are quite capable of seeing and appreciating another's point of view. This is the underpinning of empathy and ultimately of developing concern about social issues larger than the upcoming dance.

Teenagers also argue as a way of differentiating themselves from their parents. The extent to which you can stay available and involved in these arguments makes it easier for your teen to become his "own person" while remaining connected to you. Teens don't hate these arguments: parents do. If the topic is controversial and your teen brings it up, he's probably looking to clarify his feelings and proclaim his independence; shocking you is simply an added bonus. Feel free to ask your teen to clarify why he thinks heroin should be legalized. Or why hooking up is fine. Or why cheating is nothing more than a survival tool. Being curious does not mean endorsement. Listen. Ask questions. Don't judge quickly. In addition to moving his cognitive skills forward, you will become more familiar with the inner workings of the particular world your teenager inhabits. Your teen learns from these skirmishes, but so do you. It may look messy and ragged from the outside, but arguing is an expectable and healthy part of adolescence. Think of arguing as an alternative and (thankfully) time-limited way of maintaining connection with your teenager.

LEARNING TO
MANAGE SEXUALITY

The Importance of a Healthy Start

Sexuality does not begin in high school. Babies touch their genitals with apparent pleasure, children "play doctor," and older children have erotic fantasies. Long before intercourse takes place, there is a rather predictable sequence of sexual exploration that begins with activities like hand holding and kissing and moves on to touching and fondling (remember the "bases"?).

Like all of human development, sexuality proceeds in fits and starts, with marked periods of transition. Puberty is clearly the transition that moves sexual activity into a realm of far greater consequence and complexity than the sex play of earlier years. The stakes become high as pregnancy, sexually transmitted diseases, HIV, abuse, and trauma become possible outcomes of sexual activity.

For most teens, the mechanics and risks of sexuality are well understood thanks in part to the ever-present "human sexuality" class endured by most high schoolers. And while these classes are moderately successful in raising awareness of the potential problems associated with teen sexuality, they often fail to address emotional issues and give short shrift to the healthy aspects of teen sexuality. Schools, like many parents, are afraid to make sex attractive, out of a misplaced concern that they will be encouraging premature sexual activity. Forget the idea that talking about sex would be "putting ideas" into your teen's head. Once your children are in high school, the ideas have long since set up camp in their heads.

The move into adult sexuality, while normal and expectable, is still a major transition in your teenager's life. Sexual activity activates a range of sensitive and deeply felt issues. Your teen's early sexual experiences can be affirming or devastating. Girls' self-esteem, in particular, is markedly affected by their early sexual experiences. Clearly we want our teen's sexual experiences to be healthy and satisfying and advance their emotional growth. Here are some of the factors most likely to affect the quality of your teen's sexual adjustment.

Age:

The average age for first sexual intercourse among most teens in this country is between sixteen and seventeen. This is good for several reasons. First, research has shown that having intercourse at this age, rather than earlier in adolescence, increases the odds of using contraception (although typically it's still not until *after* the first intercourse that contraception is used). Also, researchers find *no negative psychological factors* associated with being sexually active at this age. However, having intercourse before age sixteen is associated with a host of concerns.

Most teens are physically capable of sexual relations long before they are psychologically ready. The fact that your teenager is physically developed or has passed through puberty (for girls this can be as young as eleven or twelve) does not alone mean that he or she is old enough to be sexually active. While early maturing boys are more likely to be sexually active because of the surge in testosterone, early maturing girls are much less influenced by hormones and more influenced by what else is going on around them. Either way, age plays a very significant role in good sexual adjustment.

Body comfort:

It's not until the relentless obsession with real and imagined physical deficits abates that teens can begin to feel comfortable living in their newly adult bodies. Young teens are still very preoccupied with the "imaginary audience." Try explaining to your teenage daughter, who is in tears because she isn't sure which is the "perfect" outfit for the high school dance, that all the other teenagers at the dance will be far more concerned with how they look than with how she looks. Early in high school, teenagers strongly (but erroneously) believe that they are the center of attention and that "everyone" is observing them with an eye toward exposing even their most hidden or minute flaws. Having sexual intercourse while still in a state of such hypervigilance about one's appearance is profoundly anxiety-provoking. Girls in particular (although not exclusively) are vulnerable to concerns about their appearance. Interestingly, concern about the imaginary audience peaks at about age fifteen for both boys and girls and then declines steadily. This fact aligns nicely with what we know about age sixteen or seventeen being a healthier time to become sexually active than earlier. The imaginary audience is on its way out by then, leaving teens much freer to more realistically and more kindly evaluate their attractiveness. Sex is much more likely to be rewarding in a body that the teenager has a positive relationship with.

Freedom to say yes or no:
Sexual activity is voluntary. For the teenager who *chooses* sexual involvement, the chances are greatly increased that the maturity and self-control needed to be sexually responsible, as well as sexually responsive, are developing. Mutuality is the cornerstone of both sexuality and intimacy. Too often teens feel coerced into having sex, either by a partner or by their peer group. Girls tend to be more vulnerable to sexual pressure than boys and can mistakenly use sexuality as a defense against feelings of low self-esteem, but boys are vulnerable as well, particularly as sexual activity becomes the norm in their peer group. The reason the ability to choose whether to engage in sexual relations is so important is that it is both protective

against coercion and emblematic of the teenager's ability to harness cognitive skills in making decisions. A teenager who knows her own mind is in a much better position to make good decisions than one who is easily swayed by others.

Being knowledgeable about sex and contraception:

Unfortunately, reliable use of protection against pregnancy is hit-or-miss among sexually active teens. About 40 percent of high school teens did not use contraception the last time they had intercourse. This is the result of several factors. First, most teens say that their sexual activity is unplanned. This is at least partly due to a reluctance to admit to being sexually active. It also explains why those teens who have taken virginity pledges (and whose rates of sexual activity are no different from those of teens who have not) are even less likely to use contraception.[1] Additionally, using contraception on some occasions is not enough to ensure continued use. Most teens who have had sex with contraception have also had it without. Kids need to be motivated to use contraception every time. The ability to talk openly and comfortably with one's partner is a good predictor of contraception use.

Finally, what is the best predictor of regular use of contraception? Age. Older teens are better at thinking ahead, feel less guilty about sexual activity, are more motivated to avoid pregnancy, and are better able to discuss contraception with their partners. Making sure that teens are prepared for the unintended outcomes of sex, for the significant role that sex will play in the consolidation of their identity, and for the power of sex to advance and cement intimate relationships is no small task. For teens to be able to manage better, we need to understand how we can be most useful to them. We're in for a few surprises.

What Does Managing Sexuality Look Like in High School?

Fifteen-year-old Jenny is upstairs getting ready to "hang out" with Justin, a seventeen-year-old boy she's seen a lot of over the past couple of months. Mom wonders whether her daughter is sexually active, but Jenny and Justin always seem to go out with a large group of friends, which is reassuring. Mom worries more about Justin driving her daughter home late at night. What if he drinks? Jenny, on the other hand, knows that although her friends generally start the evening off as a group, many of them peel away in couples and engage in a whole range of sexual activities from "making out" to intercourse. Some just "hook up," adolescent shorthand for brief nonbinding sexual forays. Jenny knows that her mom is mostly in the dark about what happens when she goes out, and she's happy to keep it that way. The last thing Jenny wants is any more questions about where she is going, what she will be doing, or when she'll be home. It already feels like the Inquisition every time she walks out the door.

Jenny and Justin have "made out" but they haven't had intercourse yet. At first they were just good friends, and it was only in the last couple of weeks that Jenny became aware of how attracted she is to him. Although Jenny is still a virgin, as are most of her close friends, there has been a lot of talk lately among those friends about whether to "go all the way." More important, though, Jenny likes Justin and thinks that maybe they can get even closer if she's willing to have sex with him. It would be awesome to be his girlfriend and Justin has hinted that he's already sexually experienced and is just waiting for her to be "ready." As she prepares to go out she thinks, "What if he wants to do it tonight?" Jenny has become rather skilled at these what-if questions, and she has lots of them on her mind. In addition to "What if he wants to do it?" Jenny is also thinking, "What if I'm not ready?" "What if I mess up?" and most disturbingly, "What if he doesn't use protection?" Jenny's not sure that she feels comfortable talking to Justin about protection. This bothers her. Sex might be cool but pregnancy or those gross STDs she's seen in sex ed class definitely would not be. Maybe oral sex would "satisfy" Justin, make him like her even more, and still keep her protected.

Jenny's newly acquired ability to think hypothetically is getting quite a workout as she thinks about her choices. She is greatly aided by her new capacity to put herself in other people's shoes. "Dad would kill me." "Mom would have a cow." "Justin would be so stoked." While all these accurate assessments run through Jenny's mind, she finds herself thinking most about her girlfriends. While she knows some girls who are sexually active, her really close friends are doing the same things that she and Justin are doing—lots of kissing and touching but nothing more. Jenny feels both "weird" and "excited" when she thinks about being the first of her close friends to have sex.

The doorbell rings and Jenny flies downstairs to make sure that her parents aren't giving Justin the third degree. She feels her relationships should be "private" and resents her parents' attempts to know more about Justin. She can't believe that he thinks her folks are "cool"; she finds them painfully embarrassing much of the time. However, she knows that they want what is best for her and as she hugs them good night, she holds on a few seconds longer than usual. Walking out the door, she is still uncertain about what choices she's going to be making in just a few hours.

How Parents Can Help

There's both good news and bad news about how we can help our kids manage issues of sexuality over the course of high school. The bad news is that researchers find that, unlike peers, parents have relatively little effect on their teens' decision about when to become sexually active.[2] This is one of many places where the friends your teen chooses are going to have a big effect on his or her behavior. Hanging out with a group of thoughtful, academically motivated kids with healthy and connected families makes early sexual experimentation unlikely for your teen. But being part of a group of kids who don't like school, who engage in risky behavior, and whose parents are "checked out" puts your teen at risk for an early and poorly managed sex life.[3]

While we don't seem to have much effect on *when* our teens choose to become sexually active, the good news is that we do have some influence on *how* they manage their sexual lives.[4] Probably the most important conversation parents can have with their teens is about contraception. This seems to be one place where warm, interactive discussion has been found to have a significant effect on increasing the odds of safe sex.[5] Discussion with older siblings about contraception also seems to carry weight.[6]

Monitoring our teen's whereabouts and activities is another way that we can limit risky sexual behavior. Verify that parents will be at home when your teenager goes to parties. Follow through on consequences for late curfews or missed phone calls. Make sure your teens, particularly during the first few years of high school, know that you are paying attention to their friends and their activities. You will get pushback on this. Young teens are heavily invested in the idea of keeping large parts of their lives "private." Sex falls squarely into this category. Remember that monitoring is only as good as your child's willingness to disclose. This willingness comes from years of good communications with your child. Do show respect for privacy in general, and certainly around issues that are of nominal concern: phone calls and closed doors for instance. But it should be clear to your teen that you are not willing to cede concern for the larger issues of inappropriate peers, drugs, or unsafe sex.

We try our best to buy our kids some time in adolescence because we know that even a year or two of life experience can make a huge difference in their ability to appreciate risk. A sexually active fourteen-year-old is at risk for a host of behavioral and academic problems; a seventeen-year-old is not. Acknowledging this to your teen can be helpful. "I think you're unsure about having sex now; if you could hold on a bit longer, then I think things will be a lot clearer to you."

Parents should be very clear with their teens that sex is *always* a voluntary act. Often girls feel pressured into having sex by older or high-status boys. This is often seen as an affirmation of the girl's attractiveness and provides a temporary self-esteem boost. Typically, but not always, it is the teenage girl with compromised self-esteem who is vulnerable to these types of imbalanced relationships. It is worth devising a creative "fallback" option should your teen find herself in over her head sexually. Remember how clear you were when it came to drinking: all they had to do was call, and you'd pick them up and bring them home, no questions asked. Sexual situations call for a similar offer. Let your teens know that if they ever find themselves in an uncomfortable sexual situation, you are available to help extricate them. In order for this to be an effective option, you have to keep your judgment in check. A good lesson for teens is that while self-reliance usually means depending on yourself, it also means knowing when it's wiser to depend on someone else.

A Note on Adolescent Sexuality

It would be naive to suggest that there are only minimal problems associated with adolescent sexuality in this country. Our teen pregnancy rate is unconscionable, the highest in the industrialized world. Rates of STDs and HIV continue to rise among teens as condom use remains erratic. There is still significant prejudice and igno-

rance around homosexuality, resulting in high rates of depression
and suicide among these teens. Sexual harassment is common and
sexual abuse is significant even though it is underreported. Some of
these problems, like pregnancy, disproportionately affect our poor-
est and most vulnerable youth, while others such as STDs and HIV
make few social or economic distinctions. Solving these problems
will take not only parental concern but involvement of all of our
social institutions: schools, religious institutions, the public health
system, and the legal system, with an eye toward what social science
research has learned about effective sex education.

However, sexual problems are not the norm; the majority of
teens are navigating their sexual awakening quite successfully. The
reality of teenage sexuality is a shock to some parents and simply a
confirmation to others. Either way, losing one's virginity toward the
end of high school is typical and not likely to be problematic either
in the short run or in the long run.[7]

Sex is a loaded and touchy topic for many parents. The notion
that we might relax a bit about our teens' sexual lives may seem
shortsighted or cavalier. But, in fact, for the most part we have
taught our teens well. Promiscuity is not the norm for teens and
most adolescent sexual relationships are characterized by warmth,
affection, and fidelity.[8] For the majority of teenagers, sexual activity
is a welcome, normal, and enriching part of adolescence.

BUILDING A SENSE OF IDENTITY

What makes preoccupation with identity such a prominent feature
of adolescence is that, for the first time, kids have the intellectual
chops, the persistence, and the creativity to think about and reflect
on the psychological reorganization that is taking place within
them. Mature cognitive skills like abstract thinking, self-reflection,
and the ability to shift perspective ensure that teens will speculate,

obsess, and experiment endlessly with shifting identities so that ultimately they can craft a coherent one. And what is a coherent identity? It is a reasonably enduring and consistent sense of who we are. When we knock on our internal door it's reassuring to find the same person home to open it. It's not so predictable for teens. Sometimes they can't find the door, sometimes the door is locked, and sometimes a stranger appears in the doorway.

Rivers of ink have been written about the adolescent "identity crisis." In spite of the long-standing popularity of this term, its meaning is hazy particularly since social scientists have discredited the notion of adolescence as an inevitable period of stress and conflict. I think the word *crisis* is a misnomer and believe that *challenge*, which suggests both difficulty and opportunity, more appropriately describes the long, uneven, and demanding project that is developing an identity. Reducing the heat on this concept should not reduce the magnitude of the task. Teens need to move from the egocentric, concrete-thinking, nonreflective person that they were in childhood toward the specific, unique, self-aware adults they will become.

While the high school years in general are a fertile period for developing identity, there appears to be heightened tension around this task early in high school. Because the development of identity is a very complex process of taking in, retaining, or discarding a whole range of beliefs, values, and goals, there are bound to be periods of hazy thinking and general befuddlement. "I think I'm pretty outgoing, but then my parents get on my case and I just want to be left alone. I'm never really sure if I'm a social or private person." With practice, teens understand that behavior can be situational and complex, and over time they experience less anxiety around contradictions. Kids who have a more complex sense of self are less likely to be depressed than those who have difficulty tolerating complexity.[9] Since building a sense of self is a work in progress, various "selves" need to be imagined before a teenager settles on a particular version. For most kids, it is not until late in adolescence or early adulthood that a consistent, comfortable, and robust sense of self solidifies.

"It's my life and I'm in charge of it," eighteen-year-old Chloe said when asked to describe how she feels about herself as she prepares to graduate from high school. I can't help but hear the echo of the two-year-old who felt pretty much the same way sixteen years earlier. And in a few more years, it is likely that Chloe will be feeling an even greater sense of control over her own life. Chloe's statement underscores the important relationship between identity and a sense of self-efficacy or personal power. To feel both authentic and capable of influencing the world around you builds both self-reliance and self-esteem and is insurance against a host of psychological problems. Most important, it allows teenagers to feel empowered to make the kinds of good choices that we lie awake at night praying they'll make.

What Does Constructing an Identity Look Like in High School?

Seventeen-year-old Josh is one of those kids you can't help but love. Athletic, charming, funny, and smart, he worked hard in therapy following a brief fling with drugs and alcohol. It was Josh himself who requested help with his drug problem, puzzled by how out of synch his excessive drug use was with his sense of himself as "a really good kid."

Interestingly, although Josh believed that he knew himself really well, his description of himself was surprisingly unenthusiastic and bland. When I pointed this out he shrugged and said, "Actually, we're all the same out here. Like those houses that are all the same, just painted different colors. Nothing really special about any of us." This was a startling statement from a boy who was an ace student and a notable athlete. Increasingly our sessions focused on how "replaceable" Josh felt. He concluded that his foray into drugs was an attempt to "feel special." While at first this seemed like a glitch in Josh's sense of identity, the more I listened to him, the more I understood that while parts of Josh's identity were strong and robust—he was proud of his good grades, of being a good son, brother, and friend—other parts that were of particular importance to him were weakly developed. Josh desperately wanted to be special, not only in expectable ways, but in ways that carried his particular signature of humor and caring. Despite being a good athlete and a popular student, Josh felt that he was meant to do something more with his life. In a community where many students are accomplished, accomplishment alone was not enough to guarantee a sense of uniqueness.

In one "aha" session, Josh said, "No one really needs me." And he was right. Even though he was seventeen, he had never worked a day in his life, as his parents urged him to devote his time to academics. Summers were spent at camps designed to hone his academic or athletic abilities. His allowance more than covered whatever material needs he had. And even though he had many friends, he often felt profoundly lonely. This was a boy who was just aching to do something that he considered "meaningful" and outside the predictable school routine he had been in for years.

Josh's mom, Ellen, approached me wanting to talk about Josh's "low self-esteem" and whether I thought a program abroad or another gifted summer camp would be helpful. Ellen, a former management executive, had poured her heart and soul into raising her three kids and was rightfully proud of the fact that in addition to being good students, all three were considered "nice" kids in our community. Ellen tended to think big, and I wasn't surprised that she had researched summer programs like Duke's and Penn's residential programs for gifted kids. But Josh didn't have low self-esteem. On the contrary, he simply recognized that having a sense of purpose was an important part of identity and that while his parents had provided many advantages, they had not provided opportunities for Josh to feel needed. I asked Josh and Ellen to give some thought to local opportunities that might help give Josh the feeling of relevance he was yearning to add to his sense of self.

Josh and Ellen came up with a terrific idea. Josh had spent a considerable amount of time at the nursing home of his beloved grandmother before she died and his sweet nature and good sense of humor made him a welcome visitor. Although his grandmother was gone, he had a "posse" of elderly ladies who adored him. He decided to begin to develop a much-needed program for some of the early dementia patients. The overworked staff appreciated his scheduled twice-weekly appearances (he actually stopped by far more often, checking up on one or another of his "ladies"). He was happy and enthusiastic about his being "a contributor." After a few months, Josh arranged for several of his friends to volunteer at the facility as well, and together they worked on researching and then expanding the dementia program he had started. This was not a calculated attempt to beef up his résumé for college; this was a heartfelt commitment to a part of growing up that is frequently ignored—the need to contribute, to feel needed. Josh's expanded identity was now grounded in meaningful social contribution, which made him feel, in his own words, "genuinely successful."

How Parents Can Help

The typical imagery of adolescent identity usually includes piercings; dyed hair, shaved hair, or Mohawks; Goth in-your-face regalia; punk's noisy indifference; hip-hop's anger and misogyny; as well as multiple other expressions of teen identity formation that drive parents wild. But if we can avoid being sidetracked by these color-

ful, temporary diversions we are in a much better position to understand the seriously demanding work of constructing an identity.

Our most important job is to be certain that we have a good
understanding of our child's basic personality, that we can "see" and
appreciate teens for who they are. At first blush, this may seem like an
odd bit of instruction. After all, isn't adolescence the period of time
when our kids are changing radically? How can you possibly keep up
with a teen who in rapid succession is a conservative, a liberal, and
an anarchist? A bookworm and a party girl. A jock and a theater
geek. You can't. At least not in any way that would be helpful. The
trying on of different identities is part of the psychological and cognitive growth that accompanies adolescence. But costumes and shifting
political affiliations aside, we need to stay connected to the core parts
of our children we have known for the past decade and a half.

Our keeping pace with the exploration of different identities
is primarily an issue when our teens appear headed for trouble. If
things are tough at home—a divorce or work layoff, for example—
and your previously well-adjusted kid falls in with a group of friends
who are uninterested students, heavy drug users, and engaged in
petty thievery, then you know that you have to be on top of any new
destructive behavior. There is a constellation of behaviors in high
school, particularly during the first year or two, that signal potential trouble—disengagement from school; early experimentation
with sex, drugs, and alcohol; minor delinquency; and a premature
push for independence. Kids may experiment with being "tough"
or being a "druggie" and if their behavior is consistent with these
self-definitions—being a bully, sneaking out of the house to sell or
buy drugs—then talk with your teen and a professional. Limits will
need to be consistently enforced to keep your child safe and it's
likely that other issues need some serious exploration.

But for the vast majority of teens, parents would do well to back
off a bit. Rather than providing a running commentary on our teens'

various incarnations, our job is to provide a "holding environment," a kind of psychological padded cell for them. This will ensure that even as they bounce around considering different identities, they feel protected, accepted, and loved. Despite endless portrayals of teens as powder kegs of volatility, the reality is that there's actually less, not more, than meets the eye. The urgency of the "Who am I really?" question dims rather quickly. For most kids the end product is not all that different from the initial prototype. Our slow-to-warm-up baby is likely to be a somewhat inhibited child, a shy teen, and a reserved adult. Temperament has been shown to be extremely stable over the course of our lives.[10] This can be hard to appreciate when our kids are in the middle of this period of intense exploration and when change and heightened self-consciousness seem to be their perpetual companions.

So, short of keeping an open heart and loving the child we've been given, are there any other ways to shore up our teenagers' healthy drive toward consolidating their identities? Parents who are warm, value individuality, and encourage appropriate independence all help make the challenge easier for their teens. "Try and figure that out. If you still need help after you've tried, let me know." Almost all coping skills are bolstered by this show of confidence in your child; it communicates faith in your teen's abilities, underscores the reality that effort is what drives competence, and provides reassurance that you remain a reliable and loving backup.

The widespread boredom reported by teens could easily be ameliorated if parents, schools, and communities provided opportunities for meaningful work for teens. Jobs, chores, mentoring, and volunteer work all contribute to teens' sense that they have something unique and important to add to their community. Participation in these kinds of activities helps teens develop competence, independence, connection, and real self-esteem. It gives them a sense of being relevant, and helps them to construct an identity greater and more robust than the sum of their test scores and trophies.

But community service is certainly not the only way that kids advance their sense of identity in adolescence. This is a time when teens actually have the physical, cognitive, and emotional capacity to embark on deep exploration of the things that interest them, whether those things are athletic, intellectual, or entrepreneurial. Summer internships during high school can strengthen an interest and bring high school students into a mentoring relationship with an adult already established in the field. My son spent two summers interning at a law firm. That convinced him that law was the profession for him. It also convinced his best friend, who interned with him, that it most certainly was not. Part of developing an identity is knowing not only who you are, but also who you are not.

DEVELOPING AUTONOMY

You've just told your twelve-year-old middle schooler, Rebecca, who is heading off to an afternoon party, that she needs to be home early for a family dinner. She stomps her feet, glares at you, and says, "You can't tell me what to do. It's my life. I'll come home when the party is over." You tell Amy, your seventeen-year-old high schooler, the same thing and she says, "I know this family dinner is important to you but this party is important to me. Can you call me just before dinner is being served and that way I can stay at my party a little longer and still be home for dinner?"

These two examples illustrate the difference between independence and autonomy. Like the two-year-old who swats your hand away and says, "I do it myself," Rebecca is asserting her independence. Her thinking is simple and egocentric: "I can" or "I can't"; "I will" or "I won't." Independence is about managing one's self. Autonomy is a much broader, tougher, and more complex task than independence. It weaves together advanced thinking, self-reliance, self-regulation, intimacy, and connection. Autonomy is the capacity to be both independent and connected to others.

Seventeen-year-old Amy, who is attempting to compromise with her mom, is able to act more autonomously because of her increased maturity. She can see the issue not only from her own point of view, but also from her mother's. This means that there are no longer only winners or losers. ("I stay longer, I win." "I come home early, I lose.") She understands that most interpersonal transactions are far more complex than the kind of rigid thinking that is character-istic of younger kids. This is why there was more outright conflict around the development of independence early in adolescence than around the development of autonomy, which comes later.

In addition to Amy's more mature thinking skills, she has gained emotional maturity. Not everything is worth a fight with her mother. Overall, Amy enjoys her mom and doesn't want to make her mad. Equally important, she knows that she is preserving some of her precious privacy by being willing to compromise. Her goodwill helps engender her mother's goodwill, resulting in fewer questions about who's at the party and why it's so important. Amy still bris-tles at her parents' rather persistent curiosity about all of her activities and knows that sometimes it's just better to avoid the discussion. Notice how many skills—cognitive, behavioral, emotional—Amy is capable of integrating in order to solve this conflict.

Several shifts in perception occur in teens that seem to herald the development of autonomy. It's always touching when one of my younger teen patients first discovers that his or her parents are flawed. Regardless of the circumstances of this recognition teens react with something bordering on disgust. Fourteen-year-old Ashley comes to an early morning session visibly shaken. She had discovered that her father left "his disgusting nose hairs in the sink" that morning. One can assume that this was not the first time Ashley's dad forgot to rinse the sink, but it was the first time Ashley allowed herself to notice. Because she had adored her father for the past fourteen years, it was indeed a great shock for Ashley to enter the stage of "de-idealization." This capacity to see one's parents, warts and all, signals the beginning of autonomy. It is both an emotional and a cognitive move away from the idealized parent of childhood, and so makes both independence and connection less conflicted.

Other indicators that the process of autonomy is under way are the ability of teens to understand that their parents are people outside their parenting roles, a lessening of dependency on parents for assistance, and an increased sense that, even within the family, the teen is becoming his or her "own person." "I'm pretty open with my parents, but there are some things that I just wouldn't share" illustrates the capacity to be both connected and independent. While we may wince at the "I just wouldn't share" part of this sentence, it is in fact an indication that we have done our jobs well, and that our teens are edging toward the autonomy and the robust sense of self that will enable them to be loving, connected partners in their own right.

What Does Autonomy Look Like in High School?

- Your sixteen-year-old daughter, Megan, is going shopping with her friends for her junior prom dress. You have not been invited on this excursion. Several hours later Megan flies in the door, shopping bags trailing, and yells with excitement, "Mom, come tell me which dress you like the best!" This is autonomy. Don't sulk about not being invited on the shopping expedition. Go enjoy her fashion show and tactfully give her your opinion.

- Your eighteen-year-old son, Chris, spends a good part of every weekend out of the house and with his girlfriend. You have taken family vacations every summer for years. This year when you talk about where to go, Chris asks if he can bring along his girlfriend. This is autonomy. Don't say that his girlfriend is not "family." Invite her along happily.

- Your fifteen-year-old daughter, Sarah, has been sick with the flu for two weeks. She failed her chemistry test the day after she returned to school. Teary and angry, she rails against how unfairly she is being treated. You agree but are shocked when she forbids you to speak with her teacher. Sarah says, "I'll take care of it." This is autonomy. Don't insist that your daughter has been victimized and don't call the teacher.

These everyday examples provide a glimpse into the complex adjustments that teens and their parents have to make as autonomy is developed in adolescence. Your teenagers' push toward independence is a given; it's in their wiring. What is less predictable is the way in which parents will react, and this is where the important component of connection comes into play. If we can "hang in" with our teens as they become more resourceful, and maintain a close relationship, the odds are that our kids will fare well. Teens who become independent but feel distant or detached from their parents score poorly on a number of measures of psychological adjustment. In contrast, kids who are independent but maintain closeness look particularly psychologically healthy. These are teens who have become not just independent, but autonomous.[11]

Of course, it's natural for us to feel a degree of surprise, exclusion, or even sadness as we are increasingly left out of territories that once belonged to us and our children—your eight-year-old wouldn't have thought of going shopping without you—but from our teen's point of view it is best to reserve your aid and participation for those things that really need parental help. Megan, Chris, and Sarah are demonstrating what healthy autonomy looks like. They each feel capable enough to handle age-appropriate challenges: picking out a dress at sixteen, making choices about a girlfriend at eighteen, handling their own schoolwork at fifteen. None of them is "dissing" parental help: they hope to maintain their connections with their parents, but on a more mature level than when they were just a few years younger.

Megan's ability to shop with her friends helps her develop many skills. She will have to consider her own preferences in dresses (individuation), budget (self-management), what other girls will be wearing (peer concerns), and how to interact with salespeople (competence). These simple acts of adolescence are wellsprings of developmental opportunity. She goes shopping with her friends because they provide support and guidance, and because she is rightfully aware that the prom is about her and her peers. Her willingness to share her excitement with her mom attests to the fact that the relationship is strong and a source of reassurance for Megan. So what if you hate the dresses? Zip it (your mouth, that is). Unless they expose your daughter's breasts, or the price tag is unsupportable, find something to like about one if not all of them. She's not coming to you as a fashion consultant; she's coming because she wants your blessing on her ability to manage this task. You've been handed a terrific opportunity to advance your daughter's self-esteem and self-reliance. Ask questions. Find out what she likes about each of the dresses. Have fun, give her a hug, and support her choice.

While some people consider "family vacations" an oxymoron, and few would deny that they can be fraught with challenges, many of us feel that they are sacred in their way. They are declarations of solidarity, unity, and common purpose. When Chris wants to invite his girlfriend on vacation, he is effectively announcing a change in his status and a shift in the composition of his family. Personal power or self-efficacy is the big player in Chris's situation. Will he be able to have some control over what his universe looks like? Assuming he's not bringing along Buffy the Vampire Slayer, his parents should be grateful that their son is showing all the characteristics of autonomy and is comfortable bringing his girlfriend into the family circle.

When my kids were little, river rafting and camping became our yearly vacation ritual. I was a born-and-bred New York City girl who believed that participating in the great outdoors meant putting the screens on the windows in the summer. So it was a testimony to the power of spending uninterrupted time with my boys that I was sleeping on the ground year after year. As they grew up, our "family" expanded to include friends and girlfriends. Did I have twinges of sadness about the change? Of course. But those twinges were mostly about the fact that I was no longer bringing along the three little boys who depended on me for so much. They had grown into young men with interests and pursuits that often had little to do with me. My being able to adapt to these changes was critical in maintaining this family tradition. To this day we still river raft every year in some combination of participants. I will do this, with whatever adaptations I have to make, until the day I can't buckle my life jacket. Adolescence is about more than our teen's ability to change; it is also about our own ability to grow.

Sarah pulls on Mom's heartstrings because she's young and upset. Mom's impulse is to protect her daughter from what appears to be unfair treatment. But Sarah is right on target. She has good reason to be upset. But by insisting that she will handle this classroom problem herself, Sarah is demonstrating that she is ready to put her newly robust skills of personal power, competence, and self-control to use. Mom's intervening would only send the message that problems of this (relatively minor) proportion are so overwhelming that only a parent can handle them. Sarah, on the other hand, needs to know that she is in charge of her own life and that while she may make mistakes, her parents are there to support her, not take over. Frustration, disappointment, and anger are inevitabilities, and our children benefit from learning how to manage these unwelcome feelings. Without practice we leave them vulnerable to mismanaging even the smallest challenges. Mom can be most helpful by showing pleasure at her daughter's autonomy, perhaps asking a few questions to help Sarah focus on what she will say, and then simply letting Sarah know that she is available should Sarah want more help.

We need to be available, to not bow out around issues of safety, to pay attention to our teens' activities—where they go, what they do, and who they do it with. But aside from a few exceptions, less is more when it comes to promoting autonomy. It's not a matter of withdrawal or disengagement. It is an active standing by, a loving holding back that allows your teen to flourish. This is not as easy as it sounds. Just as moving forward takes practice for your teen, so will holding back take practice for you.

The Challenge of Holding Back

Your daughter is seventeen and has just found out that her best friend has been seriously flirting with her longtime boyfriend. Her friend even sexted him a bare-breasted picture of herself. Your daughter comes home from school red-eyed, closes the door to her room, and within seconds is on the phone in hushed tones, crying. She has not hidden her distress from you, nor has she requested your help. You don't know if someone has died or if she wore the wrong jeans to school. Once she's off the phone, you ask what happened and get a terse explanation.

Now what? Your well-honed mother impulse, which has served you well for so many years, is to hold your daughter, soothe her, and then tell her to confront her girlfriend and talk it over with her boyfriend. But you are also well aware that while telling your daughter what to do may make *you* feel more at ease, it will not advance your daughter's maturity or capacity to handle conflict. She now has most of the cognitive capacity to figure out a problem like this, but little experience. She's good at self-regulating when it comes to homework or bedtime, but fortunately has had little experience with betrayal. You're around now to help her, but next year she'll be at college with more limited access to you; ultimately, of course, you won't be around at all. Do you stay quiet? Do you offer advice? Do you encourage her to talk?

First you have to read your daughter accurately. Closed doors mean "Leave me alone for now." Assuming there is a good relationship between you and your daughter, at seventeen she will know how to ask for help when she needs it. Your hovering around and eyeing her with constant concern is not helpful. It means you doubt that she knows how to take care of herself and makes her worry about your upset when she should be focused on managing her own feelings. This is what your daughter is likely to need:

- To feel sad and angry

- To get the facts and gain some perspective

- To figure out, on her own, the best way to manage her feelings

- To decide, on her own, how to deal with their friends

Here's how our well-intended, but excessive, involvement can mess up what our teens need most:

"DON'T BE UPSET, HONEY. THEY'RE NOT WORTH IT."

Yes they are. These kids have been her friends. What's your message about relationships? Besides, how do teens learn to accurately read their own feelings when someone else is telling them to have different feelings?

"YOU'LL FEEL BETTER TOMORROW."

How do you know? Maybe she'll feel worse. Teenagers have a complex brew of feelings, very much like adults, and need practice and time to sort out complex emotions like anger, disappointment, and betrayal.

"SHE'S A BITCH AND HE'S A LOSER. DUMP THEM BOTH."

By telling your daughter what to do, you've taken away a golden opportunity. Your advice is likely to be emotionally charged (see above) and will do nothing to further the complex interaction of skills your daughter needs to develop in order to solve these kinds of problems. Your adult perspective should tell you that this is not the end of the world and that your daughter has much to learn from this painful lesson, such as the ability to set limits or the refusal to tolerate abuse.

Having a child who is able to take care of herself well is the outcome every parent hopes for. Teens need to be able to accurately identify feelings, regulate their behavior, and rely on and comfort themselves when necessary. This is how they develop coping skills and a strong sense of self. They turn inward, call up their resources, see what is effective, and learn to tolerate unhappiness. Hopefully your teen makes mostly good calls about how to manage feelings (talk with a friend, go for a walk, write in a journal) and will only occasionally make bad calls (drink too much, get high). You can offer suggestions. But don't feel rejected if your teen just wants to be alone.

Think of a teen's bedroom as a living laboratory. Very important work is going on in there: the silent, internal, transformative process of changing from child to adult. Interrupt only when necessary.

Why Our Teen's Autonomy Can Be Tough for Us

While we all say that we want nothing more than to have our children grow up to be self-reliant, connected, and loving—the hallmarks of autonomy—the reality is that parenting in ways that advance autonomy can actually be extremely challenging for us. There is probably no other arena of teen development where parents need as much self-discipline and self-awareness to be effective. This is because our teen's growing autonomy is a mixed bag for many of us. It signals the end of an era when our kids thought we were all-knowing, when we had intimate knowledge of their lives, when we were needed 24/7, and when we almost always had the last word. Even the near-constant bickering of the middle school years is a form of intense connection. But in order to be truly autonomous, teens have to be willing to relinquish the security of an all-knowing parent, to take risks and tolerate failures, and to rely on their own, still somewhat inexperienced selves to solve problems and come up with solutions.

To effectively parent for autonomy, we need to understand how our own issues are easily activated by the child who matter-of-factly says, "I don't want to talk about it" or "It's really not your business." Certainly we've heard these kinds of statements before from our kids, usually with a great deal more vigor. But it's exactly because there was more vigor, more confusion, more upset, that we knew our child still needed our help. It's not that high school teens don't need our help, they certainly do, but they generally need less of our active involvement, fewer of our solutions, and more of our "parent presence."

When your five-year-old's best friend began saying "mean" things to your daughter, you held her while she cried, taught her to respond "I don't like it when you are mean to me," and most likely had a heart-to-heart with her friend's mom about how to resolve the conflict between the two girls. When your daughter was in middle school and the "mean girl" syndrome was in full bloom, you knew that she still depended on your counsel (although with considerable protest) to help her navigate her slippery relationships. In spite of the drama of that period, you still felt that you had some control over outcomes. You could reasonably talk with teachers or other parents if necessary and you still felt needed.

Now you may often feel that you're "not needed" anymore. While this is not accurate, it is nonetheless a creeping unease that many of us feel in our bones as our children prepare to leave the nest. We're being asked to move to the background of our children's lives when for years we've been in the foreground. It can feel like we've been "let go" from our job and sometimes even from our identity. This can feel profoundly lonely.

Part of the reason that this can be a particularly challenging time for mothers is that many of us are experiencing other losses: the ability to have more children, to turn heads when we walk into a room, the feeling that most of life is in front of us. We're entitled to grieve for the relationship that at one time had been the most intense and satisfying relationship in our lives. That being said, we also need to acknowledge that an autonomous teen is a parent's badge of accomplishment. It also presents an opportunity for us to shift gears, widen our interests, and deepen our own connections. It was only after two of my sons went off to college that I discovered that I was a writer and launched a second career. Their autonomy gave me the time and space to explore parts of myself that had been put on hold for decades. Just as there is a world waiting for our children, there is also a world waiting for us.

PART THREE

THE RESILIENCE FACTOR

Seven Essential Coping Skills

We've seen that our children's advancing maturity is an extraordinary, challenging, occasionally exhausting, and often exhilarating roller-coaster ride both for them and for us. It is by confronting and mastering the different stages of development, with appropriate help and support from us, that children come to identify their strengths and weaknesses, their interests and talents, their beliefs and values. This is how they come to know and distinguish what is "genuinely me" from what is not.

But because we are parents, we can find it difficult to hold back, to not fill in the blanks, to bear quiet witness to our children's struggles. Here's the dilemma, though. By interfering and "protecting" unnecessarily, by being unable to tolerate their mistakes and failures, we rob them of the capacity to develop and fortify the coping skills necessary for navigating their developmental tasks well and for understanding their inner selves. College admissions counselors call applicants like this "failure deprived," and know that they are unlikely to thrive under challenging circumstances. How would you ever know if you were capable or not if you didn't have the opportunity to try, fail, and pick yourself up again? How else would you figure out how to regain your equilibrium after a challenge if you weren't left alone to sort through different options? It's easy to see how a child's sense of self can wither under the well-intentioned but overprotective, even intrusive style of parenting that has become the norm today. Of course, we pay attention, advise when necessary, mitigate risk when we must, and never emotionally abandon our children. But we must allow them enough internal space, enough meaningful life experience to be able to develop the protective coping skills that are known to lead to the well-being and resilience that are the hallmarks of authentic success.

Most of us have learned to navigate through the complex and unpredictable challenges of life reasonably well. The more nimble we are in responding to both victories and setbacks, the more likely we are to feel that life is not simply manageable, but satisfying and meaningful. Given the range of challenges we face on a daily basis, we are most likely to feel successful when we can try and discard, in rapid succession, different coping skills until we find the one that is most suitable for the task at hand.

You're home alone with your two children and they're being really picky about the hastily prepared dinner you barely managed to throw together after spending an interminable day being criticized by your cranky supervisor. You can be irritable, insist your children eat, banish them to their rooms, threaten to never cook another meal, discuss options calmly, suggest they're old enough to put together an alternative, or decide you could all use a slice of your favorite pizza from the Italian restaurant down the street. There is no single "right" solution to common problems like this but you should generally know what works best. The pizza out could be a good solution from time to time, but not if your kids are making dinnertime balkiness a nightly ritual. One night telling them to eat their dinner works fine; another night you're so depleted that the only reasonable thing to do is go to your own room and let them figure it out for themselves. Many times a day you call on your coping skills to solve problems like this. It's hard to imagine running a household (or just your own life for that matter) without a generous helping of skills like resourcefulness or self-control.

These two chapters are about how we help our children develop their own set of coping skills. Sometimes we "transfer" our favored skills to our children simply by modeling them. But while our children learn from watching how we react to challenge and recover from crisis, they are not us. Genetics and temperament play a role in determining which coping skills come most easily to us. We naturally lean in to our strengths. An extroverted parent may reach for enthusiasm first, while an introverted child may opt for creativity. Both can be equally effective in solving problems. Enthusiasm, creativity, resourcefulness, and a good work ethic are looked at together in chapter 6 because they have a greater temperamental basis and are primarily the kinds of skills kids call on to help them think through problems and challenges. Self-control, self-esteem, and self-efficacy are grouped together in chapter 7 because they are skills we call upon when situations demand action out in the world (if you're wondering why self-esteem is there, you'll need to keep reading).

More coping skills means greater resilience. It is important that we understand that resilience is not something our children have or don't have. As Ken Ginsburg, one of the country's leading experts on resilience, points out, "Resilience is not a character trait." The same child can show great resilience under one set of circumstances ("My math grades are pretty bad, I'll have to study a lot harder") and limited resilience under another ("My friends didn't invite me to go shopping today; my social life is over, I'm a complete loser"). Resilience fluctuates. It depends on temperament, support, and circumstances. We bolster our children's resilience by protecting them from overwhelming risk and providing the support and the circumstances (this must include allowing our kids to struggle with manageable and age-appropriate challenge) that encourage the development of coping skills.

We have been overly focused on the "problems" of our children, our teens in particular. There seems to be endless advice on how to tell them what not to do. Don't do drugs. Don't have sex. Don't drink and drive. Don't neglect your schoolwork. But I'd suggest that we serve our children best when we don't just tell them what *not to do*, but help them figure out what *to do*. "Don't do drugs" isn't much help when you are wired to try out new and risky experiences. But by promoting self-control, modeling it ourselves, and noticing and applauding it in our children we increase the likelihood that they will be able to take care of themselves across the range of challenges and seductions that life will present.

I've chosen the seven coping skills I consider most important, but this list is by no means definitive. I can't imagine getting through life without a sense of humor; you may find a spiritual or religious practice indispensable. Every child should have some ability to draw on the seven coping skills in these two chapters. Feel free to add to and customize the list accordingly. Each section ends with a "do" and "don't" list intended to give parents practical advice on what advances and what inhibits the development of each coping skill.

• CHAPTER 6 •

Teaching Our Kids to Find Solutions

RESOURCEFULNESS
"I can handle this" instead of "Mom . . ."

May, a new undergraduate at Stanford University, walks across the campus in late September. She realizes that she has left her class schedule in her dorm room and is uncertain about which classroom she should be heading toward. So she calls her mother. In Asia. Sixteen time zones away. Despite her stellar academic credentials, May doesn't hightail it back to her dorm and check out her own schedule. Nor does she think to utilize the help of the administrative staff housed in practically every building on campus. Instead she does reflexively what she has always done. She calls her mother.

While a case could be made that this behavior is resourceful—May had a problem to solve and solved it quickly—there is something disturbing about her solution. May has not optimized her own resources. Maybe Mom isn't around. Maybe she's sleeping and has turned off the phone. Optimizing resources means that we know not just how to solve a problem but the best way to do it. This, of course, takes practice, exactly what May misses out on when she recycles the same solution she used at four or at fourteen. Many high-achieving students, because they have been urged to devote all their resources to academic advancement, lack the internal organization needed to solve the problems of daily living. While they may shine in the classroom, they can be stymied by how to approach simple novel problems like picking out a new pair of shoes alone, asking someone out for dinner, or finding a forgotten classroom. They are "book smart" but not self-reliant or resourceful.

We tend to encourage self-reliance (a good trait), but resourcefulness is even better. Why? Because resourcefulness is the ability to both *independently* and optimally solve daily problems and to *seek help from others* when we can't problem-solve independently. As our kids grow up, we want the balance of internal and external solutions to problems to increasingly tilt toward the internal. By the time our children are in college, we should expect them to be capable of solving the problems of everyday life. Depending unnecessarily on others, even capable others, does not advance resourcefulness. May might have been minutes late for class if she went back to her dorm room or walked to her adviser's office, but in turning outward rather than inward to solve her problem, she missed out on both the practice and the pleasure of self-sufficiency.

Of course it's important to know when we're in over our heads. Sometimes resourcefulness can look like pathology. The kid who cheats "to survive" is showing a kind of resourcefulness. So is the young teenager who takes a couple of hits of dope to avoid the pain of his parents' violent fighting. Many of the teens who engage in risky behaviors are doing the best they can to reduce distress in their lives. They would benefit from having trusted adults help them fill in the problem-solving blind spots that kids can have under trying circumstances. Someone to point out that if you cheat and are caught you might fail your course. Or if you smoke dope you might get suspended from school. Having sympathetic adults around, and encouraging kids to brainstorm with them when they are overwhelmed, is part of teaching resourcefulness. *Every kid should have a go-to adult outside of his or her family.* Counselors, teachers, coaches, clergy, a friend's parents often fill this role. Sometimes we feel insecure when our kids seek out the advice of other adults. Don't. It's one of the most protective factors in a child's life.

Resourcefulness is proactive, not reactive. Rather than waiting for the school deadline to sign up for driver's ed, the resourceful kid signs up in advance, ensuring himself a spot in the class. Resourceful kids plan out their activities so that they're not overwhelmed and don't find themselves double booked with SAT prep and basketball practice. Resourcefulness helps kids solve problems, but it also helps them avoid problems. Kids who are resourceful know how to make the most of the situation they find themselves in and the resources they've been given.

One of the things that make the development of resourcefulness difficult for our children is our hurried pace of life. By definition, being resourceful means trying out different ways of handling situations in order to find the most efficient and effective solution. More often our kids' attempts to problem-solve go something like this:

"Mom, I can't figure out how to wrap Grandma's present."

"Well hurry up, we're running late for her party and we still have to pick up your sister from track practice."

"I think I'll just put it in a bag and give it to her. She'll think it's funny."

"Don't be ridiculous. Wrap it and let's go."

"But it's an odd shape and I don't know how to make the paper fit."

"Jeez. Now we're really late. I'll do it. Get into the car and wait for me."

This kind of interaction is likely to sound familiar (if it doesn't, you probably should be writing your own book on parenting). Always impatient, always rushed. Not only are we perpetually stretching our own resources, but we are not allowing our children to develop theirs. There was a world of mathematical learning, of practical problem solving, of increased competence if only the child above had an extra ten minutes to experiment with rectangular sheets of paper and an irregular package. Resourcefulness develops out of multiple problem-solving attempts and the time to evaluate which are most effective, efficient, and satisfying.

No one seems to think that the world's problems are going to get any easier. And all of us know that personal challenges and problems are inevitable. One of the greatest gifts we can give our children is the time to build their coping skills. Remember that childhood is a walk, not a race. The resourceful child needs the opportunity to muddle along, in terms of both time and being left to his own devices, in order to figure out optimal solutions.

DO

- Do create a little necessity in your child's life. For example, you may always bring a snack to your twelve-year-old daughter before soccer practice. From time to time, don't. Tell her the night before that she will need to provide her own snack. Let her figure out how to get the juice and banana she usually eats before practice (bring it from home, buy it at lunch). Keep these challenges age appropriate. Be pleased when she comes up with solutions.

- Do share your solutions to your own everyday problems with your kids. If you find out at the last minute that the suit you planned to wear to work for your big presentation is still at the cleaner's, say a few words about how you feel (probably frustrated) and how you solved the problem (took a deep breath and then found something else in your closet to wear). Let kids know that minor frustrations are part of everyday life but that dwelling on frustration gets in the way of coming up with solutions.

- Do teach your children that there is no single "right" way to solve most problems. Sometimes being resourceful means plugging away at something; sometimes it means taking a break; sometimes it means figuring things out on your own; and sometimes it means consulting others.

- Do teach your child how to self-soothe (close your eyes and take a breath; count to ten; go outside and take a walk) so that emotions don't dictate choices. Lack of emotional control is the nemesis of resourcefulness. A quiet mind is able to marshal resources far more easily than an agitated mind.

DON'T

- Don't jump in too early. Of course you have the skills to be far more resourceful than your child. The point is that you're trying to *teach* those skills. This takes time and patience. It's often so much easier to just fix things ourselves. "You don't have a clean pair of socks? Here, take a pair of mine." Once in a while, sure. Any more than that and you've missed the opportunity to teach your daughter to put her socks in the hamper before she's out of clean ones. Otherwise you've taught her only that others will take care of her problems.

- Don't become so stressed yourself that your own resourcefulness is impaired. More teens than I can count have told me they started drinking because their parents seemed to reach for a drink when stressed. Since we all seem to have fairly high levels of stress on a regular basis (something to think about), don't neglect taking care of yourself in healthy ways. A yoga class is better than one too many martinis.

- Don't become impatient with your child's limited resources. The tired child who gets her older brother to finish her math homework is trying to solve the problem of conflicting demands. She knows the teacher expects the work done, you expect her to get a good night's sleep, and she wants to be both responsible and rested. Your job is to set limits ("Having your brother do your homework is not okay—it's cheating") and just as important, to teach your daughter to see a broader range of options within herself, such as finishing it during lunch, or talking to the teacher about a short extension. You don't do these things for her, but you lend your wisdom.

ENTHUSIASM
"I love this" instead of "Whatever"

It's midnight. My youngest son, Jeremy, my husband, and I have come back from one of the baseball games that have become a ritual whenever Jeremy's home from college. We sit around for a while dissecting the game. Jeremy, my generally low-key son, has had a passion for baseball most of his life and has landed a summer internship with a minor league team. He excuses himself because he needs to look at box scores and write a recap for the team's website. His best friend, Jeevan, stops by. (Yes, I know it's midnight. Try to make your house the stop-by home. You'll learn more about your children, plus you'll have the pleasure of late-night conversations with their friends, who will generally consider your advice far wiser than your own children will.) I ask him how college is going. He looks wistfully at Jeremy and says, "It's okay, but I haven't found anything I really care about. There's just nothing that excites me enough to be home after midnight on a Friday night working on something because I love it."

Enthusiasm seems like a good thing to have, but is it really necessary for healthy development? Yes, as long as we understand that kids express enthusiasm differently. Without enthusiasm, kids are just going through the motions. Think about the people in your life who are enthusiastic about what they do—those who love to talk about and share their experiences. One of my friends is an avid surfer; she positively glows when she talks about how she feels in the water. Another friend recently finished a carpentry course at the local community college and presents her slightly askew end table with the pride of a new mother. A third friend lights up when detailing the complex management issues of running his trailer park. While I had never considered any of these activities particularly fascinating (actually, I had never considered them at all) my friends' enthusiasm buoys them, gratifies them, and encourages them to become more and more competent. These activities and interests not only add to their sense of enjoyment but also confirm that meaning is actively constructed by what we do with our lives.

As long as it's a healthy activity, the benefit of enthusiasm rests not on what exactly our kids are doing, but on the fact that they are doing something with zest. We should encourage their enthusiasm around mechanical as much as mathematical ability, jump rope as much as select soccer, volunteering at the local food bank as much as interning on Wall Street. Really? Are we really supposed to be as enthusiastic about our child being the jump rope queen as being captain of the varsity soccer team? The answer is yes, because enthusiasm is the internal driver of accomplishment. There are other components, of course, such as innate talents and intrinsic motivation, that also provide the energy for skill building. But whether it's wailing along with Justin Bieber, singing in the school chorus, or performing at Carnegie Hall, continued enthusiasm is what motivates your child to keep getting better at something. This is what helps kids move from experimentation to competence to expertise.

Of course, we tend to be more hopeful when our children show signs of talent in areas that we believe will stand them in good stead as they grow into their adult selves. And part of our job as parents is to help nurture talents and provide opportunities. If your child is talented in math, then, *if he's interested*, a summer math camp can be a great idea. Your job is to point out potential benefits that make this option appealing. "I know you like math and this way you could be with a whole bunch of other kids who share your interest. You'll probably have fun and be challenged." But without his desire to participate, you are likely to be throwing water on his interest. Generally kids *want* to get better at the things they show talent for. But being *forced* to go to, say, math camp, is not the same as *wanting* to go to math camp. Your child may go to comply with you and make you happy, but being simply compliant rarely sets a child up for a lifetime of feeling nurtured by an activity. Children do need guidance, though, and we should actively participate in exposing our children to a range of interests and activities. A nudge can be helpful, a push less so, and a shove almost never. Remember, you can force your children to do something, but you can't force them to learn, to take pleasure, or to value your choices. Keep options open for your children. Don't let them quit prematurely. Check in from time to time. Enjoy your children's present accomplishments while you encourage and guide them toward future ones.

Is enthusiasm something that can be cultivated or is it largely a matter of temperament? Are some kids wired for enthusiasm while others are wired for restraint? Certainly temperament has some effect on the *expression* of enthusiasm, notably intensity and mood. Some kids are positively dynamic in their enthusiasm; others are far more subdued. Enthusiasm is measured not in decibels but in focus, engagement, and pleasure. Its development rests on our ability to allow, encourage, and take pleasure from our children's natural drive to engage the world in interesting ways. Remember when your child was an infant, and you clapped your hands in delight when he sucked his toes, swatted his mobile, or simply grinned at you? Your enthusiasm helped lay the groundwork for your child's capacity to be enthusiastic. Every time we turn away from our child's interests, dismiss them, or denigrate them, we lessen our child's capacity for enthusiasm *and* lessen the connection between us.

Kyle, one of my high-achieving but disengaged and mildly depressed teen patients, rarely showed enthusiasm for anything. Identity is typically a big issue for teens but Kyle seemed uninterested in identifying himself with any of the groups at his high school. He had little to say during his early sessions, and even after he warmed up to me, he seemed wary and genuinely surprised that I was interested in him. One day he noticed the sketchpads, crayons, and pastels I generally keep around my office for younger children. As he began sketching, it was clear that he had both interest and real talent. When I asked him why he had never told me that he was an artist, he said his professional parents considered drawing "a waste of time" and he had assumed I would feel the same way. In fact, I'm very interested in art and even brought Kyle to my house to look at some of the pictures I had collected over the years. The more I encouraged his drawing, the more enthusiastic Kyle became during our sessions. Before long we were taking field trips to museums and saw several movies about painters: *Pollock*, *Frida*, and *Girl with a Pearl Earring*, to name a few (really, being an adolescent

therapist can be such fun!). His parents, with a great deal of education and encouragement, came to see that their fears about their
son's future were only stifling his present. He went off to the Rhode
Island School of Design, a happy and enthusiastic young "artist," by
his own definition. His may not be an easy road and he may or may
not become a successful artist. But some occupations are jobs, some
are professions, and others are callings, whether that's being a nun,
a surgeon, or a performance artist. It's up to your kid to figure out
which of these categories will provide a satisfying and meaningful
life. Yes, as parents we guide, encourage, and point out challenges.
But ultimately it's their call, not ours.

Sometimes parents simply don't encourage their children to cast
their nets wide enough to find the things that really turn them on.
They dismiss as uninteresting, impractical, or silly the very thing
that will sustain their child now and in the future. And what is likely
to be valued in that future can be hard to predict. Twenty years ago
two distressed parents brought their teenage boy in for a consultation because he was spending so much time gaming. They thought
he should focus on engineering if he was so interested in computers.
Fast-forward to the present. This young man now heads one of the
gaming divisions of a high-profile Internet company. He makes a
boatload of money and is every bit as passionate about gaming as
he was the first day I met him in my office. Were his parents wrong
to have been concerned? Certainly there are more opportunities in
engineering than gaming. This young man might even have been an
adequate engineer. But it's most likely that the kind of success he
now enjoys happened only because he pursued what he loved to do.

Be less concerned about the object of your child's enthusiasm
and more attentive to her capacity to be enthusiastic. Bolster her
enthusiasm by showing your own. Any adolescent psychologist can
tell you that the toughest kids to treat are those who don't have the
energy to be engaged. Give me a tough, blustery, foul-mouthed kid

to work with. It's a much easier job than a kid who has been emptied of vigor and enthusiasm.

DO

- Do encourage your child's interests and show enthusiasm for their choices (as long as they're healthy). Your actual level of interest in salamanders is irrelevant to your daughter; your support is not. When pressed you can at least say something like "It makes me happy to see how wild you are about your salamanders."

- Do be sure to be age appropriate. For children at age seven, Prokofiev's symphonic *Peter and the Wolf* is far more likely to be a hit than Wagner's endless *Götterdämmerung*. It is easier to cultivate enthusiasm when things are fun than when they are far outside a child's range of comfort or experience.

- Do understand that kids may have many transient interests or develop a singular interest that they enthusiastically maintain for years, if not a lifetime. Remember these are their interests, not yours. Your son's passion for heavy metal music may drive you to distraction. Buy earphones (either for him or for you!) and see where his interest in music takes him.

- Do model enthusiasm by expressing it often and over a range of activities. If you don't have things in your life that you are enthusiastic about, try to figure out why. It's hard for kids to openly share the things that excite them if it feels like Mom or Dad is on a different bandwidth, or even worse, depressed. One of the most gratifying parts of family life is the enthusiastic sharing of interests, accomplishments, and dreams.

- Do remember that entitlement kills enthusiasm. If you give in to your child's demands quickly and reliably and have trouble setting limits, then you are likely to have an entitled child. *If your child wants for nothing, then there is nothing to strive for, no desire, and no possibility of feeling happily satiated.* While your children may compare themselves with a friend who "gets everything," far better for them to experience the excitement and the enthusiasm of having a goal and working to reach it.

DON'T

- Don't be disappointed when something your child was previously enthusiastic about seems to fade. One of the most critical tasks of childhood is experimenting with a range of interests and activities in an effort to align skills, interests, and capacities. This is not to suggest that flitting from activity to activity is a good thing for kids. Part of your job is to encourage persistence and responsibility. Insist that your child give his activities a good try. But don't expect that things that were engaging at eight will necessarily be engaging at twelve. Think of something you were once profoundly enthusiastic about and how that may have changed. (I once loved to use my hands to cook; now I use them to hit "reheat" on the microwave or "takeout" on my cell phone.)

- Don't expect your child's way of expressing enthusiasm to be like yours. In my überverbal household, most of us would

verbally trip over each other at the dinner table, eager to
share the things we were enthusiastic about. My youngest
son would show his enthusiasm, not by talking, but by
using any available object to construct his current interest.
We kept hundreds of sugar packets and what seemed like
millions of Legos close at hand so he could quickly assemble
bridges, fulcrums, and seemingly impossibly unbalanced
structures that somehow stayed intact. If you're particularly
verbal yourself, make sure that you notice other ways of
expressing enthusiasm, such as absorption and curiosity.

• Don't use your love or approval as a way of manipulating
your child's interests or level of enthusiasm. "No child of
mine is going to be a mechanic" is unlikely to lessen your
child's enthusiasm over *Car and Driver* or his interest
in working on cars. It is more likely to just put distance
between the two of you.

• Don't insist on "passion." For many kids, enthusiasm is
more than enough.

CREATIVITY
"Let's look at this differently" not
"What's the right answer?"

First, banish the notion that creativity is all about art and artists.
While actors and directors, dancers and choreographers, fine artists, writers, musicians, and photographers are highly creative, their
numbers are small. Places like San Francisco, Santa Fe, Los Angeles,
and New York boast the highest percentages of working artists in
the country; yet those artists represent significantly less than 4 per-

cent of the total workforce in each of those cities. Across America, artists make up 1.4 percent of the labor force.[1] They are a small and highly valuable group of hardworking people who both reflect and create our culture. They tend to be creative with a capital C.

But how does creativity become an important "tool" for the child whose interests lie far from what we traditionally think of as creative pursuits? What are the underpinnings of creativity and how do they bolster child development? While definitions of creativity may vary slightly, there is broad consensus that creativity has two major components: originality and usefulness or value. Children can develop the ability to solve problems in new and useful ways just as they can develop musical ability or mathematical skill. Too often we think of these skills as "fixed" in our children; research tells us they are not. This isn't to say that all kids are equally capable of being creative or mathematical or musical. Natural ability counts, as does parental encouragement. However, each of these skills can be developed if your child is motivated and willing to put in the effort. In general, we make sure that children put in the effort when it comes to math homework or SAT practice tests. Should we be just as vigilant about cultivating creativity? Yes. And perhaps even more so.

Think of situations where you've been unsure of yourself, maybe a job interview or a blind date. Most of us try pretty hard to adapt, to change course if necessary, and to stand out in some way. This is everyday creativity at work. Creativity encourages nimble, flexible, innovative thinking, the exact kind of thinking that business leaders regularly cite as the skill most likely to be crucial as the twenty-first-century global economy moves forward. But the capacity for creative thinking is equally important when it comes to the mental health of our children.

Thirteen-year-old Sam simply can't seem to sit still and do his homework. He fidgets, gets up to get water or visit the bathroom, taps his leg incessantly, and looks everywhere except at his work. He was diagnosed years ago with ADHD, and his mother follows the advice that was given to her when Sam was eight—provide structure and oversight. Every day she tells him that he has to sit for twenty minutes and work on his homework before he can get up. Every day this exercise fails. Sam becomes increasingly frustrated and his mother becomes increasingly angry. "Jeez, Sam, it's only twenty minutes. Anyone can sit for twenty minutes." It's clear that this particular dance with Mom setting the rule and her son "defying" her instructions will only lead to bigger battles, between a mother who doubts her parenting skills and a teen who feels impaired or stupid.

So what can Mom do? She needs to encourage Sam to "think outside the box"—something many kids with ADHD are particularly good at. Mom too needs to start thinking creatively as well; otherwise all she'll have is a headache from banging her head against the wall. Using the same solutions over and over without success is often cited as the definition of neurosis. At the very least it defines ineffectiveness. Sam and Mom need to wipe the slate clean, discard the solution she's been told to use, and see what else they can come up with. A young child with ADHD is often handled differently from a teen with ADHD. I've treated many kids with ADHD who probably never put in more than five or ten minutes in the chair in my office. We've taken "activity breaks," gone for ice cream, or sometimes put on music and danced. Typically, I let these kids take the lead on how to make the session "work" for them. One child I treated suggested straddling his bike while we talked, which we would do outside my office in sunny California. From time to time, when he needed to move, he'd scoot off on his bike. Invariably he was back within minutes. It is simply not written in stone that therapy has to take place reclining on a couch or seated in a chair.

Ultimately Sam decided that what would work best for him was not having his mother hovering around with a kitchen timer. He found it easier to sit in a rocking chair than a desk chair, and so he asked his mom to buy one. He agreed to sit for as long as he could, but he would be free to move when he needed to. For Mom's part, she gave up her persistent monitoring, didn't check on Sam's progress, and requested only that Sam show her his work when he was done. If you walked into the house, would it have seemed odd to have a thirteen-year-old boy doing sprints in between math problems while his mom went about her business in another room? Maybe. But people are productive in all kinds of different ways with all kinds of eccentricities. I work best with a decaf mocha at my side and a bunch of tulips in a glass vase on my desk. Sam figured out, with his mother's help, how he worked best. Mom's critical contribution was to allow Sam to brainstorm, to try out a number of different solutions before he hit on the one that worked for him, and most of all to let Sam know that she was confident that he "had it in him" to solve this particular problem. Allowing our children false starts and dead ends without our getting all worked up is a good way to ensure that they will keep dipping into innovative solutions.

Creativity is stifled when we value conformity over individuality and rote learning over enthusiastic exploration. There's probably no better example of the throttling of creativity than the difference between what we observe in a kindergarten classroom and what we observe in a high school classroom. Take a room full of five-year-olds and you will see creativity in all its forms positively flowing around the room. A decade later you will see these same children passively sitting at their desks, half asleep or trying to decipher what will be on the next test.

There are schools that are well aware of the cost of continuing to teach as if we're in the middle of the industrial revolution, and that choose instead to prepare their students for a very different kind of future. These schools are quick to adopt the practices known to encourage kids to be engaged in learning and enthusiastic about the process. The content is not about finding one right answer but about considering multiple solutions to complex problems. These schools practice project-based learning where kids work in groups. Collaboration, communication skills, and creativity are all skills that are valued and enhanced by working in groups. Since almost every major business sector insists that future problems will be solved using a collaborative model, that few things will evolve from a bolt of lightning striking one particularly brilliant individual, we would do well to talk with our children's teachers to see whether project-based learning is incorporated into the curriculum. If not, we need to speak with school personnel about the omission.

The opposite of creativity is boredom. The single most common word that kids use to describe their school experience is "bored."[2] Given their easy access to computers, television screens, video games, and smartphones, it is particularly interesting that the cry "I'm bored" has become louder and more pronounced. Kids simply cannot spend their days as passive receptacles of outside stimulation. They need to create, to experiment, to see the outcome of different approaches to the same problem, and to feel the pleasure that comes with tapping into their own interests and talents. Kids who are bored are not experiencing "flow," that sense of deep enjoyment, total involvement, and creative energy. As a result they are being robbed of what is one of the most gratifying parts of living—the experience of a creative and vital involvement with one's most authentic self.

Since children spend a great deal of time with their families, too often in isolation, it is important to find activities that are of interest to the whole family. This can be quite a challenge. Two of my sons loved sports; the third loved theater. Being part of a family means that there is some rotation of goals and preferences; but without attending to the needs of all, what you're likely to encounter is a splintering of the family, disrespect for each other's interests, and a narrowing of each child's domain. My husband and I tried to reframe the experiences for our kids. *Theater is about teamwork. Sports are a form of entertainment.* Now that my sons are grown up, my theater kid loves what he calls the "spectacle" of sports and attends sporting events with regularity. My sports kids, well, they go to see their brother's productions and not much else. That's okay. Not every avenue you open will be one your kids will want to go down. But the more important thing is that you've sent the message, "Look around. The world is endlessly fascinating. You can find what turns you on only if you experiment and sample." Kids start out meeting the world with wonder. It is our job to make sure that they don't lose their inborn curiosity, imagination, and creativity.

DO

- Do keep the materials that encourage creative expression around the house and easily available. Think how easily available the TV or the computer is. Keep paper, colored pencils, markers, paints (all washable!), and puppets for younger kids; add an inexpensive camera or a musical instrument for older kids. There is a reason why child therapists have offices filled with easily accessible toys and art supplies. Creativity is the language of childhood and we don't want to miss a word.

- Do encourage activities that are open-ended. The reason that many young children love building blocks and cardboard boxes is that we don't insist that there is a "right" way to play with them. As your children grow up, try to keep them interested in the process and the questions rather than always being focused on the end result. Encourage reading, journal writing, and some form of creative expression, whether that's a photography class, participation in community theater, or your child's arranging or decorating his own room.

- Do show real pleasure and enterprise when it comes to your children's creative productions. That might mean having a "concert" in the house, lining up chairs to watch a play or a dance they want to perform, or taking a piece of artwork, framing it, and putting it up on the wall with other artwork. When your children *willingly* bring you their creative productions they are gifting you with their most genuine inner selves.

- Educational projects like Odyssey of the Mind are a terrific example of how to encourage creative problem solving in kids. Do talk to your child's school about bringing this type of program into the classroom.

- Kids who have more opportunities for unstructured play develop more flexible problem-solving skills as well as higher levels of creativity than kids who don't. If you insist on structured activities, make sure that there's equal time for unstructured play.

DON'T

- Don't be passive if your child's school district cuts back or eliminates art programs (as 70 percent of the school districts in this country have done). This shortchanges all students, marginalizes those with particular strengths in the arts, and perpetuates the myth that there is some inherent hierarchy of disciplines and that math and science always trump theater. This is not to diminish the critical importance of science in the school curriculum. It is, however, an acknowledgment that most of us are glad that Arthur Miller did not become an accountant.

- Don't get sucked into a debate about whether Netflix is different from GameFly. Our children need to be unplugged in order to be creatively involved in something. This means limitations on screen time and that means all screens. Aside from homework, all other screen time is recreational and should be limited to about two hours a day, less if your child is young.

- Don't lose patience with the skeptical child. This can be trying for parents. But the skeptical child is trying to rearrange known facts into something new, a highly creative endeavor. Young children love the alchemy of mixing blue and yellow paint so that it turns green. Encourage your child to "mix it up" in order to see things differently. Bertrand Russell noted that Einstein had "the faculty of not taking familiar things for granted." Children who are able to step back from obvious explanations and consider alternative ones are cultivating creativity and positioning themselves to be tomorrow's innovators.

- Don't expect your child to be notably creative without putting in the time. Almost all people who have made noteworthy creative contributions have worked very hard at mastering fundamental principles in their field. If your child shows a talent and a passion for a creative endeavor—computer design, architecture, ballet, photography, singing—encourage a greater understanding through mentors, classes, and exposure. Don't do this prematurely.

Wait until your child signals that she's ready and wants help cultivating her particular talent.

A GOOD WORK ETHIC
"I'm going to keep at it" instead of "I quit"

There is a consistency to the questions I field from parents who are disappointed by their child's grades. "My kid is really smart but just doesn't care about school. What can I do?" "My kid is really smart but cares more about her friends than her grades. What can I do?" "My kid is really smart but spends more of his time playing World of Warcraft than studying. What can I do?"

While "What can I do?" is a good solutions-oriented question, it's usually directed at the wrong problem. Most parents assume that if they could only get the children to care more about their grades, then their grades would most certainly improve. Perhaps. Sometimes grades measure content in ways that indicate robust learning and sometimes they measure content in ways that are shallow and easily forgotten. The endless rounds of debate about grades and standardized testing that have taken center stage for the last decade are primarily an indication of uncertain science and a lack of consensus about how to best keep American students competitive in the global economy. It's an odd use of energy and resources because the countries that lead on international test scores are working overtime to get rid of the standardized, centralized concept of education that has turned their students into very good test takers and very poor innovators. It should be noted that since international testing was introduced, some fifty years ago, American students have never fared well on these tests. In spite of this we are still the country that turns out the most patents, wins the most Nobel Prizes, and introduces most of the major technological advances to the world. Of course, we must teach our children content, and content lends itself to measurement, although we might do well to consider alternative assessment strategies. But in terms of our global standing, it is America's capacity for innovation that we should be paying attention to in spite of the fact that it doesn't lend itself to easy measurement.

Our children are not learning well, not because they haven't put enough time into test preparation, but because, in some cases, excessive test preparation has gotten in the way of what we have traditionally done best. Teach content. Engage students. Encourage curiosity. Value creativity and innovation. Children learn when they are engaged in the process of learning. By *engaged* I mean interested, invested, and internally motivated. Engaged students have higher grades, better mental and physical health, and a greater capacity to work diligently, cooperatively, and with optimal effort. In other words, academic engagement and a good work ethic go hand in hand. The effort and persistence needed to learn well come from *caring* about both the material itself and its relevance to self-image.

People with a good work ethic generally feel good about themselves, are capable and thorough, don't need constant positive feedback, and have notably good relationships with peers and colleagues. Having access to the components of a good work ethic when faced with problems keeps kids solution focused and wards off giving up prematurely. We are thinking too narrowly when we think about work ethic only in terms of school or grades; our work ethic is part of what makes us successful across a range of activities, from gardening to playing Scrabble to raising children. It is our basic approach to the inevitable challenges of life. It's about hanging in and doing our best.

The definition of a good work ethic seems to be the province of business books. This is odd since our kids' attitudes toward work starts well before kindergarten. When he was four, my oldest son, Loren, set up his first business endeavor. Selling rocks outside our house must have seemed a natural to him since our front lawn consisted entirely of rocks. Like the proverbial lemonade stand, Loren's rock stand taught him most of the basics of a good work ethic. He noticed that people bought more rocks when he was talkative and enthusiastic about his product. He was careful with other people's money and thanked them for their purchase, and if they didn't purchase, for their interest. Did he do this all on his own? Of course not. While the idea of the rock stand was his, at four he needed help with the arithmetic, signage, and some of the niceties of social interaction. This is how we reinforce a work ethic in our children. Start early, stay focused on process, and don't overvalue the end results. The twenty-four dollars he collected over the course of that summer was the best educational bargain imaginable.

But what about the child who works one day at the rock stand and then declares his business "closed"? The child who wanders off while customers hang around and becomes crabby or teary when you remind him to stay at his stand? Or the child who begins adding an impossible number of other salable items to the table, including your new shoes and old lipsticks? In junior form, these are the issues that arise often when parents wonder about how much to insist on sticking with a task, how much energy needs to go into a task, and what to do when kids get off track. What happens when your soccer player decides he's done with soccer, when your pianist refuses to practice, or your previously diligent student decides that his girlfriend matters more than his homework? If it's persistence, diligence, effort, and the ability to delay gratification we're after, how do we know how much to push and when to back off? Clearly we would prefer that our children become competent, responsible workers as opposed to pursuit-revolving dilettantes.

So do we let the four-year-old close down shop or the fourteen-year-old skimp on his studies? It depends. Part of our job is to teach our children the importance of a good work ethic, to have high expectations for them, and to make sure that we provide a warm, supportive environment for our kids as they wrestle with impulsivity and pleasure on the one hand and responsibility and diligence on the other. No one has ever developed a good work ethic by being berated or by being confronted consistently with overwhelming tasks. If something's not working, you need to find out why. Is your youngster just too young and too physically active to spend hours sitting at a "rock stand"? Is your fourteen-year-old really messing up in school or age-appropriately dividing his energies between his academic life and his newfound social life? Assuming that your child has generally maintained zest for learning, what aspect of a particular activity is making him want to throw his hands up? If it's extracurricular, after a reasonable effort, maybe it's just not right for him. The world is full of opportunities—find ones that fit with your particular child's talents and interests. If it's academics, talk to the teacher. See if you can pinpoint the problem before it turns into "I'm just stupid at math." Be on your kid's side even as you set and enforce expectations. "I know it's hard to practice every day, but I admire your tenacity. It will pay off down the line." As I said earlier, kids tend to live up or down to the expectations we set for them. Keep your expectations high. Tolerate the anger your kids may direct at you when you know they can do better and insist on greater effort. And, most important, make sure your kids know that it's their work ethic and not simply how smart or talented they are that will ultimately determine their success.

DO

- Do model enthusiasm around hard work. Some parents are so overwhelmed that their kids get the message that all hard work brings is stress and tension. Who wants to join that club? Let your kid know that when you work hard, you feel a sense of accomplishment and pride. Not every moment, but often enough to make your hard work feel worthwhile.

- Make sure that the work your child is expected to do is reasonable. If a task is overwhelming, and no amount of effort will make it doable for your child, then the benefit of expending effort will be lost. Too many kids end up in tears several hours into homework that is totally overwhelming in either content or amount. Talk to your child's school if the amount of homework your child is given seems out of line. Guidelines are ten minutes per grade in elementary school, about an hour in middle school, and not more than about two to two and a half hours in high school.

- In addition to focusing on effort, persistence, and discipline, do make sure to notice other components of a good work ethic like integrity or the ability to communicate and collaborate. Often kids with good social skills are thought of as simply popular, and parents implore them to socialize less and study more. But these same kids generally are good collaborators and communicators. They are likely to be sought after in the work world.

- Do notice the activities that your child is willing to put effort into and the solutions that work well for him. Let your child know that many skills can be carried from one type of endeavor to another. "I notice you go into your room and put on music when you need to focus on your tough math problems. Maybe you should give that a try with those Spanish verbs you're having trouble with."

DON'T

- Don't expect all your kids to put in the same kind of effort. Intensity and persistence are both parts of temperament and will vary significantly from child to child. There are so many components to a good work ethic. Focus on strengthening the ones that come more easily to your child.

- Don't worry that your child will be "mad" at you when you discipline. Stay away from humiliation and harsh, arbitrary punishment. But keep in mind that your capacity to discipline ensures that your child will have the capacity to self-discipline. Children aren't born with a programmed understanding of rules and regulations. They are taught what to value and how to value by their parents and their community through a combination of praise/encouragement and disappointment/discipline. Your love helps your children develop connections; your discipline helps them to self-manage. It's often easier for us to love our kids than to discipline them. But both are critical components of a good work ethic.*

- Don't insist on your child's "best effort" at absolutely everything. Somehow we've gotten the idea that kids have to be great at so many things, when out in the world, most of us are really good at a few things and not particularly notable at many other things. Talented people lean in to

---

* If this chapter hasn't fully convinced you of the benefit of parental discipline in order to further your child's self-discipline, consider this: self-discipline is a far better predictor of academic success than IQ is. Twice as good, as a matter of fact. See A. Duckwork and M. P. Seligman, "Self-Discipline Outdoes IQ in Predicting Academic Performance of Adolescents," *Psychological Science* 16:12 (2005): 939–944.

areas of strength and have hobbies where standards are less exacting. Focus on the things that matter most both to you and to your child. Too often good kids are being criticized for not putting their "best effort" into the most trivial things.

CHAPTER 7

Teaching Our Kids to Take Action

SELF-CONTROL
"It just doesn't feel right" instead of
"All the kids are doing it"

- The ruckus downstairs lets you know that your four-year-old son and his six-year-old brother have morphed from being companionable siblings to being mortal enemies once again. Not unexpectedly, your four-year-old is crying in the corner, massaging his head where his older brother undoubtedly popped him one. Your older son is triumphantly brandishing Talking Buzz Lightyear, the toy you bought for your younger boy after seeing *Toy Story 3*. When you ask, "What happened?" your younger son continues to sniffle and your older boy simply says, "I wanted it."

- Your twelve-year-old daughter surprises you by saying that she plans on babysitting Saturday night instead of hanging out with her girlfriends. Since Saturday night sleepovers have been a weekly ritual for the last couple of years you ask her about her change in plans. Clearly reluctant to have any discussion, she mumbles something about not "liking" her friends so much lately. As she retreats into her room she impatiently says, "Besides, I thought you wanted me to be responsible and earn some money." Her door clicks shut.

- Your almost eighteen-year-old son is holding down the fort for the weekend while you and your husband get away for a night. Your two younger daughters have been farmed out to friends' houses but your son stays home. When you return Sunday, he is sitting outside on the steps, clearly waiting for your return. Before you're out of the car he's apologizing. Apparently he invited "a few" friends over and that gathering quickly escalated into a drinking party he couldn't control. He called a trusted neighbor and asked for help, fearing that the police would turn up. With your neighbor's help, he dispatched the crowd, but not before a lamp was broken and some red wine was spilled on your hall carpet. While you are angry with him, he seems even angrier with himself. "I should have known better. I'm really sorry, Mom. I was an idiot. I'll pay for what got trashed." He doesn't protest his grounding.

Issues of self-control dog us throughout life. The six-year-old hits out of frustration; his self-control repertoire is still very limited. But the twelve-year-old and the eighteen-year-old use words, distraction, common sense, and outside help to reinforce their not entirely successful attempts at self-control. The twelve-year-old is not comfortable around the straying hands of the young boys who, of late, are showing up at the slumber parties. She doesn't know how to confront the situation so she opts out and in the process learns one effective way of maintaining self-control. The eighteen-year-old overestimates his self-control, finds himself in a pickle, but has the wherewithal to reach out for help and to think deeply about consequences. He is learning how much he can trust himself, who he can depend on, and who he can't. He's unlikely to need many repeat performances to convince him that there are certain situations that remain beyond his control. All of these kids are fortifying their repertoire of self-control skills in age-appropriate ways. It is to be expected that kids' best intentions regularly run up against their lack of experience and their imperfectly controlled selves.

I have spent much of my life working with teens, most of whom have run into trouble of one sort or another. Some have had serious emotional problems like depression, anxiety, and substance abuse; others have just been mouthy, not as academically inclined as their parents wished, or stuck in a difficult family situation. But all of them have had issues with self-regulation. The kid who self-mutilates, who drinks too much, who shoplifts, who is too vulnerable to peer pressure, who constantly needs to be reminded to do homework, take out the garbage, or get to sleep at a reasonable hour is wrestling with self-control issues. One of our most important jobs as parents is to help our children construct and strengthen a range of self-control strategies for dealing with both incidental and serious threats to their well-being. The importance of the internal ability to say no, to control impulsivity, to delay gratification cannot be overestimated as a protective factor in child and adolescent development.

Here's the problem, though. When our kids are not exercising self-control, we are typically disappointed, worried, and angry. We tend to miss these important teaching opportunities because we are so upset, and catastrophize the situation. Your kid is hitting his brother. *Maybe he has no conscience. Maybe he'll grow up to be a bully, or worse, a sociopath.* Your preteen daughter's peer group is experimenting with sexuality. *Maybe next time she'll join them, get pregnant, catch a venereal disease, or, God forbid, HIV.* Your teenage son is at a party at a friend's house. *What if he's drinking? What if the police drop by? What will happen to his college acceptance? To his life?* Our first impulse is often to set limits that will "protect" our children from ever walking close to this imagined level of danger again. Most of us have instituted irrational and unhelpful consequences that needed to be rescinded the moment our sanity returned. "You hit your brother again? Let's see how it feels when Dad hits you." "How could I have been so stupid to trust you alone in the house? Don't you have any judgment? You're grounded for the rest of the year." We all know the feeling of having to come back with a cooler head and undo our own impulsivity. It would work better for us, and for our children, if we could see their lapses in self-control as inevitable and challenging but actually welcome opportunities to teach strategies for handling impulses while they're still under our roof.

The part of the brain that is responsible for self-control, the prefrontal cortex (or more specifically, the dorsal fronto-median cortex), is not fully developed until your child is in her mid-twenties. This gives us lots of years and plenty of opportunities to help our children find ways to shore up their strategies for self-control. Getting from "all the kids are doing it" to "it just doesn't feel right" will be a two-steps-forward, one-step-back process because we are fighting biology. However, it is quite doable as long as we keep in mind that if we get completely bent out of shape when our kids do stupid things we are in a much weaker position to teach the skills that ultimately will lead to internal restraint rather than dependence on external monitors.

Too often we confuse compliance and self-control. While compliance is the precursor to self-control, it is not the same thing. Compliance is about following someone else's rules. Self-control is about developing, fortifying, and internalizing your own rules. If your child complies but hasn't learned real self-control, then when the "rule-maker" isn't around—you're distracted on a phone call, the teacher has left the room, your teen has just gone off to college—the rules are nonexistent, poorly internalized, or, most often, constructed by peers. While much of our job is laying down and enforcing rules, we also need to help our children understand the rules, practice them, and to feel, *over time*, that their behavior will be directed by their own good choices. Our external "no" has to ultimately become their internal "no." How do we help that happen?

In psychology there is the classic Marshmallow Test. Conducted fifty years ago, it is still the gold standard experiment for illustrating the enduring value of self-control and the strategies that help strengthen it.[1] Strikingly, this experiment used very young children, traditionally not considered exemplars of self-control. Four-year-olds were put in a room each with a bell and plate with a single marshmallow on it. The researcher explained that he would leave the room. If the children wanted to eat the marshmallow, they could ring the bell, the researcher would return, and they were free to have the marshmallow in front of them. However, if they waited for the researcher to return on his own, they would get to eat two marshmallows. Many children were able to wait, even when the researcher was out of the room for as long as fifteen minutes. In addition to the surprise of finding that some hungry four-year-olds already have enough self-control to wait for a single extra marshmallow, the long-term follow-up from this experiment could hardly have been anticipated. Twenty-five years later those youngsters who had been unable to delay gratification turned out to have higher rates of behavioral problems both in school and at home. They did less well academically and in their relationships. In contrast, the youngsters who had been able to call up an internal "no" in the face of great temptation grew up to have a host of personal and academic advantages—greater academic achievement, higher self-esteem, lower rates of substance use, and more satisfaction with relationships.[2]

How did those young kids manage to control themselves in the absence of an adult's watchful eye? The kids who were best able to delay gratification not only distracted themselves by singing or turning their backs to the marshmallows; they also lessened the seduction of the marshmallows by thinking of them, not as delicious treats, but as clouds or cotton balls. This all seems like pretty sophisticated behavioral and cognitive maneuvering for a child who often still sleeps with a teddy bear. But these children did not exhibit self-control in a vacuum; they exhibited it when they had a meaningful goal in mind—twice as many marshmallows.

As we look at ways to further our children's self-control, it is important to remember that in order to give something up, we all need to keep our eye on a greater goal. I love desserts, but when I'm geared for battle with the perpetual five pounds I'd like to lose, I manage (well, sometimes manage) to settle for a cup of coffee after dinner. Children need to be reminded of the greater goal in order to show self-control. "I know you want to stay up late studying tonight but you've already studied hard for your test. It's more important to be rested so that you can do your best." "I know you don't feel like going to practice today, but Monday is your big game and your team's success depends on everyone being fully prepared." These are reminders to your child that, while short-term solutions may look attractive, thinking of the big picture is usually the way to go.

Another way to help children learn self-control is to help them develop ways to wait. Learning to wait, to divert attention, to change focus, and to switch from one activity to another is not a skill that children pick up without our active teaching and modeling. We begin this process in infancy when we don't run into our baby's room at the first whimper, and we continue it with older kids when we emphasize the value and rewards of waiting: "You can spend your allowance now, but if you save for a few weeks you'll have enough for that video game you've been wanting."

All kids start with a limited capacity for discomfort—remember the frustrated, stomping preschooler who demands candy at the grocery checkout—but we need to help them learn that they can tolerate discomfort, that it helps to be distracted or to switch focus and that delayed gratification often brings greater rewards than does impulsivity. This is a long, slow process with forward progress, meltdowns, and more progress. The child who can hold off—whether it's marshmallows at four, or Buzz Lightyear at six—is in a much better position to hold off on drugs at twelve or sex at fourteen.

DO

- Do make sure that you expose your child to good self-management strategies by modeling them yourself. Don't cut in line, don't impatiently refuse to wait, and don't "lose it." Having an involved father is a protective factor when it comes to children's development of self-control.

- Do allow your child to experience moderate levels of distress. We have to allow our children to be exposed to increasingly difficult challenges that are manageable or almost manageable for them. One of the most painful parts of being a parent is seeing our child struggle while we hold back. Your third grader left his homework assignment on the kitchen table and is angry that you didn't bring it up to school for him and that he received a zero for the assignment in spite of having completed it. Don't call his teacher and "explain" the situation. Kids need "successful failures," that is, failures that serve the function of strengthening coping skills. A missed third-grade homework assignment is a tolerable "failure" for your young child.

- Do show that you value your child's ability to "go against the crowd." The first time your child says "Everyone was ——— [fill in the blank: cheating, drinking, smoking] but I just didn't feel it was right" is an occasion worthy of (quiet) celebration. Your child's attemps at self-control, whether that's not kicking a friend who snatched his favorite toy, or not having sex with the "stud" at school, deserve your quiet admiration. Don't overplay your hand; moments like these need to fully "belong" to your child.

DON'T

- Don't expect your children to learn without your guidance how to show self-control. Children need to be shown how to change focus, how to shift activities, how to divert their attention. "Why don't we read this story while we wait for the doctor." "I know it's been a long ride; let's see who can spot the first license plate from another state." "Sometimes when I'm frustrated going for a run really helps." We want to help our children manage their distress before it becomes overwhelming. Intolerable distress is a very poor teacher.

- Don't minimize or be dismissive of your child's negative feelings. A large part of self-control rests on the ability to manage uncomfortable feelings while searching for healthy solutions. An anxious child who is tempted to cheat on a big test will be less likely to do so if he has alternative ways of handling his anxiety. This is not the time to say, "Oh, don't be silly. It's just a test." Take your child's concerns seriously and help him come up with ways to lessen his anxiety (make a study schedule, sign up for teacher office hours). You will help him strengthen the likelihood of his being able to exert self-control even if others are cheating.

- Don't back off emotionally when your child becomes a teenager. It is critical that we stay involved and supportive even as our teens begin crafting more autonomous lives. Continuing to monitor your teens' friends and whereabouts has been shown to protect them from peer pressure and self-destructive behavior. This, in turn, allows them the psychological space necessary to think about and develop strategies for self-control. Remember that learning self-control is a lifelong assignment and always takes energy. A home that is a safe haven helps kids recharge their batteries.

SELF-ESTEEM
"I feel good about myself" instead of "I suck"

Molly is twelve years old and a naturally talented athlete. She plays several sports, but her passion is for swimming. Molly has advanced to the regional swim meet several years in a row and has consistently moved up in the rankings. Last year she placed third in her age group and vowed to come in first this year. While she practiced hard for this year's event, she also had become increasingly social, spending time that she used to devote to practice to hanging out with her girlfriends. She is frustrated when she comes in second. Her parents give her a big hug, point out how much she has improved, and end by saying, "If you want to come in first, you'll have to work harder."

My audiences don't like this story; neither do many of my colleagues. They take issue with the last line, seeing it as nonsupportive and potentially harmful to Molly's self-esteem. I disagree. Our efforts at bolstering our children's self-esteem are likely to be discounted if we aren't honest. Molly is a gifted athlete who is finding, quite appropriately at her age, that competing demands are cutting into her practice time. She will have some hard decisions in front of her as her social life may trump her desire to become a top swimmer.

The point here is that Molly, who excels at her sport, wants to come in first. Since self-esteem comes not from being gushed over but from being competent, Molly's desire to become more competent needs to be acknowledged and supported just as her current accomplishment needs to be acknowledged and supported. She's frustrated but not thrown into a tailspin by her second-place showing. Her parents have simply underscored the reality that she increases the chances of reaching *her* goal if she increases her effort and practices more. Their big hug communicates that their love or pride in her is in no way conditional on her performance. We risk damaging our children's self-esteem only when we are disingenuous, unrealistic, or overly invested—when we tell a child who's practiced herself into near exhaustion that she needs to work harder or a child with poor motor coordination that she's a "terrific athlete," or when we express disappointment in spite of a child's best effort.

Self-esteem, a valuable and protective attribute, has unfortunately been popularized in ways that have stripped it of descriptive accuracy. Popular notions would seem to suggest that self-esteem can be manufactured out of thin air. That if you tell your child often enough that he is smart or talented or special, somehow this will translate into just that. *Self-esteem is not bestowed, it is earned.* We help our children cultivate healthy self-esteem when we encourage them to set meaningful goals and then to work toward them with effort and perseverance. One child's goal is to swim the length of the pool; another's is to come in first at the regional competition. As parents, our job is to help our children set goals that are realistic, challenging, and safe.

Real self-esteem, the *feeling* that one is worthwhile, has been tied to positive outcomes almost too long to list. Children with high self-esteem have more friends, do better academically, have a wider range of coping skills, and are more resilient, to name a few advantages. The word alone should alert us to the fact that *self*-esteem is cultivated internally. It is the result of two things—*competence* and *confidence*. I have included self-esteem in this section on more active coping skills because few of us need encouragement to check out how our kids are feeling about themselves, but it would be wise to begin to pay more attention to what our children actually can *do* to advance their sense of self-esteem. This shift in emphasis should help take us away from the excesses associated with self-esteem and return us to the active drivers of self-esteem.

Competence, the ability to do something well, is often described as an "inherent need." It is what enables us to adapt to different environments and helps us determine where to put our energies. Our children are *driven* to be competent. They go through the same motions, repeat the same words, listen and look at the same stories over and over as they learn to walk, learn to talk, and learn to read. Competence is in our genes. If your ancestors weren't competent— didn't know how to effectively forage for food, construct shelter, or stay ahead of danger—then it's unlikely you'd be reading this. Our children may no longer have to scan for tigers, but they do have to develop other, equally important and timely skills, such as critical thinking and the ability to collaborate, in order to successfully navigate their contemporary lives.

Competence begets confidence. Your child may need your steadying hand on the back of her bicycle many dozens of times before she can maintain her balance. Kids will pull you outside to practice for hours, days, or weeks until they have learned the incredibly complex set of tasks that are necessary to master bike riding—balance, coordination, visual awareness, and a host of motor skills. If you want to know what confidence looks like, conjure up your child's face when he first realized that your hand was gone and he was riding *on his own*.

It is important that you and your child set reasonable goals. Riding alone down the block inspires confidence because it is doable for children. Yes, it takes a lot of motivation, practice, and effort, but it is well within the realm of what most children can do. In encouraging this kind of challenging but manageable skill development, we help our children look forward to greater challenges like riding around the block and then around the neighborhood. Confidence is built from the hundreds of small successes that are part of daily life, and not from great leaps, which are few and far between. High self-esteem, just like a robust sense of self, should not be vulnerable to temporary setbacks. This doesn't mean kids aren't going to feel disappointed when they don't live up to either their expectations or ours. It simply means that they will recover quickly and learn from their experience.

How do we help our children to become competent in the things we anticipate will be most important in their lives, while respecting their natural interests, capacities, and skills? We hope to see our children become competent in many arenas, from brushing their teeth to being a good friend to driving safely. Some of the motivation to accomplish these things will come from our insistence that they brush their teeth before bed, or help a friend in need, or have conditional driving privileges. Children internalize parental values and directives particularly when they're accompanied by warmth, support, and firm limits. Competence becomes its own reward and most of us can rest assured that when our children go to college they will continue to brush their teeth in the absence of our reminders.

Yet when we think about competence, most of the time we think about academic competence: good grades, top schools. These are major accomplishments, and kids who have this kind of academic competence are to be congratulated for their hard work and perseverance. But we've lost sight of the fact that, besides the highest level of academic achievement, kids can develop an array of additional competencies that help them become thriving, contributing people.

There is little disagreement about the skills that will be essential for our kids in order to function effectively in the world: creativity, critical thinking, and the ability to collaborate. Sometimes these traits come from really academically talented people, but just as often they can be found in the "average" state school student (check out the Fortune 500 and note that many of this country's CEOs have been educated in our state schools). My fear is that as we limit the competencies we value and try to fit a majority of students into slots that belong to 5 or 10 percent, we do two things. First, we unnecessarily stress a group of academically talented students, and second, we marginalize the talents of an even greater group of students. They too need to benefit from the protective factors that competence and confidence can bestow.

What about kids who aren't great students, who are interested in people, in the arts, or in practical matters? These kids also need to be encouraged to follow their passions. There are dropouts who go on to be highly successful in business, creative kids with mediocre grades who end up blessing us with their art, and tinkerers who are happy working as mechanics. There are as many ways to be competent in the world as there are children blooming. Each and every one of them should be nurtured, should feel that his or her skills, gifts, and interests count for something. When we can broaden the tent so that a full range of competencies are welcome, we are likely to see far more children blessed with genuine self-esteem.

DO

- Do encourage your child to work just outside his or her comfort zone. If your child is solidly reading at a fourth-grade level, have him or her read a few fifth-grade-level books. Provide a dictionary and be available for clarification if needed. The way to increase ability is to be challenged— not to endlessly repeat what one is already good at. Self-esteem is a function of *increased* competence. Kids seem to thrive when they are given tasks that they can successfully complete about 50 percent of the time.

- Do let your children know that you have confidence in their abilities and that restrictions tend to be self-imposed. This doesn't mean that your child can excel at absolutely anything, but much of what our kids accomplish in life depends on what they believe they can accomplish. Confidence comes from the steady accumulation of skills. The steady accumulation of skills comes from interest and practice. Interest typically takes care of itself; practice more often needs our encouragement and oversight.

- Do help children break their goals down into smaller goals. Kids can become easily discouraged by early failures if goals are unrealistic. If your daughter's goal is to learn how to play soccer, start with the basics. Pick up a video on beginning soccer and watch it together. Invite her to go to the park for some physical activity; running or sprints is a good start. Let her practice just kicking a soccer ball around on the grass. Make sure you notice the small improvements in your child's abilities.

DON'T

- Don't pounce on every activity your child enjoys with an invitation to take lessons. If your daughter enjoys pirouetting around the family room, it's not necessary to say, "Why don't we sign you up for ballet lessons?" One of the quickest ways to discourage a child's budding interest is to take it out of the realm of play and turn it into one more organized activity. Allow your children the opportunity to signal you when they want help moving to a higher level of competence.

- Don't allow your child to shift responsibility for difficulties to others. Don't aid and abet your child when he fails a test "because the teacher's an idiot," doesn't get the pitching position on the baseball team "because the coach always picks his own son," or gets a speeding ticket because "the cops are always after kids." Remember that competence and confidence are internal states. When you allow your child to palm off responsibility you encourage the idea that someone else is responsible both for the problem and for fixing it.

This attitude is bound to make your child less competent and therefore lower his self-esteem. Even when others have a hand in your child's distress, which will happen, teach your child to take responsibility for his own life.

• Don't praise indiscriminately if you feel your child needs a "boost" in self-esteem; it's likely to have the opposite effect. To be most effective, praise needs to be specific, and focused on effort, perseverance, and practice. If your daughter is having difficulty with her piano technique, instead of "You played terrifically today," try "I could really hear that you've been working on that left hand. Good for you." Keeping the focus on hard work and improvement means that kids can feel confident even when they are challenged.

SELF-EFFICACY
"I can make a difference" instead of
"Nothing I do matters"

Self-efficacy, the name for our *belief* that we play a significant role in determining how things will turn out for us in life, is at the heart of all success. *Agency* is the word psychologists use to describe how we put that belief into *action*. "If I study harder I think I can pull my grade up." "If I shoot a hundred free throws a day then I'll be a better free throw shooter. "If I get a good night's sleep, I'll be fresher for the SATs tomorrow." All three of these ordinary examples illustrate the power of self-efficacy and agency. These kids are thinking about what they need to do to improve their chances and then acting on their conclusions. Of course, there will be trial and error here, not all solutions will be equally effective, and your kids will get to compare results. "I have my math final tomorrow and the best thing I can do is":

a. Study and get to bed early
b. Stock up on Red Bull and pull an all-nighter
c. Cheat

Many of our kids will try some variation of each of these solutions over the course of their school years. Experience will hopefully teach them that the first option is the most effective. Of course we will guide and counsel. Remind them of the consequences of cheating, educate them about stimulant drugs and ban those drugs if necessary, and reaffirm the value of sleep and hard work. But it is their *experience* that will teach them that the first is the better choice. Whenever our children feel that outcomes are up to them, they are more likely to feel optimistic and enthusiastic about their lives, as opposed to apathetic or defeated.

Repeated positive experiences of self-efficacy help kids move from being dependent on others to trusting their own judgment. Every time your children think about future events and accurately predict how they can increase their chances of being successful they take a step toward independence. "My big piano recital is next week. Think I'll cool it with my friends Friday night and get in a couple of extra hours of practice." These kinds of opportunities to advance a sense of personal control begin very early in life and build upon each other. Infants who have mobiles in their cribs that move when struck, as opposed to a windup mobile, are found to be quicker learners.[3] (Don't get bent out of shape by this finding. Most of us had windup mobiles for our babies. The point is just that kids learn best when they're actively involved.) Overall, we want to provide safe opportunities for our children to feel that they are the agents of their own lives. We help them move in that direction every time we gradually withdraw our aid as they become increasingly competent.

Dan is sixteen years old and has essentially dropped out of school. He turns up irregularly and his parents' best attempts to sympathize with Dan or discipline him are met with indifference. Dan's high school is known to be particularly competitive, and Dan, an average student, finds the competitive atmosphere "suffocating." My sense is that what is being suffocated is Dan's sense of having anything of value to contribute. The school's unwavering attention to test scores and rankings makes it difficult for students to focus on their progress and personal standards as opposed to how they stack up against their classmates. Schools like Dan's often promote a winner-take-all attitude, with top students being victors and less academic students suffering demoralization. Too often, teenagers like Dan are labeled "bad kids," who hang out with other struggling kids and passively make choices that often land them in trouble.

In fact, Dan has simply given up trying to make better choices because in schools that emphasize comparative progress, reputations, once established, are very hard to change.[4] He's likely to feel that he is no longer in control of his own life and to allow it to proceed without thought to consequences. "Nothing I do seems to matter" is a frequent and worrisome comment of children and teens who feel that their personal power has been usurped. It is exactly the ability to feel that what you choose matters, and that these choices will reasonably predict how things will turn out for you, that enables most of us to face the challenges of the day with some degree of confidence and optimism. Giving Dan a fresh start in a school that is more cooperative than competitive, that does not teach in a lockstep fashion that leaves behind children who work at a slower pace, and that does recognize a wide variety of skills and interests helped Dan to feel more in control of his life both academically and socially. While Dan has some catching up to do, he no longer feels that nothing he does matters. An additional benefit of finding the right school is that as he gains a sense of efficacy about his life, he finds it easier to make friends and is less likely to hang out with troubled kids.

Much of what we do as parents relates to clarifying and underscoring the likely consequences of our children's behaviors. We implore our children to "make good choices" and to "think ahead" in order to consistently highlight the relationship between the actions they choose and the results they are likely to get. Smack your best friend and you've lost a playmate; practice and you're more likely to make the team; come in past curfew and you may spend the next weekend watching movies on the couch with Grandma. We highlight consequences and back off when our kids understand the effect of their actions on outcomes. On occasion this means holding our tongue (and our breath) when our children make bad choices, but this is how they learn. We need to be interested in those things that not only protect our children but also enable them to move forward into more advanced and rewarding territory. The tougher class, the harder practice, the more demanding physical activity can give our children a tremendous sense of pride once they've mastered the material or met the challenge. Research tells us that self-efficacy is one of the key factors in developing resilience in children.[5] It is what protects us from feeling like victims and allows us to feel that we are masters of our own fate.

Children benefit in significant ways—academically, personally, and socially—when parents provide them with opportunities to advance their sense of agency. How do we do this? From our children's earliest days we react quickly and with enthusiasm to their attempts to put their stamp on the world. The baby maneuvers a spoon into his mouth, the toddler takes his first few steps, the child finds his balance and skates down the block, the teen gets his first paycheck. Every time children attain a goal because of a choice they made, their sense of agency is enhanced. We really don't need to do much; the pleasure of mastering a challenge is enough for kids.

The consequences of bad choices also have to be made apparent. If your daughter is desperate for the latest designer jeans and you find out that she secretly has pulled a twenty out of your purse, then the jeans are off-limits. Always underscore the relationship between behavioral choices and the end result. "I know you really wanted those jeans but stealing money is unacceptable, not only at home, but anywhere. You might think about what other choices you could have made to get those jeans. Let's talk about that tomorrow." (Give it a day—it allows your daughter to mull it over, and you to calm down.) Give your daughter the opportunity to make amends—run some errands, cook a meal. She will be in a better position to tolerate setbacks and failure, and to be thoughtful about her choices, because you believe in her ability to turn things around.

DO

- Do help your children to appraise their capabilities realistically. Kids who act on faulty self-evaluations are likely to fail. It is much better for kids to be realistic so they know to put in extra effort rather than to overestimate their abilities and expend less effort than is needed. This point need not be made critically, it can simply be noted matter-of-factly. "I know you wanted to be in advanced math. But you've struggled with math this year. Take regular math, and if you work hard and do well, we can reevaluate with your teacher next semester."

- Do provide opportunities for your child from a very early age to be able to contribute successfully to the family. A two-year-old can follow you around with a rag, helping to "clean up." A ten-year-old can mow the lawn. A fifteen-year-old can wash the car. Interacting effectively with the environment is the basis of agency. Although there's no need to swoon over these incremental advances, do make sure that your child knows that you are proud and that you enjoy his or her increasing competence.

DON'T

- Don't project your own anxiety as your child moves forward. Part of a sense of agency comes from pushing past the boundaries that have already been mastered into less certain territory. You've taught your child to cross the street. He's done it a hundred times with you. Now he's going to do it without you. No mother lets go of her child's hand that first time without holding her breath until he's safely on the other side. But just like our confidence, our anxiety is easily communicated. Clearly we never put our children in danger, but when they are ready, we should send them off, whether it's across the street or across the world, with enthusiasm and confidence in their abilities. I'm not suggesting that this is easy. Still, it's the right thing to do.

- Don't protect your child from failure. Failure is both inevitable and desirable. It is how children learn what works and what doesn't. It helps them hone the skills that will be most effective in meeting challenges. Thomas Edison was fond of saying, "I have not failed, I have just found ten thousand ways that don't work." Home run legend Babe Ruth struck out 1,330 times. That's nearly twice as often as he homered. "Every strike brings me closer to the next home run," he often said. Depending on my kids' interests, I kept rotating chestnuts like these on the refrigerator door or their bathroom mirrors. Let your children know the reality—that mistakes, setbacks, and failures are ways to advance knowledge—and that successful people have always experienced more than their share of failure along the way. A diet of easy success ensures being discouraged at the first whiff of challenge.

• Children, particularly adolescents, need to feel a sense of self-efficacy not only about their academic life but also about their relationships and emotions. This means you will need to step back as your teen manages new and difficult feelings. But don't simply hand over control and disengage. Maintaining close and supportive relationships keeps our kids feeling connected, protects them from depression, and advances self-efficacy.

The coping skills that we've looked at in these last two chapters help our children stitch together a highly individual way of dealing with adversity, recovering from challenges, and advancing healthy psychological development. Taken together, they help ensure that our children are resilient in the face of setbacks and optimistic about their current lives as well as their future potential. Hopefully you've gained some ideas about how to help further these protective factors in your children while attending to their genetic and stylistic differences.

But parents' practices and coping skills are not cultivated in a vacuum. They are embedded in our values. We want our children to have a strong work ethic, to do well in school, but not to cheat. We want them ot feel competent to compete on the playing field but not to take illegal substances to gain an advantage. We should never separate our values from the ways in which we encourage our children to become effective family members, friends, collaborators, and citizens. The next chapter of this book will be about our values—which ones are most important to us, the ways to strengthen them, and how to avoid the traps that can make us vulnerable to unintended compromise.

PART FOUR

WALKING THE TALK

CHAPTER 8

Defining and Living
Your Family Values

A Paper and Pencil Exercise

No ordinary parent has ever said, "I hope my child's not successful." Regardless of what our particular version of success emphasizes—a good education, money, satisfying relationships, status, meaningful work, a robust sense of self, service to others—*we are all doing the best we can* to give our children the opportunities and help them develop the skills and the values that will lead to the kind of success we envision for them. The way each of us has constructed a version of success is a combination of many factors: our own parents' attitudes about success; our interests, competencies, and sometimes deprivations; the values we hold; the communities we live in; and the cultural zeitgeist.

Our own values and histories play a particularly important role in what we are likely to emphasize to our children. "Your father worked construction every summer in high school and we'd like you to do the same. It builds character and teaches you independence" or "I don't care what sport you pick, but it would be a good idea to pick a team sport. It will teach you leadership skills and how to work well with others." The effectiveness of these kinds of interventions in promoting success will depend heavily on what is being asked for, how it's communicated, and, especially, how well it fits your particular child. Telling a quiet, artistic child with poor motor coordination that he has to play a contact sport is not likely to make him more successful. Telling the same thing to an active, athletic, socially skilled boy may be a perfect way for him to hone his skills.

Parenting, unfortunately, does not come with an instruction booklet. Some of us have the advantage of having been well-parented ourselves. Others bring little of use from their own upbringing to their new job as parent. We need to keep an open mind about what is in the best interest of our children and be willing to tack this way or that when blown off course. This works best when we're not afraid of capsizing. Children are remarkably forgiving and my own bias is this: if you can see your child clearly, love that child unconditionally, set limits when necessary, and hold fast to a core set of good values, then your boat is sturdy enough to withstand the inevitable squalls of parenthood.

The fact is, parenting isn't *a* job, it's multiple new jobs every couple of years. You're the parent of an infant, a toddler, a child, a preteen, a teen, a young adult, and an adult. While there are great commonalities to the job description at each of these stages, there are also profound differences. Even our love, the greatest commonality of all stages of parenting, frequently needs to change form and expression. Just try hugging your fourteen-year-old son the way you hugged him at four. The mere possibility of his "junk" coming anywhere near yours is enough to send him into a panic. And the curfew that was just fine for your ten-year-old daughter has become the subject of unimaginable histrionics at thirteen.

There seem to be millions of books written on child development and virtually none on parent development. But just as our children's needs change, so do ours. Our interests, attachments, health, and emotional well-being all shift significantly over the course of the two decades or so of active parenting. And of course we spend a great deal of time and energy accommodating to our children's different stages of development. Getting it right when our child is an infant is a good start. But it's just a start and we can expect to get some things right and other things wrong at regular intervals. Mistakes, as we've seen, are the foundation of competence. Our kids need to tolerate, even welcome mistakes, and so do we. It's hard to help your child grow when you've stopped growing yourself. Don't just try to mold your child to be the adult you'd like her to be, work on being that adult yourself.

Donald Winnicott, the well-known English pediatrician and psychoanalyst, formulated the idea of the "good enough mother"[1] after years of observing mothers and their children. He did not mean that a good mother was indifferent, but rather that "the ordinary mother in her ordinary loving care" lays the foundation of emotional health for her child. Imagine thinking that "ordinary loving care" is sufficient to ensure a happy, well-adjusted child. I'm quite certain by *ordinary* he did not mean being a chauffeur, tutor, coach, personal chef, publicist, or best friend. Since Winnicott considered the mother's capacity to be responsive to her child the most important contribution she could make to her child's emotional health, I suspect he would be appalled at the running around that most of us do, which leaves little time for the kind of quiet observation necessary to truly "get" another person. Remember staring into the eyes of your first love, or your infant. It takes calm, unhurried time to learn how to tune into and accurately read another human being.

A common complaint I hear from my young patients is "Nobody knows me." This is true in profound and unsettling ways. We know the outside of our children, how they present themselves, and how they perform. But many kids feel completely unknown to the people who are supposed to know them the best—their parents. Their false selves are on display, but their authentic selves, generally marginally developed, are scarcely glimpsed. A false self, something I see regularly in the teens I treat, can project confidence and competence but in fact feels neither. These are the kids who look like they "have it all" but experience mostly feelings of unreality, unhappiness, and even "deadness." *The Price of Privilege* opened with a successful-appearing teen who had used a razor to incise the word *Empty* into her arm. She is still the model for me of what it feels like to have a false self. Of course, no one feels successful all the time. But there is no real success for any of us if we don't know ourselves in deep, realistic, and appreciative ways.

Understanding that success always needs to have an underpinning of emotional authenticity should make it easier for us to broaden our ideas about what success might look like for our children. Just as colleges, marriages, and friendships need to be a good "fit" to make them comfortable and sustainable, ultimately our ideas about success have to be a good fit for our particular child in order to endure. Best-case scenario: we're clear about our values, we live by them, our children adopt many of them, and they are supported in their particular choices about how to live out those values. There is a big difference between values and school or occupation choices. Depending on your child's interests, skills, and capacities, he can be a compassionate teacher or a compassionate venture capitalist. Your job is to instill compassion; his job is to figure out the arena where he is best suited for, and most interested in, exhibiting compassion. This doesn't mean that we don't have feelings about the choices our children make; it just means that we know the difference between the person and the packaging.

Before we can think about a definition of success, we need to be clear about the things we value. Let's take a closer look at the values we think are important, and whether or not we're satisfied with how these values are lining up with how our families function. If they're not, let's consider what changes we might make. I hope this chapter reassures you about some things, clarifies others, and seriously challenges you on still others. Before delving in, though, you need to make sure your mind is open and your internal critic is caged. The point of looking deeply at what you value, how you define success, and how you hope to put your particular definition into effect is to give you a little breathing space to think through the wisdom of your choices unfettered by blame or faultfinding.

Most of us are so busy trying to meet multiple and often over-whelming demands that we neglect to carve out the time and space we need to weigh different options, clarify our own values, and find the information we need to help us make decisions. This is that time. It is not a time to be critical, to point fingers at yourself, your spouse, or anyone "out there." This chapter is for you. It is designed to help you structure your thinking around what you mean by "success" for your particular child, knowing full well that every child is different and that success for one may look nothing like success for another. However, in some way this is about the details—one child shows an aptitude for math, another for writing, and a third for science and music. Regardless of your child's interests and capacities, I'm betting that you want your future mathematician, journalist, or jazz-playing surgeon to find meaning in his work and to be a person with good values. You may value entrepreneurship, but I doubt that you'd be happy if your child became a heroin distributor or a pimp.

We simply do not pull the strings on the life choices our children will ultimately make: the careers they pick, the spouse they choose, or the communities they will become part of. However, our children's choices are informed by what we believe constitutes a life well lived and what doesn't. Once you determine which values are most important to you, this chapter will help you develop an action plan that focuses more fully on integrating these values into your parenting. If you have a spouse or partner, it's probably best to do these exercises separately since they take introspection and reflection. Come together to discuss differences and similarities and work on compromise if your values or strategies are at odds. There are bound to be some differences of opinion. You are not clones, and your own histories are apt to be different. However, most couples find that the *majority* of their core values are quite aligned even if they have somewhat different ideas about how to put them into action. Do not be dismissive. Try to learn from each other.

WHAT ARE YOUR CORE VALUES?

One of the most interesting and provocative discoveries I have made as I travel around the country is the degree of disconnect between what parents and children say defines success. Ask any audience of parents this question: "How would you define success for your children when they've grown up?" Without fail the responses are primarily internally cultivated qualities like independence, integrity, generosity, passion, self-confidence, and healthy relationships. A notably healthy list of attributes. But when children and teens are asked, "How will you define success when you grow up?" the answer is quick and inevitable—"Making lots of money." Now, I have no doubt that we are all sincere when we say that our most important goal for our children is for them to be emotionally healthy, responsible, and contributing members of society. Yet somehow our children are taking in a very different message. Making lots of money is fine, but as a definition of success it is likely to leave our children, and the adults they will ultimately become, disappointed and disengaged. Money buys many things, but typically not a sense of either authenticity or meaning.

Of course, we are not the only influences in our children's lives. Messages about the importance of money are both explicit and implicit in our culture. Television shows focus on extravagant parties, multimillion-dollar "cribs," and tricked-out cars. Americans have long been notoriously poor savers, predictably choosing to consume rather than save. And our recent financial troubles have under-scored the relative invulnerability of the wealthy and the extreme vulnerability of the less well-off. Small wonder that our kids come to see money as the greatest indicator of success and security.

Although culture certainly influences our kids' beliefs, when it comes to core values, parents generally exert a stronger influence. So why aren't our beliefs about what it takes to have a successful life getting through to our kids? Are we sending mixed messages, telling our kids to be responsible, while at the same time giving them a pass from responsibility every time they have a test because it might affect their GPA? ("Forget about doing the dishes tonight, honey. Go study.") When we pay for tutors and turn a blind eye to irresponsible behavior, whether it's cheating or not getting adequate sleep, are we fooling ourselves? When we tell our children we want them to have "options," is that really another way of saying that we want them to get the best possible grades, so they can go to the best possible college and graduate school, to prepare them for the best possible jobs, which disproportionately seem to be in the field of finance?

Among the tens of thousands of parents I have spoken to, not a single one has said "money" in answer to my question about what success would look like. The closest anyone has come to this admission are the two parents who said "off my payroll." I appreciate these two brave souls who dared to bring the issue of money into the discussion particularly in front of an audience of hundreds of other parents! Kids laugh when I tell them that their parents don't mention money as a measure of success; they think I've been snowed. And I know I can't be the only parent who has applauded financial achievement: I was thrilled the first time our oldest son took his father and me out to dinner and paid with *his own* credit card. Of course, being financially independent is part of being successful and our hesitancy to name this as part of success highlights our ambivalence. Money increases well-being. It's just that a modest amount of money buys an awful lot of well-being, while lots more money is of little added benefit. We need to make this clear.

In order to strengthen our messages to our children about our core values, we need to make sure that our core values are aligned with our parenting practices. For example, if you say you value physical and emotional well-being and your middle school child isn't getting at least nine hours of sleep a night, then you have to either rethink how much you really do value well-being *or* consider rectifying some of your parenting lapses on this issue. Talking about values can become an almost endless diversion from actually living them. The point here is to get clear on what we value so that we can translate values into actions.

I never much like "exercises" in parenting books and typically skip over them. But the thousands of parents who have used these exercises as part of our Challenge Success parenting course developed at Stanford University have found them to be profoundly helpful.* Grab a pencil and paper. Take your time. This process can take place over a day or a month. Reminisce about your own childhood and the things that helped to make you the person you are today. When my husband, our young children, and I had dinner together almost every night during the week, it wasn't because of the research on how protective family dinners are for children's academic and emotional success. I was recapturing the warmth and joviality of that tiny kitchen where my parents, my brother, and I ate a celebratory meal of roast beef, potatoes, and artichokes every Thursday night, the one weekday my mother didn't have to work. Mine your own history for experiences that still make you smile.

---

* Much of this curriculum was developed by Denise Pope, senior lecturer at Stanford University, and Jim Lobdell. I'm grateful to them both for allowing me to present this material here.

Defining Core Values

What is important to you? It's something most of us know on a gut level but rarely formalize. It's important to be genuine and clear on what matters most to you if you're committed to the idea that authentic success always includes good values. Below is a list of words and phrases that many parents associate with success. There are some blank spaces at the end for any additional items that are important to you. Think about how important each of these qualities is to you. Put a 1 next to those things that are very important, a 2 next to things that are moderately important, and a 3 next to those less important items.

CORE VALUES

Popularity ____	Being reflective ____
Being a go-getter ____	Being generous ____
Conscientiousness ____	Being responsible ____
Being a good problem solver ____	Empathy ____
Industriousness ____	Being attractive ____
Competitiveness ____	Contributing to the community ____
Good relationships ____	Having deep interests ____
High grades ____	Being relaxed ____
Elite colleges ____	Making a lot of money ____
Being athletic ____	Being a team player ____
Having a family ____	Communicating clearly and well ____
Creativity ____	Being self-directed ____
Independence ____	Adaptability ____
A strong sense of self ____	Having a prestigious job ____
Having power over others ____	Being collaborative ____
Religion ____	Honesty ____

Individuality ____	Being aggressive ____
Enthusiasm ____	Curiosity ____
Social consciousness ____	Confidence ____
Self-control ____	"Pillar of the community" ____
Physical well-being ____	Optimism ____
Emotional well-being ____	Financial independence ____
Being a people pleaser ____	Having a sense of humor ____
Putting in best effort ____	Resilience ____

As you do this exercise, withhold judgment. This exercise is not about political correctness or about endorsing only altruistic characteristics. That would be your internal critic saying, "Endorse everything that looks like I'm a really, really good parent and stay away from things like money or elite colleges; they make me look superficial." Actually, every one of these qualities can be a plus in your child's life. Right now we're just trying to get clear on your particular vision at this moment. You will have plenty of time to change your mind or tweak your value system.

As you look at your rankings, there will probably be some combination of internal and external qualities. Internal qualities such as being generous or empathic are what help our children become good, well-adjusted people; external qualities such as being aggressive or wanting high grades help them reach goals by being active participants in their lives.

Sleep on this exercise.

FAMILY VALUES STATEMENT

Welcome back. Look at your values rankings again. Look at those characteristics to which you gave either a 1 or a 2 and choose the four or five that seem most important to you. You are not discarding the others; you are simply trying to hone down and make manageable a very complex idea—what are my strongest values, the ones that I believe are most likely to faciliate authentic success for my child? Take the characteristics you've chosen and put them into a couple of sentences.

For example, if you've chosen:

- Having deep interests
- Self-control
- Empathy
- Being responsible

then your statement would look something like this:

The things that I value most are empathy, self-control, having deep interests, and being responsible. I will feel that my child is successful if these qualities are well developed when she leaves the nest.

Post this Family Values Statement where you and your family will see it every day—the refrigerator, a kitchen bulletin board, a home office. Revisit it from time to time and talk about it with your family.

There are two alternative ways to do this exercise that I have found to be useful:

- Do this exercise as a family. Once your children are about eight years old they can contribute to the process, often including values like "having fun" or "hanging out" that might indeed be important values that are flying under our radar. Their language will be different from yours and you may want to edit the list accordingly ("not taking stuff that isn't yours" instead of "self-control" or "staying healthy" instead of "physical well-being"). But the collaborative experience of working out what family members see as most important shines a lot of light on your family as a whole and the individuals within it.

- After you've narrowed your list to five values, narrow it to three and then to one. While this may seem silly—no family functions on just a single value—it is a good way of seeing what you consider absolutely essential for your children to thrive.

YOUR GUIDING PRINCIPLES

Now that you've had a chance to write down, think about, and prioritize your core values, you need to start thinking about how to translate those values into broader "guiding principles." What exactly do these values mean to you? Having a set of guiding principles makes things easier when you are faced with the decisions, challenges, and compromises that are part of daily family life. Guiding principles are not written in stone; they may differ slightly from child to child. But in addition to helping you clarify the "how" of parenting so that your values are explicit, they serve as a bulwark against bad decisions made out of exhaustion or anger. Use them to help sort out alternative solutions to problems, to lessen the wear and tear of constantly figuring out how to be a "good parent," and to help structure family life in a way that actively reflects your values.

So, using the example above, where "having deep interests" and "self-control" are both core values, your guiding principles would look something like this:

I believe that having deep interests will help my children be successful. For me that means:

- *Exposing my children to a wide range of different experiences*
- *Following my children's lead about what is interesting*
- *Allowing my children to opt out of activities when they lose interest after some sustained effort*
- *Modeling the pleasure of deep interest myself by making sure there are things in my own life that I care deeply about*

I believe that self-control will help my children be successful. For me that means:

- *Not doing for my children what they can do for themselves*
- *Generally making sure that responsibilities are attended to before free time*
- *Discussing strategies for dealing with inevitable frustrations*
- *Privileges are earned by responsible behavior*

THE FAMILY ACTION PLAN

So far we've mostly relied on our good angels, the ones in our heads that tell us it's good for our children to be responsible or empathic or capable of managing themselves well even when challenged. Aside from thinking, and thinking hard, you haven't had to *do* anything yet. Now we need to translate our values and our guiding principles into actions. This final exercise, the Family Action Plan, will help you formulate *specific* ways of encouraging the values that *you* have identified. Above all else, the Action Plan is intended to be a practical tool, something you can return to when you're feeling muddled about some parenting dilemma.

If you've been anxious to see some real shifts in focus, some significant changes in the tenor and pace of your household, and greater attention paid to those things that you believe in, then you will need to put your heart and soul into this plan. And you will need to devote some real time to doing this. Many of us spend quite a bit of time every day checking on homework, inquiring about grades, and discussing potential colleges but we find ourselves short on time when it comes to emphasizing the effect of personal qualities and good values on our children's ultimate success. Now is the time to shift focus.

Here's an example to give you some ideas about how different parents have chosen to shore up the value of "deep interest."

I believe that having my children find deep interests is an important part of success. This means:

Exposing my children to a wide range of different experiences:

- Once a month we will have a family outing to a place we (preferably but not necessarily) haven't visited before. We will rotate choosing the type of outing.

- Twice a week an hour is taken for every family member to concentrate on an activity that interests him or her. (Social networking and television watching are excluded, but learning how to write a television script is not.) I'll try to make this the same time for all household members, including myself, to pursue their interests; modeling that deep interests are a pleasurable part of life whether you're a kid or a grown-up.

Following my children's lead about what is interesting:
- Once a week we'll set aside ten to twenty minutes at dinner for each child to "teach" the family something that interests him. One child at a time will have the privilege of being the teacher.

- Once a week I'll spend thirty minutes to an hour with my child at the library or on the computer to help him research his particular interest.

Allowing my child to opt out of a couple of activities that no longer interest him after some sustained effort:
- Barring unusual circumstances, after two to three months of being unhappy with an activity, my child can opt out. (Shorter if it's a contact sport, longer if you went into hock for the baby grand.)

- As long as my child is not overscheduled, I will ask him to come up with an activity to replace the one that no longer interests him. This can include nonstructured activities like reading or guitar strumming. If he is overscheduled, I will congratulate him for keeping his life balanced.

Modeling the pleasure of deep involvement in activities by making sure there are things in my own life that I care deeply about:

- Do something that matters to me that I've been putting off. Talk about it at the dinner table so everyone understands the importance of my commitment to myself.

- Twice a month I will do something outside of the house with a friend or friends. It's important that the kids see me live the value of good relationships and it's important to me that I maintain my connections in spite of the multiple demands on me.

It's easy to see from this example how healthy families can see issues completely differently. In some families being miserable at a sport is reason enough to quit immediately (an unhappy kid can be a preoccupied kid, not an optimal state of mind on the football field). In another family, a perfectly reasonable response might be that the family schedule has been changed to accommodate the football schedule and the team depends on your child, and therefore the season gets finished out. It's likely that the first family puts a higher value on individuality and the second family on being a team player. What matters is that we express our values consistently enough to make them important and with enough flexibility to make them meaningful. So, the kid who's given a pass on sticking with the team should be called to account if not honoring commitments becomes a pattern. And the kid who is expected to honor his commitment should never feel that his safety is a secondary issue.

Hopefully this chapter has given you some idea of how to effectively align your values with your actual parenting practices in order to promote authentic success. This is hard work in the short term but it will yield a great payoff in the long run. Your kids will know where you stand and you'll have a reference guide around tough decisions. Once a year revisit the work you've done. While your values are likely to stay constant, the ways in which you teach them to your children will change as they grow. One of the greatest thrills of being a parent is witnessing your child, out in the world, behaving in accord with the values you treasure most.

• CHAPTER 9 •

Editing the Script

Becoming the Parents We Want to Be

Every psychologist knows that there is a point in therapy when you and your patient have looked at all the facts, turned over as many stones as you both could find, and analyzed (maybe even over-analyzed), each and every relevant piece of information. There is always a moment when you are sitting across from each other and, whether you've sat in the same room together for five months or five years, this fact becomes inescapably clear: you have done the work, the problem is reasonably well understood, and all that remains is whether or not your patient can act on his or her accumulated knowledge. Can the alcoholic executive give up drinking? Can the depressed mom walk away from an abusive relationship? Can the angry teen express herself with words instead of cutting her wrists or throwing up her food? When all is said and done, are they willing and able to make the necessary changes?

If thirty years of being a psychologist has taught me anything, it is that it is much easier to talk about things than to change them. But the potential for change is always present. We are at that moment of change now—with our children, our education system, and our willingness to alter some of our parenting habits in order to protect our children from the worst excesses of our culture. The authentic success we want so desperately for our children can't possibly come out of a system that feeds itself and starves our children. As you come to the end of this book, you've read the statistics around our current education system and its effect on our kids' well-being. You've heard from experts in the fields of education, psychology, and business. You've been asked to consider their analysis and how well it fits with what you observe in your own home, in your children's schools, and in your particular community. And most of all, you've heard the voices of many different children and teens, perhaps heard them in ways that make it easier to hear your own child. You've met kids who have thrived in the current system but more kids who have been damaged by it. And you've been asked to consider your role and your contribution to both the problems and their solutions. You've understood that the coping skills in your child's repertoire must also be in yours.

I'm well aware that being a reader is not the same as being a patient. All kinds of things that nurture change in the therapeutic relationship are missing in the reader-writer relationship. I don't know your particular story or what challenges you the most. I haven't met you or your family, looked into your eyes, or walked in your shoes. The best I can do is summon my knowledge and experience and suggest that while all families are different, there are similarities in the challenges they face as they try to make changes. I also know two steps forward and one step back is the rule, not the exception, as people work on change. So, even if you're convinced that changes need to be made—that you will insist on a good night's sleep for your child; that you will discuss homework policy with your child's school and set limits on homework time; that you will encourage play, downtime, and the value of family time; that you will be careful to keep clear the difference between your interests and abilities and those of your child; and that you will refocus on your child's character and values as you lessen your persistent concern about his or her grades—there are still bound to be moments of uncertainty and backsliding. Education and business researchers call this the "implementation dip"; psychologists call it "regression." The point is that you should be prepared to find that your good intentions will, from time to time, be frustrated and that this is normal. In order to keep your commitment to change lively and fully charged, you need to expect both opportunity and challenge.

Undertaking a process of change demands several things from us. First, we need to understand and anticipate the kinds of situations that are likely to make us feel uncertain or helpless. We need to inventory our strengths and weaknesses so that we have a pretty good idea of what parts of our psychology slow us down, and what parts get us moving again. Every one of us walks around with emotional vulnerabilities. Some of us are nervous or sad, whether we're simply the "worried well" or suffer from full-blown anxiety or mood disorders. Some of us don't trust our own judgment, and fear that we might be holding our children back if we follow our instincts or defy peer or community pressure. And others of us have not yet made our peace with our histories, our "ghosts in the nursery," whether those were minor missteps of our own parents or full-blown traumas that continue to haunt us. Being human means being vulnerable but it also means having the capacity to modify our responses and to make different choices. This chapter will look at those troubling but commonplace obstacles that get in our way, or even take us by surprise, as we go about our job of parenting. It is also about how we can maintain our own values and authenticity in the face of competing psychological, social, and cultural demands around parenting.

I'm going to start by describing a parenting challenge of my own, and for two reasons. First, *everybody* runs into parenting problems. Experts are no more likely to be immune from mistakes than anyone else. After all, we also have family histories that play out in our own families, with our own children. As a psychiatrist recently said to me, "We really don't do much better. We're just a lot guiltier when we make mistakes." Sure, it helps to have an understanding of child development; but that's in our head, and the places we tend to run into trouble usually come from the heart. Second, I'm asking a lot of you. To really dig down deep, to find the places where your own limitations, vulnerabilities, wounds, and defenses keep you from being the best parent you can be. We have much to learn from each other if we are willing to be open and honest about our successes and failures. This example is a little bit of both.

I was eighteen when my forty-seven-year-old father died suddenly of a heart attack. He was a New York City policeman, and I adored him. Neither of my parents had been particularly happy with my decision to go to the University of Buffalo, because it meant being away from home. He died several months into my freshman year. I didn't make it home in time to say good-bye. This tragedy has in many ways defined my life, in terms of both my anxiety over separation and my choice to work in a helping profession as he did. It certainly has informed my worldview that the moment matters far more than whatever plans you may make for the future. It is hardly surprising that I have devoted a great deal of time and energy in my professional career to encouraging parents to be present with the child right in front of them rather than being overly focused on the future. In this respect, I think I was an effective parent—one who understood that family time was precious, and unrecoverable—and so in my own family a lot of time was spent in family rituals and encouraging each other's particular skills and interests. When my three sons were young, I had a lot of control over what we did, and where we went. So planning the yearly whitewater rafting trip, or piling everyone in the car for the theater production or the lacrosse playoff was generally well received, kept me happy, and kept my anxiety about separation at bay.

As my sons grew up they naturally became increasingly interested in experiences outside the family. Most of this involved local
activities, Indian guides, Boy Scouts, and athletics, and this was
all quite comfortable for me. At about nine, my oldest son decided
he wanted to go to sleepaway camp. I knew that there was a well-
regarded sleepaway camp some twenty minutes from our home and
I happily enrolled him. Each of my sons in turn chose to attend
this camp, confirming for me that they wanted to be close by and
would have been anxious at a distance. It wasn't until my middle
son, Michael, wanted to go to Stagedoor Manor, a well-known performing arts camp on the other side of the country, that I realized
the extent of my separation anxiety. My eleven-year-old was excited
beyond words at the prospect of being in a place filled with theater
geeks just like him. I was panicked beyond all reason. The plane
would crash, he'd drown in the lake, or he'd be bitten by a rabid ani-
mal in the woods. Although I was accustomed to walking around
with high anxiety, even I found my preoccupation with catastrophe
unsettling. I was suffering and knew that my anxiety was crushing
my son's enthusiasm. Something had to change.

So, thirty years after my dad died I went back into therapy.
I sorted out the distortions I had carried for decades. It was an
unfortunate coincidence that my dad died shortly after I left home.
No, going away and into one's own life doesn't kill anyone. No,
I wasn't protecting my children by keeping them so close. I was
actually impairing them by preventing the development of the very
skills they would need to manage out in the world, such as independence and confidence. And probably most painful of all, no
matter how much control I thought I had over my sons' destinies,
life in fact can be random and unpredictable. Getting a handle on
the distortions that had become an invisible but potent part of my
parenting was emotionally demanding but ultimately extremely
valuable. It helped me transform my father's legacy from one of

fear to something far closer to the zestful and enthusiastic way he had lived his own life.

This honest and difficult example of what gets in the way of our best parenting intentions should have a familiar ring. While your family story may be quite different, it is likely that the things that get in your way share some commonalities with the things that got in mine. Busy raising three children and having a career, I didn't have time (more accurately, didn't make time) to think about, let alone work on, my own issues. Because my children were young, they didn't confront my decisions, something older children or teens might have done. And finally, when we've lived a good part of our lives with a particular narrative, it's very difficult to see it as anything but ordinary. It takes some kind of kick, a major uptick in anxiety like I experienced, perhaps a spouse who reaches the end of his rope, or a child who becomes symptomatic, to shake us up and make us decide that a change is necessary. We will find ourselves most capable of making real change, change that benefits ourselves and our children most directly, but also our families and our communities, if we inventory those things that get in our way and figure out how to turn down their volume so that we are free to act without distraction, distortion, or unnecessary anxiety. Here are some of the most common psychological stumbling blocks that get in our way.

DENIAL: "PROBLEM? WHAT PROBLEM?"

Whenever I speak about the wave of stressors on young people and their often less than optimal coping skills, I ask the following question of my audience: "How many of you don't really see this as a problem?" Invariably about 10 percent of hands shoot up. When I ask a couple of these parents what they think is different in their house or community, the answer is always the same. "My kid is fine. Likes school. Doesn't have too much homework. Gets a good night's sleep. I'm just not seeing any of the symptoms of stress you're talking about."

I have no reason to doubt the accuracy of these reports. Increasingly, there are schools that are committed to reviewing homework policy, to limiting AP courses, and to reevaluating things like start times and test schedules. However, these schools are still a small minority, and change comes slowly in educational institutions. More important, there are kids who have the capacity to thrive in highly competitive environments, and parents who are capable of bucking the tide and enforcing reasonable limits that protect their children from excessive stress. Generally this is more easily done when children are younger. But what interests me most about those who don't see our current system as dysfunctional is the fact that they're not really looking past their front door. And as soon as our children enter school, much of their day is spent past that front door.

My question is intentionally framed broadly as an invitation for parents to consider their own home as well as the larger world that their children participate in. The end result of not considering everything that affects our children—school, advertising, peers, and culture—is parent after parent sitting in my office, genuinely appalled that a child has become obsessed with her GPA or her chances of getting into a top-tier school. "But we never made an issue out of grades. Never. How can she possibly think it's the end of the world if she doesn't get an A in history?"

Your child lives in your house but participates in the larger culture that frames education as a "race to the top," that emphasizes "right" answers and not good questions, and urges parents to worry ferociously about whether their children need tutors, coaches, or other forms of enrichment. In many middle schools the only list of names in the school's weekly paper is of the students who have made the honor roll; most high schools give students class rankings. The media and popular culture are obsessed with money, status, and early achievement. An advertisement for a state educational project shows an infant wearing only a diaper, crawling toward an inverted job pyramid with a copy line reading, "The Race for the Best Jobs Starts Earlier Than You Think."[1] So even if you've managed to fend off some of the worst offenses to child development, short of keeping your child chained to her bed you cannot fend off all forms of influence, indoctrination, and even coercion.

The point is that our children are not exclusively ours for long. To be unimpressed with the problems in our communities and schools is to leave our children vulnerable to influences few of us would embrace in our homes. It is a form of denial to think that what happens "out there" will leave our children unaffected. On the contrary, if you think that your family really can function as an island of sanity in a sea of crazy, you probably haven't gathered life jackets. And life jackets, protective factors like resourcefulness and self-control, are exactly what kids need to navigate successfully through intense pressures and conflicting messages. The parents who sit in my office stunned that their daughter is so anxious about her SAT scores that she has started cutting herself, or that their son is staying up late on a combination of Adderall and Red Bull so that he can pass an AP exam, have unwittingly missed the vulnerability of teens to outside influences.

What fuels denial? Most of us are vigilant, often hypervigilant, about our children and their safety. Take a moment to think about some area of your own parenting where you might be pushing aside doubt, where others may have pointed out a problem that you've handily dismissed, or where there is an obvious lack of communication between you and your child. Here are some ordinary examples of denial drawn both from my clinical practice and from everyday life in my community.

- The school calls and tells you that your ten-year-old son has been involved in several bullying incidents. You meet with the counselor and while you're not thrilled to hear that your son is pushing kids around, your husband is irritated at having his day disrupted by this meeting. As you walk out, he shakes his head and says, "Boys will be boys." There's so much going on at home right now that you decide there's nothing urgent here and put the whole incident on the back burner. After all, your son's a great kid and you've never seen him being overly rough with either of his siblings.

- You notice that the level of a couple of bottles of liquor you keep in the house seems to be going down slowly but surely. You ask your twelve-year-old son about this and he suggests that perhaps there's some "evaporation" going on. You doubt that he would drink; he's just too young. Besides, you can't be absolutely sure that evaporation isn't the problem since the tops are not fully screwed on. You tighten them and forget the incident.

- You bring laundry into your fifteen-year-old daughter's room and find a birthday card sitting on her desk. You debate whether to open it, but curiosity (and a vague unease) gets the better of you. It's from her best friend and is essentially covered with sexual references, most of which you need Urban Dictionary to translate. You know your daughter will have a fit if she finds that you've been "snooping" in her room. Besides, the two of you have talked about sex previously and she promised to tell you when she becomes sexually active. You opt not to talk to her, fearing that her accusations of not respecting her privacy will derail the conversation.

- Your seventeen-year-old has been cited for speeding. Because she is under eighteen, this means her license will be revoked for a year. She explains that she was speeding because she was going to be late for curfew and didn't want you to worry. You know that this is not the first time she's been stopped for the same offense, but unlike several of her friends, she's never tested positive for alcohol. The drama in the house is too much for you to bear as she believes her entire social life will come to a screeching halt if she loses her license. Besides, you would then have the added burden of taking her to school in the morning. A friend puts you in touch with a lawyer who is "good at getting kids off because cops are too busy to show up in court." You decide that the punishment is too stiff, and, after all, no one was hurt. So you hire the lawyer to contest the ticket.

When we turn away from evidence that seems relatively straightforward to others we are using denial. Often there is more than meets the eye when we make these choices. For example, the mom who lets her son's bullying go may be afraid to confront the fact that she is bullied in her marriage, much as she was bullied by her own father. The parent who passes on confronting a child about drinking may have had an alcoholic parent and may have worked overtime on educating her children about the dangers of alcohol abuse. She may find it unbearable that in spite of all this she may not be able to protect him from a genetic disadvantage. And so it goes whenever we suspect that our lack of concern may relate to issues in our own lives that either are unresolved or raise our anxiety so high that we'd just as soon walk away.

It's important to be aware of the times that we choose not to engage and why. There's a big difference between deciding to ignore your teen's T-shirt emblazoned with a marijuana leaf and ignoring a veritable head shop in his bedroom. If you were raised with little warmth, strict rules, and excessive punishment, you may be committed to a more accepting household for your own children. However, we need to be clear enough about our motivation so that we can evaluate whether we're trying to undo our own past hurts or providing a healthier and more appropriate environment for our children. This ability to see our children clearly, and the world they live in clearly, is the best protection we can offer them against competitive excesses, counterproductive educational and psychological fads, and unrealistic expectations.

The first step in being able to make effective parenting changes is the ability to recognize problems. We need to be alert to the power of our own history in shaping what we pay attention to and what we find difficult to confront. If we can keep this in mind, we are in a far better position not to miss the early, often subtle, warning signs of emotional distress in our children.

PROJECTION: "YEAH, THEY'VE GOT A PROBLEM, NOT ME"

When I am invited to speak at schools and parent groups around the country, most often they want help addressing specific problems like cheating or too much homework, or want me to more broadly address the competitive, pressure-cooker atmosphere their kids are trying to manage. Sometimes it is faculty members or school administrators who bring me in, hoping to improve a particular aspect of curriculum or student behavior, such as bullying, or to examine the general climate of the school. Sometimes I'm in Tennessee with a bunch of kids, sometimes in Hawaii with administration and faculty, sometimes in New York with parents. So while I'm never certain what problems my next speaking engagement will address, I am quite certain who will be blamed. If I talk to parents, the teachers

272 • Teach Your Children Well

and school administrators will be blamed for too much homework and too much pressure. If I talk to teachers and school administrators, the parents will be blamed for being too involved, too anxious, and too competitive. If I talk to parents and school professionals together, they will both attack the college and university selection process, believing that if higher education took a more reasonable position, then schools and parents could as well. The kids? Well, the kids don't typically blame anyone. They're too busy trying to keep their heads above water to worry about who's at fault. They just want me to help them find a way to cope with it all.

It is generally psychologically easier to identify external contributors to a problem than it is to tease out our own contributions. "The homework policy at my kid's school is just crazy" is simpler than wondering why you tolerate, perhaps even encourage, a "crazy" system. Yet *crazy* is the word I hear most often when parents talk about homework time, pressure to take multiple AP courses, or the entire college application process. When apples were sprayed with a chemical at my local supermarket, middle-aged moms turned out, picket signs and all, to protest the possible risk to their children's health. Yet I've seen no similar demonstrations about an educational system that has far more research documenting its toxicity. We have bought into this system not because we are bad people or are unconcerned about our children's well-being, but because we have been convinced that any other point of view will put our children at even greater risk. We assess the problem as being "out there," which is to say, out of our control. It isn't.

Projection is an unconscious defense mechanism. When we "project," we deflect an uncomfortable thought, feeling, or impulse by saying, "I can't possibly be having this thought, feeling, or impulse; therefore it must be you." The cheating husband starts to suspect that his wife is having an affair, the depressed shopaholic mom brings her daughter to my office claiming she is "too materialistic," the insecure dad blames his wife when he takes a wrong turn because men are never directionally challenged—these are all examples of projection. Projection ranges from the devastating to the trivial, but all acts of projection reduce our anxiety and help us keep our image of ourselves intact. Remember that projection is an *unconscious* way we have of handling distress and anxiety, so we need to be gentle with ourselves when we start investigating the ways in which we protect ourselves from uncomfortable feelings.

So, how exactly do parental projections contribute to the high levels of stress documented among kids? Here are just a few examples from the hundreds I've collected in my practice. "My mom thinks I'll go crazy if I don't get into Michigan. I really don't care. Besides, I'd rather go to Wisconsin. What's with her?" "My dad tells me I'll be 'left behind' if I don't do better in math. Math just isn't my thing. Why doesn't he focus on the subjects I'm good at like English or journalism?" "My parents say I'm afraid to succeed because I'd rather take regular history instead of AP history. They were never into all this competitive stuff but now that I'm a junior they're acting totally whacked. How can I convince them that I haven't turned into a slacker, that I'm just giving myself a bit of breathing space?"

The first thing to notice in these examples is the disconnect between what the child is feeling and what the parent assumes the child is feeling. Let's look at the first example in more detail.

Why does Mom think her kid will "go crazy"? He gives no indication of going crazy so he is confused by Mom's assessment. If your child is genuinely baffled by something you feel strongly about, think about where your insistence is coming from. In this case, Mom, a conformist by nature, and her two siblings had been Wolverines, and she simply couldn't imagine that her son could be okay in a school other than Michigan. A "march to his own drummer" kind of kid, her son felt little pressure to continue the family tradition but was quite upset both by his mother's agitation and by

274 • Teach Your Children Well

her completely missing the mark about what kind of school *he'd* prefer (from his point of view, this rightfully means "My mom doesn't know who *I* am"). If Mom could understand that she was projecting, she might be less insistent and less off the mark about her son.

Projection always involves some distortion. Make as few assumptions as you can about what is driving your child's behavior. Don't assume that your issues are the same as your child's. "Being team captain was the most important thing in the world to me when I was in high school. I know my son must have been devastated when someone else was picked for the position." He may have been, but he may just as easily have been relieved. If you're stuck in your own head, you can't really get into your child's.

The best way to avoid projection and distortion is to spend as much time reflecting on our own psychology and motivation as we do on our children's. As the boundaries between parents and their children have collapsed—"*We're* going to the lacrosse finals"; "Is *our* homework finished?"; "*We're* trying to get into Tulane"—so has our ability to differentiate between the needs of our children and our own needs. Rarely are both sets of needs the same. The needs of middle-age adults are quite different from the needs of children or teens. Be alert to signs from your children that you are misreading them. Typically, they are only too happy to let you know. "You don't get it." "Earth to Mom." "*What* are you talking about?" Once you are alerted to a disconnect between what you think is true and what your child thinks is true, that's your opportunity to do some deep thinking.

One of my patients had been sexually abused as a young girl. She was certain her sixteen-year-old daughter was terrified to be home alone at night. If Mom had to go out for the evening, she would call home every hour or so to "make sure things were all right." One day in my office her daughter (who did not know Mom's history) exploded, saying, "I don't know what you think is going to happen to me. But you're making me crazy calling all the time." Mom's job then was to make the connection between her own early trauma and the assumptions she was making about her daughter's state of mind. She had to own the fear she had felt as a terrified young girl, be clear that she and her daughter were two separate people with very different life experiences, decide how much of her history to share with her daughter, and, finally, commit to changing her own behavior.

Over time, and with considerable support and effort, Mom learned techniques to help control her anxiety so that she no longer felt compelled to check in on her daughter inappropriately. Once we're aware of the ways that we project onto our children, most of us are quite willing to make adjustments. No parent wittingly chooses to traumatize his or her own child.

Not all projections are negative. Our kids may or may not be smart, athletic, musical, or good-looking, but we may see them that way because they remind us of a beloved parent, grandparent, or friend. "You're just like my grandmother, the kindest lady who ever lived." But if you're just like saintly Grandma, it makes it harder to take the last cookie or insist that it's your turn to choose a movie. The problem with all projections, good, bad, trivial, or significant, is that they confuse the reality of who our child actually is with who we wish him or her to be. Our job is to see our children clearly. Regular, thoughtful introspection is our most potent weapon against the unwitting damage that projection can inflict.

PEER PRESSURE: IT'S NOT JUST FOR TEENAGERS

I sit in an office surrounded by books on teenagers. Flip through the index of any one of them and you will find an entry for "peer pressure." Long thought to be one of the major issues, if not the major issue, of preteens and teens, peer pressure is really a life-span issue. We are, after all, social animals, and so by definition, we are going to be influenced at all ages by the people and the culture around us. What Erik Erikson described as "a uniformity of differing" in the ways teens dress, the music they listen to, and the language they use can just as easily be found in our neighborhood driveways' propensity toward Ford Explorers, Honda Accords, or BMW 3s. Depending on where we live, we might as well carpool to Target, Macy's, or Barneys for our jeans and boots. In my community Louis Vuitton "speedy" purses look like they've been bought in bulk.

Communities have norms, and there is always an interaction between the places we live and the norms we are expected to follow, from how we dress, to what we drink, to our political leanings, to how we raise our children. Unlike denial and projection, which are largely unconscious, peer pressure is generally experienced consciously. "My daughter enjoys playing piano and she's definitely talented. My friends think I should send her to a music camp. I have great memories from childhood of my own days at just a regular camp. Do kids always need to 'specialize' these days?" "My son's counselor says kids with B averages are 'a dime a dozen.' She thinks we need to get him a tutor so he can bring up his GPA. He's a great kid, works hard, and is just pretty much a B student. Do I really need to push him harder?" Clearly, these types of norms are typical of middle-class, upper-middle-class, and affluent communities. Some first-generation immigrant communities have even more exacting standards for their children. "I came to this country and worked my whole life so that you could go to college and become a doctor." "We could have stayed back home if you wanted to be a musician. In this country you will be an engineer." By contrast, there may be a lack of exacting standards for some inner-city kids. "Don't give him any big ideas. Nobody here makes it through college."

The point is that regardless of where we live, most of us and most of our children are aware of what our community values and what it devalues. While my community's high school offers several courses in building materials, construction, and computer-assisted drawing, it has never gone through the necessary paperwork to make them courses that are counted toward University of California credits. Therefore the hands-on kind of learner, who is likely to do well in courses like these, can't use his particular strength to bring up his GPA. This makes it painfully clear to the pack of boys who live for these kinds of classes that their strengths and ambitions are out of synch with the values of their community.

It's one thing to understand teenagers' vulnerability to peer pressure. After all, they are new to the experience of depending on people outside their family for support, direction, and information. The peer group serves as a kind of way station for teens who are leaving childhood but are not yet young adults. With peer support, teens feel comfortable trying on different identities, considering different choices, and generally distinguishing and separating themselves from their families. But why should peer pressure play that much of a role in our parenting? For the most part we've established our identities and have considerably more experience and, hopefully, more confidence in our adult choices than we had in our adolescent choices. Yet many of us still seem overly vulnerable to the opinions of others. The mom who just wants her kid to have a good time at summer camp or the mom who's perfectly content with her son's academic performance would be unlikely to struggle with her decision if she lived in a community that shared her values. There is probably no place where we are more vulnerable to criticism than our parenting skills. After all, this is where many of us pour our hearts and souls into doing the best job possible. We read and hover, discuss and keep track of how our kids are "doing," and unfortunately end up equating our child's "success" with our own.

And this, of course, is where we run into trouble. A bright young man named Alex is fascinated with cars. When he was young, he and his father spent hours in the garage tinkering with a clunker his dad had bought for a few hundred dollars. Sometimes Alex's grandfather would join them. He lived locally and had shared the same passion with his own son when Alex's dad was young. Knowing about cars was a family tradition that bound three generations of these men together. When Alex was younger, he and his dad made "house calls" to help neighbors who had a dead battery or just a finicky car. It was a source of great pride to Alex's father that his son had such a "knack" for car repair. Fast-forward a few years and Alex is now starting his junior year in high school. He has really good grades but hasn't lost an iota of his passion for cars. As the college application process nears, Alex seems surprisingly noncommittal about his plans. He mentions "hands-on industrial programs" and his parents are dismissive. His father, a physician, is terrified that Alex will "settle" for being a car mechanic. Dad wants to know what he "did wrong."

In fact, Dad did everything right. He was close with his son and spent considerably more time with him than most dads do. They had a strong bond, they shared interests, and his son was an awfully nice kid with good grades. Yet Dad was feeling criticism from all sides. His wife accused him of not setting "high standards" for their son. His friends faulted the amount of time they spent in the garage when he could have taken his son "to the hospital for rounds" and thereby encouraged an interest in medicine. The school counselor suggested that they "take it out of Alex's hands" and insist that he apply to the top-tier schools for which he had the grades. Dad felt that he had "failed" his son by ignoring his potential. Alex became more withdrawn; he was uncomfortable and angry about being the center of so much discussion.

Let's get a few things straight here. First of all, Alex hasn't decided where to go to school. But the amount of turmoil he's experiencing around this decision is not going to make it any easier for him. He's getting all kinds of messages about the various mistakes he and his dad have made, and no recognition of his passion and competence. He may be a mechanic, or he may be an engineer. He doesn't know and neither should anyone else assume that his path is set. It's a rare teenager who has his life plan firmly in place. Alex needs support for who he is in order to go about finding a college that will be a good fit for him. He likes working with his hands, he's mechanical, he has good visual-spatial abilities (no coincidence that his father, with these same traits, is a surgeon), and he's curious. He will find his way. His parents will have to disregard the peer pressure that makes them feel that somehow their son is not measuring up, and by extension, that they're not, either.

The amount of pressure that parents are experiencing to have their children be outstanding performers in multiple areas is positively staggering. Eavesdropping on the conversations at the grocery checkout counter is like entering a parallel universe where all children are uncannily brilliant and preternaturally talented. The oddest part of this is that I know many of the kids who are being discussed. Some are my sons' friends, some I see in therapy, and some are just neighborhood kids. Most are bright, a few notably so. They certainly have talents, interests, and a few passions. Some of them also have significant problems. One or two might end up at Carnegie Hall; the rest will likely be strumming guitars in their dorm rooms. They are far more likely to play in rec leagues than in the big leagues, and the best thespians among them will be lucky to do community theater. This is not a put-down. I like to think of it as the wisdom accumulated by working and living with kids for more than three decades. It simply is real life. And yet parents everywhere seem to believe that their child is different, more special, smarter, and more talented. Which is to say that they, the procreators of these extraordinary children, are more special, smarter, and more talented.

The poet Khalil Gibran wrote, "Your children are not your children."[2] We delude ourselves when we think that our parenting is the singular engine behind our child's development. Your children come hardwired with interests, abilities, capacities, and temperament. They will grow, more or less, into the person they are meant to be whether they have one tutor or two, go to math camp or computer camp, work out twice a week or daily. I'm not saying that the opportunities that we provide our children are meaningless. On the contrary, I'm asking you to consider the types of opportunities you are providing, what is motivating you, and how well these opportunities fit with your child's particular nature. I'm asking you to do all this while putting aside the peer pressures that make you question whether your child's doing enough, whether you're doing enough, whether you *are* enough.

Challenging peer pressure takes courage. It did when we were teens and it still does now that we're middle-aged. What makes peer pressure such a formidable opponent is the comfort it provides when we go along with the group and the alienation we feel when we take a stand in opposition to the group. The fear of rejection is very powerful for most people, and it drives our constant self-questioning, and often bad parenting decisions, too. Insisting on another AP when your daughter has headaches and stomachaches before school because, in addition to raising her GPA, it secures your position as a mother who has raised a "gifted" child, is not acceptable. This isn't to say we aren't entitled to feel some glow around our children's achievements. Often we have put in a lot of time and effort and money helping our children cultivate their skills. But the operant word is *their*. Their accomplishments are not our accomplishments. In this respect, it is important to have interests and accomplishments of our own so we don't need to leech from our children.

If you live in a community where accomplishments mean almost exclusively academic or athletic success, try to think more broadly. Of course we're proud of our kids when they do well in school, make the honor roll, bring home trophies. Celebrate these accomplishments with them. But every kid has a place where he or she excels. A very important part of our job is to find those places. The workplace is saying look for honesty, character, the ability to get along with people, to be an accurate reader of social environments, to think outside the box, and to find new ways to connect the dots. While peer pressure might suggest that these are "soft" skills and that without a degree from a top-tier school your child will be at a disadvantage, it is much more realistic to say that without creativity, collaboration, integrity, and communication skills, it doesn't matter where your child goes to school: he or she won't be optimally prepared for the demands of our new century.

Finally, you will be asking your teenagers over and over again to stand up to peer pressure. You will want them to stay out of cars with drivers who have been drinking, to say no to sex when they're not ready, to resist easily available drugs and a host of other risky adolescent behaviors that could pose real threats to their well-being. We should be asking no less of ourselves. Question aggressively a system that seems to sanction excessive homework, competition over collaboration, sleep deprivation, and choosing activities based solely on their résumé-enhancing potential. Show your child that values need to be acted on, not just espoused. And just as you tell your teen that there are plenty of kids who don't do drugs or don't have casual sex, I can assure you that there are plenty of parents out there who are just as concerned, frustrated, and anxious to change the system as you are. Find them and start exerting a little peer pressure of your own.

IS PARENTING HEREDITARY? "I CAN'T
BELIEVE I SOUND JUST LIKE MY MOTHER"

I used to think that we inherited a parenting style from our own parents, and that most of us parented much the same as we had been raised. A body of research, called attachment theory, confirmed that if you were securely attached to your mother, your own child was likely to be securely attached both to you and to others. Children develop secure attachments when parents show warmth, support, stability, and emotional attunement. Under these circumstances kids feel confident about venturing out in the world and confident that a secure base awaits them in times of stress. Securely attached kids feel good about themselves and worthy of being loved.

Other, less capable parents formed insecure attachments with their children. These parents were too anxious, unavailable, poorly attuned, or disturbed to provide a secure base for their children. As a result these children were impaired in their ability to form healthy relationships or to feel worthy of being loved. Needless to say, children classified as being insecurely attached were not expected to do well, either in their relationships with others or in their ability to feel good about themselves. This classification system was a rather neat and easy way to think about parenting. It suggested that we are likely to turn out to be more or less the same kind of parent that our own parents had been. And it made the common epiphany "I can't believe I sound just like my mother" a predictable extension of our particular history.

Attachment theory continues to play a very significant role in the way psychologists understand both how we form relationships in the outside world and how we feel about ourselves in our inside world. However, it is no longer a static system of classification but rather a dynamic one. Our early relationships with our parents do leave strong, often indelible, marks on the person we grow up to be.

But life also intervenes in countless ways. Good things happen to insecure children and they evolve into secure kids. They're smart or talented and some reliable adult takes them under his or her wing and provides the warmth, reliability, and support they've been missing. Bad things happen to secure kids and they grow into insecure adults. Throw a secure young child a major curveball in life—a life-threatening illness, the early death of a parent, economic disaster—and that child's trajectory is likely to falter or be altered. Yes, our parenting style greatly affects our children, but many other factors do as well. This is a painful realization since it means our children can be at risk in ways we can't even foresee. On the other hand, it also means that nothing is written in stone, and we can change how we parent regardless of our own early experiences.

A friend of mine who is a wonderful mother, loving, supportive, and disciplined, looks for all the world like she inherited the good parenting gene. While she and her husband both attended highly selective universities, I've never seen either of them push their kids inappropriately or hover over their schoolwork. This isn't to say she doesn't have high standards for her kids. She does. But her two kids are notably different from each other and so the standards are very much in keeping with the temperament, interests, and capacities of each child. Instead of prestige schools for them (of which there are plenty in her community) she has chosen schools that are less pressured, more project based, and decidedly focused on the development of the "whole child." Her kids have thrived, and while her kids' interests often didn't align with hers, she was always enthusiastic even if occasionally baffled. For years I had used her as a parenting model, and a trusted friend to confer with when I faced difficult parenting decisions. I assumed that she had "inherited" a high degree of good "motherliness" from her own mom. As in most friendships during the years of intense mothering, we talked mostly about our kids, our husbands, and our work.

As our kids grew and we had a bit more free time, we found out more about each other's histories before we had kids. One afternoon over coffee she told me, "My mother never made me feel valued or validated as a person separate and apart from her own hopes and dreams for me. Rather than feeling proud of me for hard-won accomplishments, she seemed much more interested in accruing glory to herself through the kudos she received from friends. I suspect this is because her own role model was an extremely austere mother whose love was both conditional and self-referential." My mouth dropped in astonishment. One of the best moms I knew had been raised not by an equally competent mom, but by a poorly attuned mom who apparently was following in the footsteps of her own poorly attuned mom. My "hereditary" notions were both confirmed and disproved in a single story. "But you're so sensitive to your own kids. How did you turn things around?" With the thoughtfulness I had come to appreciate in my friend, she said, "Unless we make a conscious decision to change, it's all too easy to become prisoners of our past." No, she's not a shrink. But she is reflective and introspective and was determined not to repeat a relationship that had served her so poorly.

If warmth, support, stability, and emotional sensitivity are the "magic bullets" of parenting, what if, like my friend, you didn't grow up in this kind of environment? Maybe your parents had a tumultuous marriage, or your mom was depressed or your dad was an alcoholic. How do you learn to develop the skills that come naturally to parents who came from healthier backgrounds? Is it even possible? The answer is a resounding and reassuring yes. We are never "finished" products. We are always capable of greater understanding and change. We can learn to be warmer, more stable, more supportive, and more attuned to our children regardless of our own backgrounds. This is not easy work, but there are few things you can do as a parent that have a bigger payoff.

All of us have days when all our emotional resources are at our disposal and days when we feel depleted; we are all people in addition to being parents. Perfect is not something parents are, nor something they should strive to be. Striving for perfection is bound to end in disappointment and often in depression. We do, however, want to be the best parent we can be and we don't want to have our histories necessarily dictate our parenting skills or choices. This means taking an inventory of both the positive and the negative parts of the way you were parented. You are not betraying your parents when you think long and hard about their strengths and weaknesses. It took me years to allow myself a critical thought about my own mother. She was widowed at forty-two; how could I fault anything she did? But I came to understand that in the process of thinking about how I was parented, I was actually doing what my mother would have wanted most: becoming a more capable mother myself.

I hear endlessly from parents that they want their children to have "better" lives than they have. Sometimes this is about money or status. But for most of us, it's not about having our kids out-spend us. We want our kids to be just better—better people, better citizens, better parents. So assume that your parents will bless your work here, and take an objective look at their parenting skills; then take the same objective look at your own. Write down your thoughts. Identify one or two things that you feel compromise your parenting most. Anxiety? Depression? A difficult marriage? Trouble with closeness? Being easily overwhelmed? Trouble reading emotions? By writing it down, you've overcome denial, challenged projection, and become poised to think about the kinds of change you need to make.

THE TRINITY OF CHANGE:
SELF-REFLECTION, EMPATHY, AND FLEXIBILITY

You've already written down what you think is most likely to get in your way when you're tackling tough issues. Now jot down the particular parenting issues, big or little, that you find most difficult: letting your young child make her own decisions ("You can't wear stripes and polka dots together"), bugging your middle schooler to be more "friendly" because you're afraid she won't be popular, staying out of your adolescent's room day after day when the door is closed even though you worry about what he's doing in there, insisting that your child study harder because you fear that his grades won't allow him the "choices" you see as being critical to his future. Put these two lists aside, to be returned to later.

The job of understanding our own lives is the project of a lifetime. We are never really finished, because life ebbs and flows and change is inevitable. What feels tolerable one day—your three-year-old's pouty "I hate you"—may be intolerable a decade later when your twelve-year-old looks straight into your eyes and spits out the same words. Parenting continually asks us to grow and develop. There are three things that stand out as being critical to our ability to adapt and grow along with our children. The first is self-reflection, that is, truly understanding our histories and ourselves. The next is the ability to tune in to another's state of mind, or empathy. And finally, flexibility ensures that we have a repertoire of parenting skills so that we can bring our best game to the parenting table. While I'm writing about self-reflection, empathy, and flexibility as if they are separate categories, in fact they are more like a web than a list. Each of them depends on the others for maximal effectiveness.

Self-Reflection

If there's a heartbeat to this book, it's about the value of self-reflection. As a psychologist, I'm trained to help people turn inward and think about the circumstances and feelings that drive their thoughts and behavior. One piece of advice inscribed on the temple of Apollo at Delphi was "Know thyself." There is a reason why self-reflection is such a positive and critical part of human development. Without it we are not free to make *choices*. Forces that are unclear, or even unknown to us, drive us instead of our own considered decisions. What allows us free choice, as a parent, a partner, a friend, and an individual, is having "digested" our own experiences. Self-reflection or introspection is not navel-gazing. It is the challenging task of taking in our history, our life experiences, and our feelings, processing them, and integrating them into a clear and coherent story about our lives. You need to be able to make sense of your own life in order to help your children make sense of theirs.

Go back to your lists. How do you make a deeper, more mean ingful story of your life, one that sheds some light on both the parenting problems that are toughest for you and the ways of coping you use that are less than successful? Start by taking some quiet time just to think about what's on your lists. Most of us have given considerable thought to our parenting issues, sometimes talking them over with spouses and friends until we're blue in the face. While talking with friends and partners can be extremely helpful, suspend your reliance on others for a bit, as you turn inward to collect your own memories and feelings. Many people find writing in a journal helpful. This allows you the opportunity for intimate expression as you write, as well as objective reflection as you read what you have written. For example, you might write something like "I know I'm way too anxious and pushy about my kid's grades. But what if she falls behind and loses out on all kinds of opportunities. I couldn't bear to see all my friends' kids marching off to top-tier schools while my kid goes to the University of No Stature." This is a good start. You've identified a difficult parenting issue—how best to manage involvement with your child's schoolwork. And you're aware of the parts of you that get in the way of optimal parenting (anxiety, vulnerability to peer pressure). Now your task is to see if you can discover, in your own history, what makes this issue both so vital and so draining. Were your parents' expectations for you high or low or in line with your capacities? Were they interested in your educational progress or indifferent to it? Were they concerned with your feelings of accomplishment or defeat or more concerned with how others might judge you? Were you made to feel proud of your progress or ashamed of your mistakes? I can't possibly list all variants, since every family is different, and the reasons behind anxiety or depression or vulnerability are different for each reader. But exercises like meditating, journal writing, reviewing family photos, or simply talking to oneself all help to bring our particular issues and challenges forward, broadening our understanding of ourselves and helping us to make clearer and better parenting choices.

We are never free of our past, but we can be free of its unwanted intrusion into our relationship with our children and the ways in which we choose to parent. Being a parent gives us the extraordinary opportunity for a "do-over." Once again we are in a parent-child relationship, but this time we hold the cards. We can use the best of what we learned from our own parents and change the things that were out of synch or hurtful. This time around, we get to choose.

Empathy

I've long held this particular notion, a perhaps idiosyncratic one, that given a choice between being loved and being understood, most of us would choose to be understood. Of course, most of us want both. But while it hurts not to be loved, it can be unbearable not to be understood. We seem to have a profound need to have our deepest selves be seen, acknowledged, accurately understood, and embraced. We can be in a "love relationship," but if we're not understood or, worse yet, if we are misunderstood, the relationship ends up feeling profoundly lonely. Of course, you could argue that love without a clear understanding of the other person isn't really love at all. But as we've looked at things like denial, projection, or family history, it's also clear that seeing the people we love accurately and without distortion can be a tall order.

I've never met a parent who didn't love his or her children in profound and well-meaning ways. Ask any group of parents what they want for their children when they grow up, and the universal answer is "to be happy." Most of us believe we are empathic parents and believe that the empathic bond we have with our child will have a great effect on how they develop. And yet most kids I see feel anything but understood. So many of the issues we're currently facing as parents will be resolved either successfully or unsuccessfully depending on our capacity to be accurately attuned to our children.

Because we are social animals, we have a biological need for connection. The neuropsychiatrist Daniel Siegel calls this our need to "feel felt" and traces its origins to how our brains are wired for connection.[3] Much of this connection goes on nonverbally; just remember the back-and-forth of smiling at your infant's face and her smiling back at you. This is called resonance and it's a critically important way of communicating throughout our lives. Think lover's eyes, mother's hand, child's hug.

Parents today have become great talkers with their children. They discuss, debate, argue, and explain endlessly. This certainly is a change from how much our parents talked things over with us, and it has its benefits as well as its limitations. But talking to your child does not ensure that you are being empathic or even on the same wavelength. Generally children feel talked "to," not with. Their assessment is often accurate. You do not build your connection with your child through verbiage; it is built through an accurate understanding of your child's emotions and point of view. This is where parents sometimes get off track. They confuse empathy with sympathy, discussion, or friendship.

An empathic connection with your children is probably the single most advantageous and protective factor in their development. It encourages everything from good mental health to academic performance. Since empathy is also a silver bullet, let's take a moment to fully understand it. *Empathy is the accurate understanding of another person's internal experience.* It has nothing to do with agreeing or disagreeing with that experience. Unlike sympathy, it makes no assumption about how the other person is feeling. When you are being empathic with your child you are joining him in *his emotional* experience. If it's a positive experience *for him* you share his enthusiasm and amplify his good feelings. If it is an unsettling or distressing experience *for him* you comfort and soothe him.

Entering into another human being's internal life is a delicate business. Clearly we have great advantages with our children. We've known them from birth. We've had lots of practice learning the meaning of their various gestures and can generally read their signals rather easily—hair twirling means "I'm tired," a quivering lip means "I'm upset," foot tapping means "I'm anxious." But here's the caveat. They change. And so do we. Going down the slide may have been terrifying to your three-year-old and tuning in to him would have meant comforting him. Six months later going down the same slide is positively exhilarating and you get to celebrate his accomplishment with him. All the while you need be attuned to his nonverbal communication so that you're not telling a terrified child that he did a super job or gathering a competent child in your arms to reassure him.

It is easier to be empathic when we have had empathic parents ourselves. We've been tuned in to and generally know how to tune in to others. But just as self-reflection was a road to clarifying and, in some cases, undoing damage from our past, so is it a way to build our empathic capacity. We first need to know what pleases us and what disappoints us. These may or may not be the same things that please or disappoint our children. While we certainly hope that our children grow up to share our basic values of respect, kindness, and service to others, we simply can't expect them to grow up with the same likes, dislikes, preferences, and talents that we have. Our job is to produce and guide our children; not to reproduce ourselves. Nor should we want to. One of the absolute miracles of life is the profound uniqueness of each person.

All three of my sons went to the same local public high school. In my community that meant a demanding curriculum with high expectations and a narrow view of what success looks like. This worked fine for my oldest boy, who was competitive, extremely hardworking, and high-achieving. If he came home with less than an A on a test he would be frustrated with himself. My job was simply to tune in to his frustration, not to talk him out of it, give him a pat on the back, and let him know that I was available if he wanted to talk more. He had no disturbing symptoms (for example, stomachaches, headaches) for me to worry about. So because I was a high achiever myself, it was easy to empathize with him over what to him was a disappointing grade.

My middle son couldn't have cared less about his grades. Through some process of osmosis he maintained a high GPA; he never actually knew what it was until he had to fill out college applications, because he didn't care about numbers. He was all about creativity and looking at things in different ways. Often he would crumple up a test as soon as he received it and toss it in the class wastebasket, occasionally to his teacher's chagrin. He never understood how this could be considered "disrespectful"; he always scored well; his grades just weren't that interesting to him. Empathizing with him about school was just a bit harder for me because his disregard for grades and scores was foreign to me. When he came home upset about a detention because he once again had tossed out his exam, I had to be empathic in an entirely different way than I had been with his older brother. Encouraging him to help me see the world through his eyes made all the difference. "There are so many more interesting things than grades. I see amazing things that other kids barely notice. Grades are just kind of boring." That was all it took. The great thing about empathy is it helps our kids yet it helps us, too. Seeing the world through his eyes was part of what transformed my own views about the current state of affairs in education.

And finally, my youngest son was a perfectly average student (exactly in the middle of his class), which in our community, with its unrealistic zeitgeist of "excellence," meant that feeling good at school was a real challenge. The things that interested him and that he was good at, such as using his hands, building, or landscaping, were scarcely given a nod at his high school. To his credit, he understood early on that if he solely focused on academics, he was going to have a tough few years. So he found courses that interested him at the local community college and took several of them with considerable success. This is how you turn a C student into a B or an A student. Not with tutors, but by helping your child find what he is good at and interested in. (I don't mean to dismiss all tutoring; I just think it's *greatly* overused. And while it may help some children, it makes many more feel that they can't learn without constant oversight.) As a PhD and a type-A high achiever, could I really empathize with a child who was on a different path? Absolutely. I chose to see all that was good about him—the most genuinely kind kid I've ever known—and when he was frustrated with his school's constant drumbeat about grades, I was perfectly capable of empathizing with his difficulty and supporting his strengths. After a couple of false starts (pretty miserable misreads on my part), I don't think I ever challenged him about his grades again. He was working to capacity and he was happy. Good enough. More than good enough. Terrific.

This is what I mean by tuning in to your child to help make decisions about pressure, school, sleep, homework, and extracurricular activities. My sons are mostly grown now. The oldest predictably went to a powerhouse school. My middle son went to a school known for the arts and my youngest is at a polytechnic. They have all been happy with their schools. In order to help your children maintain optimism and enthusiasm and eventually make good choices about what college to attend you need to crawl up behind their eyes and look out at the world from their point of view. It takes an open mind and an open heart. It takes practice in listening and an awareness of the knee-jerk reactions we may have that prevent us from listening closely and seeing clearly. It doesn't mean that we don't have our own viewpoint or preferences. But it does mean that in addition to being able to share our perspective and maturity with our kids, we can "feel with" them as they try to sort out their lives.

Empathy is the glue that holds together our most important relationships. This is what ET meant when he pointed to Elliott's forehead and said, "I'll be right here." Empathic connection is stronger than distance or separation. It is what keeps our children alive in us as long as we live, and what keeps us alive in our children even as they set off into the untraveled territory of their own lives.

Flexibility

Flexibility is a frame of mind. It is what allows us to choose the best response from a raft of different possibilities. Flexibility in parenting does not mean you should become a pushover. There is a delicate tightrope to be walked between your child's need for structure and the importance of considering content and context when you make decisions. But without flexibility, you are unlikely to be a successful parent and will certainly not be an empathic or introspective one. A lack of flexibility makes us vulnerable to poor decisions because we've defaulted to an unthinking, nonempathic, automatic response. When it comes to our kids, this is not the way we want to make decisions. Actually, it's not the way we want to make decisions at all.

Marilyn wants her youngest son, Ryan, to attend the same private elementary school her two older daughters attended. It is a well-regarded, academically focused school, and Marilyn's two older daughters thrived there. Marilyn's active son hated the school as soon as he walked in the door. The halls were hushed and when he peered into the classrooms, he could see kids quietly working at their desks. At his preschool there was a lot of action, kids running around, noisy chatter in the classroom. When the headmistress brought him into her office for an interview, he was told to stay in his seat and she reprimanded him for touching the objects on her desk. When Ryan and his mother got home, Ryan burst into tears. "I'm never going there. I hate it. You can't make me." Marilyn took offense at this last comment and responded angrily, "You're just a kid. You don't know what's good for you. You'll go wherever I decide you should go." Harsh, huh? But Marilyn isn't an evil mother. While she couldn't be empathic with her son, we can afford to be empathic with her. What was going on?

First of all, the headmistress spoke with Marilyn after interviewing Ryan and suggested that while her two daughters had been terrific students at the school, perhaps Ryan wasn't "ready" for its rigor. This made Marilyn feel humiliated and ineffective. A reserved woman herself, she had been happy with her two quiet girls; but her husband had pushed for a third, hoping to have a son. While he was thrilled with Ryan's arrival, Marilyn felt different. What little time she had shared with her husband was now taken up by Ryan. From the beginning she felt confused by her son and his constant activity. Whether it was colic as an infant, two visits to the emergency room before he was five for tumbles that he took at the playground, or the fact the he was never quiet, always humming or singing even while he was playing alone in his room, Ryan felt alien to her. She worried that maybe he had ADHD, even though his pediatrician said he was just a normal, active boy. Marilyn wasn't sure she believed him. He'd never seen Ryan madly whip through the house trailing a cape of towels shouting at the top of his lungs, "Beware my superpowers!"

Marilyn had seen Ryan as a problem from day one, and the headmistress' comment at school only reinforced this feeling. Here is an example of why self-reflection, empathy, and flexibility are a web and not stand-alone characteristics. If Marilyn had been able to be self-reflective, she would have had more awareness of both her resentment toward Ryan and the shame that she defended against by being angry with him so frequently. This in turn would have made her more likely to feel connected to Ryan and empathize with his view of the school as being rigid, unwelcoming, "not me." If she could see the school through his eyes, she might decide that flexibility was in order, and while it was a good school for her daughters, perhaps it wasn't the right school for her son. Instead of seeing this as a deficit in Ryan, she might have felt some pride at his ability to figure out how wrong the school was for him.

Is flexibility something that you can develop? Aren't some people just rigid in their thinking? Besides, isn't consistency supposed to be good for children? The answer to all three questions is yes. But flexibility gives us the opportunity to exercise free choice.

If you always respond in the same way, you are being driven; you are not driving.

There comes a point in parenting where we must decide whether to maintain the status quo or, armed with new information, choose a different course. There is little question that our children are living in a world that is not simply oblivious to their needs, but is actually damaging them. Given the amount of research documenting how our current narrow version of success is exhausting the resources of a small group of highly academically talented students and diminishing the potential of a far larger group of students, our failure to act, to demand change both from our institutions and from ourselves, is inexcusable.

We are at a tipping point. Either we will continue to show a lack of courage, or we will become proactive and decide that our children deserve a reasonable childhood, schools focused on the joy of learning, empathic parents, and protection from the excesses of a culture defined by materialism. I know that you're worried about your child. Worried that he or she might get left behind, not have the stuff it takes to compete, lose out on opportunities. *But we do not have to choose between our children's well-being and their success.* The very things that promote your child's well-being and happiness are the same things that will promote his or her success in the world. Enthusiastic kids who feel loved and valued for their particular skills and interests, who are both self-aware and aware of the needs of others, who can work hard, delay gratification when necessary, and reward themselves when appropriate, who find life both fun and meaningful, are kids who are most likely to be both happy and successful. Deeply happy and authentically successful.

I know that it takes courage and discipline to fight an uphill battle, to compete with market forces that have unlimited resources, and to take unpopular stands. But here's the reality. Every measure of child and adolescent mental health has deteriorated since we've decided that children are best served by being relentlessly pushed, overloaded, and tested. *Our current version of success is a failure.*

Yes, we are all facing an uncertain future—technologies that we can barely imagine and jobs that have not been invented yet. Uncertainty is difficult to tolerate and our anxiety about how well our children will do in this only partially imagined world is understandable. However, the needs of children were, are, and will be irreducible. They need to be unconditionally loved, allowed to have an active and curious childhood, encouraged to challenge themselves, disciplined when necessary, and valued for the unique set of skills, interests, and capacities they bring to this world. If we can return to these essentials of healthy child development, then more than any tutor, prep class, or prestige college can do, we will have prepared our children to lead satisfying, meaningful, and authentically successful lives.

ACKNOWLEDGMENTS

One hand writes a book; many hands guide it. For all the help, mentoring, and guidance that were so generously offered to me by colleagues, researchers, family, friends, parents, and kids, I am deeply grateful. This book owes its vitality to the collaboration of different stakeholders who are justifiably concerned about how our current version of success is impairing our children rather than preparing them to navigate the increasingly complex world they will inherit.

My colleagues at Stanford University deserve special thanks. In 2008, when Denise Pope, Jim Lobdell, and I started Challenge Success, a project of the Stanford School of Education, we had no idea that within a few years we would be speaking to thousands of parents at hundreds of venues around the country. Working intensely with more than a hundred schools we have seen firsthand both the toll that our narrow definition of success takes on children, and the changes that are possible when parents, educators, communities, and kids commit to healthier and broader notions of success. Jim and Denise's contributions to this book, particularly to chapter 7, are immeasurable. Maureen Brown, our indefatigable executive director, somehow managed to take this small group of "do-gooders" from a well intentioned but scrambling "start-up" to an effective and efficient project capable of effecting robust change.

Amy Alamar, our schools program manager, and Gina Morris, our parent education manager, both added breadth, depth, and vigor to the project.

Dozens of people added information, research, experience, and wisdom to this book. Notably, I depended heavily on the work of Laurence Steinberg, Robert Sternberg, Wendy Grolnick, Peter Salovey and Jack Mayer, Ken Ginsburg, Carol Dweck, Howard Gardner, Roy Baumeister, Albert Bandura, and the ever generous David Elkind.

To my best friends, Bonnie Caruso and Ann Buscho, your love and support are with me always. No one could ask for more loving or constant friends. And to my good friends Merla Zellerbach, Phyllis Kempner, David Stein, Michelle Wachs, and Susan Friedland, thank you all for tolerating my distractibility, unavailability, and disappearances. To my good friend Dagmar Dolby, thank you for facilitating those disappearances and being a willing, thoughtful sounding board. And to my dear friend Lisa Stone Pritzker, thank you for coming into my life and being the most truly generous person I have ever known. It's been a privilege.

Great appreciation and respect go to Gail Winston, my editor at HarperCollins. It is neither exaggeration nor false modesty to say that this book would not have seen the light of day without her conviction that it needed to be written, and her patience with its endless iterations. There is no more supportive or more talented editor out there. To Eric Simonoff, my "star" agent, whom I was lucky enough to snag when he was a newbie. There are many days when I still can't believe how fortunate I am to have you not just as an agent, but as a friend as well.

To the rest of my support team at HarperCollins, from production to design, thank you all. To Caitlin McCaskey, my speaking agent, for always getting me where I belong in good spirits and on time. To Maya Ziv for her patience and diligence in attending to the mandatory details. And to my astonishing copyeditor, Tom Pitoniak, who kept me laughing at all hours with his far-ranging knowledge of everything from grammar to Prokofiev to whether Babe Ruth or Hank Aaron deserves the title of home run "king."

Several people in my life deserve special recognition. First to Margarita Sanchez, who takes care of me, my husband, my mother, my boys, or anyone else who needs a hand. Your kindness and endless optimism are a daily tonic to my genetically installed pessimism. To Tom Hutchman, who does his best to keep my sedentary, computer-glued body in something resembling reasonable shape. To Cheryl Belitsky, who kept me hidden and happy with an endless supply of blackberries, Greek yogurt, and chocolate. To Jeff Snipes, who reminds me that men can struggle just as mightily as women. And a million, billion thanks (no exaggeration!) to Scott Wood, the world's most savvy computer guy, who humored me out of my panics and fixed my recalcitrant computer often in the wee hours of the night.

Finally, and especially, to the center of my life: my husband, Lee Schwartz, and our three sons, Loren, Michael, and Jeremy. Lee, my lifelong editor, does his best to keep me clear and concise. This is not always an easy job. You have met my sons often in these pages. I am grateful for their generosity and good humor in letting me use their stories and in correcting me on those occasions when the writer in me got ahead of the facts. Thank you for your remarkable openness and grace, for tolerating my total devotion to this project, and for allowing me open access to your friends for ideas, anecdotes, and endless discussions. You've made it so easy to love you all exactly as you are.

NOTES

INTRODUCTION: Courageous Parenting—Taking the Long View

1. S. Reardon, A. Atteberry, N. Arshan, and M. Kurlaender, "Effects of the California High School Exit Exam on Student Persistence, Achievement and Graduation," paper presented at the American Educational Research Assocation in San Diego, April 2009, James Irvine Foundation, California High School Exit Exam Study Coverage Report.
2. "Kids and Stress, How Do They Handle It?" KidsHealth KidsPoll, October 12, 2005. Poll questions retrieved June 19, 2009, from the National Association of Health Education Centers database.
3. "The NIMH Blueprint for Change Report," Research on Child and Adolescent Mental Health, National Intitute of Mental Health, *Journal of the American Academy of Child and Adolescent Psychiatry* 41, no. 7 (July 2002): 760–66. (U.S. Department of Health and Human Services, 1999.)
4. Ibid.
5. W. S. Grolnick and K. Seal, *Pressured Parents, Stressed-Out Kids* (Prometheus Books, 2008).
6. J. P. Hunter, and M. Csikszentmihayi, "The Positive Psychology of Interested Adolescents," *Journal of Youth and Adolescence* 32, no. 1 (2003): 27–35.
7. S. P. Suggate, "School Entry Age and Reading Achievement in the 2006 Programme for International Student Assessment (PISA)," *International Journal of Educational Research* 48 (2009): 151–61.

CHAPTER 1: The Kids Are Not Alright (and Neither Are Their Parents)

1. J. Mosley and E. Thompson, "Fathering Behavior and Child Outcomes: The Role of Race and Poverty," in *Fatherhood: Contemporary Theory,*

Research and Social Policy, edited by W. Marsiglio (Thousand Oaks, CA: Sage, 1995), 148–65.

2. "IBM Capitalizing on Complexity," Insights from the Global Chief Executive Summary, 2009.

3. Stacy B. Dale and Alan B. Krueger, "Estimating the Payoff to Attending a More Selective College: An Application of Selection on Observables and Unobservables,"*Quarterly Journal of Economics* 117, no. 4 (2002): 1491–1527.

CHAPTER 2: How Did We Get into This Mess?

1. L. B. Ames and C. C. Haber, *Your Eight-Year-Old: Lively and Outgoing* (New York: Dell, 1990), 2.

2. L. B. Ames, F. L. Ilg, and S. M. Baker, *Your Ten- to Fourteen-Year-Old* (New York: Delacorte, 1988), 23.

3. Ibid., 157.

4. "The Home Media Use of Children Age 6 to 12 in the United States: 1997–2003," www.popcenter.umd.edu/people/hofferth_sandra/; Sandra L. Hofferth and Jack Sandberg, "Changes in American Children's Time, 1981–1997," in *Children at the Millennium: Where Have We Come From, Where Are We Going?* Advances in Life Course Research, vol. 6, edited by S. L. Hofferth and T. J. Owens (Oxford: Elsevier, 2001), 193–229.

5. S. Carpenter, "Sleep Deprivation May Be Undermining Teen Health," *APA Monitor* 32, no. 9 (October 2001).

6. National Archive of Criminal Justice Data, www.icpsr.umich.edu/icpsrweb/NACJD/; retrieved 9/12/10.

7. J. Twenge and W. K. Campbell, *The Narcissism Epidemic: Living in the Age of Entitlement* (New York: Free Press, 2010).

8. *A Nation at Risk: The Imperative for Educational Reform*, April 1983.

9. 2009 United States Census, www.census.gov; retrieved 2/11/10.

10. G. Tononi and C. Cirelli, "Sleep Function and Synaptic Homeostasis," *Sleep Medicine Review* 10, no. 1 (February 2006): 49–62.

CHAPTER 3: The Tasks of the Elementary School Years

1. B. R. Burleson, J. D. Delia, and J. L. Applegate, "Effects of Maternal Communication and Children's Social-Cognitive and Communication Skills on Children's Acceptance by the Peer Group," *Family Relations* 41 (1992): 264–72.

2. R. R. Sears, E. E. Maccoby, and H. Levin, *Patterns of Childrearing* (Evanston, IL: Row Peterson, 1957).

3. R. Larson, "Toward a Psychology of Positive Youth Development," *American Psychologist* 55, no. 1 (2000): 170–83.

4. C. Dweck, *Mindset: The New Psychology of Success* (New York: Ballantine, 2006).

5. R. J. Herrnstein and C. Murray, *The Bell Curve* (New York: Free Press, 1993).

6. F. J. Sternberg, "The Theory of Successful Intelligence," *Review of General Psychology* 3 (1999): 292–316.

7. K. Bradshaw, D. L. Martin, and R. Gill, "Assessing Rates and Characteristics of Bullying Through an Internet-Based Survey System," Johns Hopkins Bloomberg School of Public Health and the Johns Hopkins Center for the Prevention of Youth Violence, 2006.

8. L. A. Sroufe, B. Egeland, E. A. Carlson, and W. A. Collins, *The Development of the Person* (New York: Guilford Press, 2005).

9. L. J. Walker and K. H. Hennig, "Parenting Style and the Development of Moral Reasoning," *Journal of Moral Education* 28 (1999): 359–74.

10. D. L. Rosenhan, "The Natural Socialization of Altruistic Autonomy," in *Altruism and Helping Behavior*, edited by J. Macaulay and L. Berkowitz (New York: Academic Press, 1970), 251–68.

11. Office of the United Nations High Commissioner for Human Rights, Convention on the Rights of the Child, General Assembly Resolution 44/25 of 20 (November 1989), available at www. unhchr.ch/html/menu3/b/k2crc.htm.

12. D. Johnson, "Many Schools Putting an End to Child's Play," *New York Times*, April 7, 1998, A16.

13. A. Pellegrini and C. Glickman, "The Educational Role of Recess," *Principal* 68, no. 5 (1989): 23–24.

CHAPTER 4: The Tasks of the Middle School Years

1. L. Steinberg and J. Silk, "Parenting Adolescents," in *Handbook of Parenting*, vol. 1, edited by M. Bornstein (Mahwah, NJ: Lawrence Erlbaum, 2002).

2. L. Steinberg and A. S. Morris, "Adolescent Development," *Annual Review of Psychology* 52 (2001): 83–110.

3. R. Larson and M. H. Richards, *Divergent Realities: The Emotional Lives of Mothers, Fathers, and Adolescents* (New York: Basic Books, 1994).

4. B. Goldstein, *Introduction to Human Sexuality* (Belmont, CA: Star, 1976).

5. J. Graber, P. Lewinsohn, J. Seeley, and J. Brooks-Gunn, "Is Pubertal Timing Associated with Psychopathology in Young Adulthood?" *Journal of the American Academy of Child and Adolescent Psychiatry* 43 (1997): 718–26.

6. H. Peskin, "Pubertal Onset and Ego Functioning: A Psychoanalytic Approach," *Journal of Abnormal Psychology* 72 (1967): 1–15.

7. A. Booth et al., "Testosterone and Child and Adolescent Adjustment: The Moderating Role of Parent-Child Relationships," *Developmental Psychology* 39 (2003): 85–98.

8. J. Brumberg, *The Body Project: An Intimate History of American Girls* (New York: Random House, 1997).

9. Body Mass Index, Livestrong.com (accessed October 6, 2010).

10. M. Richards, A. Boxer, A. Petersen, and R. Albrecht, "Relation of Weight to Body Image in Pubertal Girls and Boys from Two Communities," *Developmental Psychology* 26 (1990): 313–21.

11. J. Mendle, E. Turkheimer, and R. E. Emery, "Detrimental Psychological Outcomes Associated with Early Pubertal Timing in Adolescent Girls," *Developmental Review* 27 (2007): 151–71.

12. E. Stice, K. Presnell, and S. Bearman, "Relation of Early Menarche to Depression, Eating Disorders, Substance Abuse and Comorbid Psychopathology Among Adolescent Girls," *Developmental Psychology* 37 (2001): 608–19.

13. R. Silbereisen, A. Petersen, H. Albrecht, and B. Kracke, "Maturational Timing and the Development of Problem Behavior: Longitudinal Studies in Adolescence," *Journal of Early Adolescence* 9 (1989): 247–68.

14. A. Caspi, D. Lynam, T. Moffitt, and P. Silva, "Unraveling Girls' Delinquency: Biological, Dispositional and Contextual Contributions to Adolescent Misbehavior," *Developmental Psychology* 29 (1993): 19–30.

15. E. Ozer and C. Irwin, "Adolescent and Young Adult Health: From Basic Health Status to Clinical Interventions," in *Handbook of Adolescent Psychology*, 3rd ed., vol. 1, edited by R. Lerner and L. Steinberg (New York: Wiley, 2009), 618–41.

16. American Academy of Pediatrics Patient Education Online, Teen Sleep Patterns, patiented.aap.org/content.aspx?aid=6776 (accessed October 28, 2010).

17. Dr. William L. Coleman, pediatric professor at the Center for Development and Learning, University of North Carolina–Chapel Hill and member of the American Academy of Pediatrics Committee on Psychosocial Aspects of Child and Family Health. From iParenting, "Is Your Teen Sleep Deprived?" family.go.com/parenting/pkg-teen/article-781220-is-your-teen-sleep-deprived--t.

18. K. Fredriksen, J. Rhodes, R. Reddy, and N. Way, "Sleepless in Chicago: Tracking the Effects of Adolescent Sleep Loss During the Middle School Years," *Child Development* 75 (2004): 84–95.

19. J. A. Owens, K. Belon, and P. Moss, "Impact of Delaying School Start

Time on Adolescent Sleep, Mood and Behavior," *Archives of Pediatrics and Adolescent Medicine* 164, no. 7 (2010): 608–14.

20. American Psychiatric Association, *Diagnostic and Statistical Manual of Mental Disorders*, 4th ed. (Washington, DC: American Psychiatric Association, 1994).

21. www.kidshealth.org/parent/general/body/overweight_obesity.html (accesssed October 29, 2010).

22. American Academy of Child and Adolescent Psychiatry, "Obesity in Children and Teens," May 2008, www.aacap.org/cs/root/facts_for_families/obesity_in_children_and_teens (accessed 9/5/11).

23. Monitoring the Future Survey, Survey Research Center, University of Michigan, 2005.

24. S. Paxton et al., "Body Image Satisfaction, Dieting Beliefs, and Weight Loss Behaviors in Adolescent Girls and Boys," *Journal of Youth and Adolescence* 20 (1991): 361–80.

25. L. A. Ricciardelli and M. P. McCabe, "A Biopsychosocial Model of Disorder Eating and the Pursuit of Muscularity in Adolescent Boys," *Psychological Bulletin* 130 (2004): 179–205.

26. L. Steinberg, *Adolescence* (New York: McGraw-Hill, 2011).

27. L. Steinberg and J. Belsky, "A Sociobiological Perspective on Psychopathology in Adolescence," in *Rochester Symposium on Developmental Psychopathology*, vol. 7, edited by D. Cicchetti and S. Toth (Rochester, NY: University of Rochester Press, 1996), 93–124.

28. M. Ernst et al., "Amygdala and Nucleus Accumbens in Response to Receipt and Omission of Gains in Adults and Adolescents," *Neuroimage* 25 (2005): 1270–79; L. Spear, *The Behavioral Neuroscience of Adolescence* (New York: Norton, 2010).

29. L. Wang, S. Huettel, and M. D. De Bellis, "Neural Substrates for Processing Task-Irrelevant Sad Images in Adolescents," *Developmental Science* 11 (2008): 23–32.

30. L. Steinberg and S. Silberberg, "The Vicissitudes of Autonomy in Early Adolescence," *Child Development* 57 (1986): 841–51.

31. Steinberg, *Adolescence*, 291.

32. J. Jaccard, H. Blanton, and T. Dodge, "Peer Influences on Risk Behavior: An Analysis of the Effects of a Close Friend," *Developmental Psychology* 41 (2005): 135–47.

33. H. C. Rusby, K. K. Forrester, A. Biglan, and C. W. Metzler, "Relationships Between Peer Harassment and Adolescent Problem Behaviors," *Journal of Early Adolescence* 25 (2005): 453–77.

34. J. Wang, T. Nansel, and R. Iannotti, "Bullying Victimization Among Underweight and Overweight U.S. Youth: Differential Associations for Boys and Girls," *Journal of Adolescent Health* 47, no. 1 (2010): 99–101.

35. J. Payton et al., *The Positive Impact of Social and Emotional Learning for Kindergarten to Eighth-Grade Students: Findings from Three Scientific Reviews*, Collaborative for Academic, Social, and Emotional Learning, December 2008.

36. J. E. Zins, M. R. Bloodworth, R. P. Weissberg, and H. Walberg, in *Building Academic Success on Social and Emotional Learning: What the Research Says*, edited by J. Zins, R. P. Weissberg, and H. J. Walberg (New York: Teachers College Press, 2004).

CHAPTER 5: The Tasks of the High School Years

1. J. Rosenbaum, "Patient Teenagers? A Comparison of the Sexual Behavior of Virginity Pledgers and Matched Nonpledgers," *Pediatrics* 123 (2009): e110–20.

2. B. Miller, B. Benson, and K. A. Galbraith, "Family Relationships and Adolescent Pregnancy Risk: A Research Synthesis," *Developmental Review* 21 (2001): 1–38.

3. S. Small and T. Luster, "Adolescent Sexual Activity: An Ecological Risk-Factor Approach," *Journal of Marriage and the Family* 56 (1994): 181–92.

4. C. B. Aspy et al., "Parental Communication and Youth Sexual Behavior," *Journal of Adolescence* 30 (2007): 449–66.

5. Ibid.

6. A. Kowal and L. Blinn-Pike, "Sibling Influences on Adolescents' Attitudes toward Safe Sex Practices," *Family Relations* 53 (2004): 377–84.

7. C. Bingham and L. Crockett, "Longitudinal Adjustment Patterns of Boys and Girls Experiencing Early, Middle, and Late Sexual Intercourse," *Developmental Psychology* 32 (1996): 647–58.

8. J. S. Singh and J. Darroch, "Trends in Sexual Activity Among Adolescent American Women: 1982–1995," *Family Planning Perspectives* 31 (1999): 212–19.

9. A. Jordan and D. Cole, "Relation of Depressive Symptoms to the Structure of Self-Knowledge in Childhood," *Journal of Abnormal Psychology* 105 (1996): 530–40.

10. R. McCrae et al., "Personality Trait Development from Age 12 to Age 18: Longitudinal, Cross-Sectional and Cross-Cultural Analyses," *Journal of Personality and Social Psychology* 83 (2002): 1456–68.

11. J. Allen et al., "The Relations of Attachment Security to Adolescent's Paternal and Peer Relationships, Depression and Externalizing Behavior," *Child Development* 78 (2007): 1222–39.

CHAPTER 6: Teaching Our Kids to Find Solutions

1. National Endowment for the Arts, *Artists in the Workforce 1990–2005*, Executive Summary.
2. *The Gallup Youth Survey, January 22-March 9, 2004*. Retrieved June 24, 2009, from www.gallup.com/poll/11893/Most-Teens-Associate-School-Boredom-Fatigue.aspx.

CHAPTER 7: Teaching Our Kids to Take Action

1. W. Mischel, Y. Shoda, and M. L. Rodriguez, "Delay of Gratification in Children," *Science* 244 (1989), 933–938.
2. W. Mischel, Y. Shoda, and P. K. Peake, "The Nature of Adolescent Competencies Predicted by Preschool Delay of Gratification," *Journal of Personality and Social Psychology* 54 (1988): 687–96.
3. J. S. Watson, "Depression and the Perception of Control in Early Childhood," in *Depression in Childhood: Diagnosis, Treatment, and Conceptual Models*, edited by J. G. Schulterbrandt and A. Raskin (New York: Raven, 1977), 129–39.
4. S. J. Rosenholtz and S. H. Rosenholtz, "Classroom Organization and the Perception of Ability," *Sociology of Education* 54 (1981): 132–40.
5. E. E. Werner, "The Children of Kauai: Resilience and Recovery in Adolescence and Adulthood," *Journal of Adolescent Health* 13 (1992): 262–68.

CHAPTER 8: Defining and Living Your Family Values

1. D. W. Winnicott, *The Child, the Family, and the Outside World* (Middlesex, UK: Penguin, 1973), 17, 44.

CHAPTER 9: Editing the Script

1. ExpectMoreArizona.org.
2. Kahlil Gibran, *The Prophet* (New York: Knopf, 1923).
3. D. J. Siegel and M. Hartzell, *Parenting from the Inside Out* (New York: Penguin, 2003), 64.

INDEX

resourcefulness, 189–94
  development of, 189–92
  parenting for, 192–94
  resilience and, 187
  unstructured play and, 26–27
reward. *See* discipline
risks
  assessing peer group, 138–39
  valuing academic, 67–68
risky behavior
  brain development and, 125
  cognitive revolution and, 153–57
  health and, 104
  parental denial about, 269–70
  resourcefulness of, 190
romantic feelings, 101. *See also*
    puberty; sexuality
rote learning, 204
rules, self-control vs., 220–21

sacrifice, parental, 39
sadness, 39–40, 53–54
safe sex, 165
safety
  autonomy and, 180
  bullying and (*see* bullying)
  independence and, 48
  outdoor play and, 83
  parental monitoring for, 128
  personal space and, 23–25
schools. *See* educational systems
screen time
  limiting, 82, 208
  play vs., 80–81
  sleep hygiene and, 110–11
selection, cliques and, 133
self, sense of. *See* identity
self-consciousness, 150–51
self-control, 217–25
  authentic success and, xvii
  development of, 217–23
  guiding principles for, 254–55
  independence, coregulation, and,
    46
  parenting for, 223–25
  resilience and, 187–88
self-criticism, 84–85, 236

self-discipline, 214. *See also* work
    ethic
self-efficacy, 232–38
  autonomy and, 178–79
  development of, 232–36
  identity and, 169
  independence and, 128
  parenting for, 236–38
  resilience and, 187
self-esteem, 225–32
  autonomy and, 178
  concepts of, 28–30
  development of, 225–30
  of early maturing girls, 97–98
  girls' sexuality and, 160
  identity and, 69–72, 170–71 (*see
    also* identity)
  parenting for, 230–32
  resilience and, 187
  self-criticism and, 84–85
self-evaluation, 84–85, 236
self-mutilation, xiv, 104
self-reflection
  metacognition and, 150–51
  parental, 274–75, 286–88, 295
self-regulation. *See* self-control
self-reliance, resourcefulness vs., 190
self-soothing, 193. *See also* emotional
    intelligence
self-worth. *See* self-esteem
SEL (socio-emotional learning)
    programs, 143
sense of humor, 100, 127, 188
sense of self. *See* identity
separation
  adolescent issues about, 5
  parental issues about (*see* loss,
    parental sense of)
  unstructured play and, 26–27
serotonin, 125
sexting, 180–81
sexuality, 159–67. *See also* puberty
  age of first sexual intercourse and,
    83, 160
  appearance of management of,
    163–64
  body comfort and, 160–61

ABOUT THE AUTHOR

Madeline Levine, PhD, is a clinician, consultant, and educator; the author of *The Price of Privilege;* and a cofounder of Challenge Success, a project birthed at the Stanford School of Education that addresses education reform, student well-being, and parent education. She lives outside San Francisco with her husband and is the proud mother of three newly minted adult sons.